THE SPECIALIST

THE
Revelations
of a
Counterterrorist

SPECIALIST

Gayle Rivers

STEIN AND DAY / *Publishers* / New York

First published in the United States of America in 1985
Copyright © 1985 by Littopus S. A.
All rights reserved, Stein and Day, Incorporated
Printed in the United States of America
STEIN AND DAY/Publishers
Scarborough House
Briarcliff Manor, N.Y. 10510

Library of Congress Cataloge Card Number 85-4690

CONTENTS

AUTHOR'S NOTE

Every incident in this book is true and the people are all real. Necessarily the names, including my own, have been changed for security reasons and in some cases minor changes have been made to dates and circumstances to avoid identifying those who worked with me on the operations. Many members of the counter-terrorist community mentioned in this book are still active and many of the situations described are continuing in other forms. My aim has been to protect existing security networks and to avoid damaging the never-ending task of counter-terrorism.

The counter-terrorist agencies are not seeking recognition but there is a general feeling amongst my colleagues that the public will be heartened to learn that the authorities are capable of tackling terrorism with its own weapons.

This book is about the world of counter-terrorism as it really is – and has to be.

THE
SPECIALIST

ONE

KIDNAP BRIEFING IN BEIRUT

The call from Lebanon came as I was driving along the shore of Lake Geneva, on the dramatic, elevated stretch of autobahn where the mountains start to close in as you head into the Valais Pass.

It is amazing what can be transacted in a simple phone call. To anyone watching from the roadside, it was a very routine glimpse of affluent Swiss life: the driver of a Pacific blue Porsche Targa, with the local VD licence plates of the canton of Vaud, casually taking a call on his car phone without even slowing down. My unit is a Motorola – very easy to handle, fully duplex, no press-to-talk; just a bleep and a red light and Beirut was on the line. I could have been chatting to my stockbroker or making a date for lunch at the Café du Lac. In fact, the caller was U.S. Marine Major Tom Udall, asking me to go to Lebanon to lead a special covert operation to kidnap a Syrian intelligence officer in Beirut.

'Hello, this is Tom,' he said. I knew the voice well; it was the only identification he would give. 'Gayle, there's a matter we'd like your help with again, concerning our blue guests. Could you manage a quick trip?'

Each of the factions in the Lebanese civil war is colour-coded. Blue denotes the Syrians, from the blue flashes some of their special units wear. Their Druze allies are red, the Christian Phalangist militia green. Yellow means the Israelis or, as they're often referred to in coded conversations, 'our pale friends'.

Nothing was said during the phone call about the mission itself, but I could guess easily enough. At that period, in the final months of 1983, the Syrians and the Druze, together with their Shi'ite allies, were the biggest threat to the safety of the 1,500-strong Marine garrison which was the American contingent of the multi-national force, and most of Tom Udall's efforts were directed at trying to neutralize them. I had already been to Beirut three times to help in various ways.

Tom was calling me in as a mercenary but money was not mentioned on the phone. These matters are too urgent to bargain about. It is rather like a Lloyds salvage transaction, certain basics are without question. For this kind of mission, I charge the Americans a basic retainer of $75,000 plus expenses, which is paid by direct transfer from an American or Swiss-owned private company into one of my offshore holding companies and is described usually as a consultancy or survey fee. That figure gets me to Beirut for a briefing. At the briefing I will decide whether to accept the final mission and a full fee is agreed. Even assuming it was a solo mission, Tom had probably committed at least $120,000 by picking up the phone to me, but that is less than the cost of a salvo fired into the Shouf mountains from the 16-inch guns of the U.S. battleship *New Jersey*, off Beirut harbour, and Tom knew that I would probably give him better value for money. The Americans are good to work for because they have a money-no-object mentality. They pay for what the job needs, and I am careful not to overprice my services; my aim is to be the man they feel they really have to have.

I have known Tom Udall since Vietnam where we both began our careers in special warfare – he was with the Marines and I was with the Anzac special forces, attached to the U.S. Special Forces. Now, he was with what were known as the U.S. Special Assignment Groups in Lebanon – in other words, he was the liaison man between the Special Forces and the Central Intelligence Agency in Beirut.

Before he was posted to Beirut, we had worked together at Quantico, the huge Marine base outside Washington. He was an acting rangemaster there, supervising a series of firing ranges, and he had been responsible for the trials of some special explosive equipment I was selling to the Special Forces.

Tom is also one of the select group of people in several countries who know that I do a great deal more than sell specialized military hardware. I also carry out special operations. Beneath the surface of my civilian career, I have been engaging in various forms of active service ever since Vietnam, first as a regular with the Anzac special forces, then as a reservist serving with the British S.A.S. and as a contract mercenary specialist in covert warfare, working for a number of governments, including the Americans, the British, the South Africans, the Spanish, the Germans and the Iraqis.

When Tom was assigned to Lebanon, one of the first things he did was to call me up. We met for dinner at a quiet, elegant little restaurant in Old Town, Alexandria, across the Potomac river from Washington DC, and during a pleasant evening of social chit-chat, we nailed down the nitty-gritty in short bursts.

'Is your number in Switzerland still valid?'

'Yes.'

'Can I use it?'

'Yes.'

'Can you make equipment available?'

'Sure.'

'Will you come with it, if I need you?'

'Of course.'

I gave the last answer with a grin because Tom knows very well that I enjoy going on operations far more than I enjoy selling equipment, though unlike most mercenaries I am a fully commercial animal. I have run and still do run a series of successful businesses, including my own aviation and air freight company, as well as firms which sell military hardware and provide specialized military services. But covert operations are my real business. Quite frankly, I find ordinary business childs' play. It's hard work only because there is too much trivia. The workload builds up because most businessmen seem to revel in trivia, in fact they seem to have a trivial attitude to life in general.

By comparison, getting involved in covert operations really clears the mind. Once I'd put down the receiver after Tom's call, I instinctively started to drive the Porsche even faster. It wasn't excitement. I never get excited in advance about an assignment. The excitement begins once I'm there and operational and the adrenaline is running because it is needed. The speeding up of the car simply reflected the speed at which my mind was suddenly working. For the rest of the drive, I was already in Beirut, planning, anticipating, reviewing likely options.

A week later I flew to Cyprus – with $75,000 already in my account – and began the procedure for arriving at Larnaca airport, which I had established on the three previous trips to Lebanon for the Americans.

If I am carrying anything the Cypriot authorities wouldn't take kindly to, like explosives, I arrange to be met on the arrival side of Customs. If not, I go through Customs and Immigration myself and walk out to be met in the mêlée of people looking for taxis. Often, though, even if I do have some dubious stores to bring in, I prefer to go through Customs on my own – it makes me far less obtrusive. I have gone into several countries carrying some pretty heavy hardware and Customs didn't bother me. I guess I must have an honest face. I suppose my great advantage is that I look ordinary – I am medium height, clean-shaven, with neatly trimmed hair and no distinguishing marks. I make a point of dressing conservatively and if you saw me in a restaurant, you would probably think I was just a business executive. I might even be in insurance!

This time, I had no equipment and I walked straight through, carrying only a small holdall. Beside the taxi queue, I immediately saw a familiar face: Bill Lundin, a tall, blond, Scandinavian-born captain in the U.S. Special Forces, another well-tried veteran I have known since Vietnam. After a quick exchange of greetings, we drove in a hired car round the perimeter of Larnaca airport to a section of the field the Americans used for their military traffic. The Americans ran shuttles, mostly by helicopter, to their garrison in Beirut and to the ships of the U.S. task force lying offshore. Within minutes, Lundin had me on board a big CH-46 chopper, which is very similar to the Chinook, and we were heading for Beirut. On board, the routine continued.

So that I wouldn't be too conspicuous on arrival, I changed into a set of olive-green fatigues I had brought with me. They were very similar to the U.S. standard issue and though I wore no unit markings or badges of rank, I didn't look out of place when we landed at Green Beach.

Green Beach is the beachhead the Marines have established as a safe channel for men and supplies moving in and out of their main garrison, near Beirut airport, very close to the shoreline. The beach is heavily defended with Stinger man-portable anti-aircraft weapons, backed up by well-dispersed machine-gun positions and beach radar units, with more firepower on board landing craft moored inshore.

As soon as I stepped off the chopper at Green Beach, I was back in the environment I like best; the last traces of civilian life were gone and I was a fully military creature. I have always had the gift for making these instant transitions. It is one characteristic of the Special Forces soldier that he can psyche himself up for combat much faster than the regimental soldier, but I don't think that many people find the switch as easy as I do. I have the ability to pick up on a new situation like turning the page of a book. There is no transitional period at all. Once I'm on Green Beach, I am instantly attuned to the military atmosphere, not to mention the warm Lebanese sunlight, and the crisp winter chill of Switzerland is forgotten. This time, as always, I felt completely at ease. I tuned in automatically to the sound of shelling beyond the city in the Shouf mountains, routinely checking on what kind of heavy weaponry was being used in the latest exchanges between the Druze militia and the Lebanese army. It also seemed right that there should be Israeli jets flying a reconnaissance mission over the city to inspect militia positions; their trails in the sky fitted into my natural landscape. This is how I have lived most of my life and, quite honestly, it was a real relief to be away from businessmen for a while and back among military professionals.

We didn't linger at Green Beach. One of the features of these trips to Lebanon is the speed at which they move. I usually arrive in mid-afternoon, and on a couple of occasions I have been hiding out, alone, in a bomb-shattered building in Syrian or Druze territory on an intelligence-gathering mission by early evening. This time, the mission was more complex and there was to be a longer briefing stage, but we still moved quickly, first to a building on the airfield perimeter, where I met a few more old friends, then, discreetly, in a civilian car, Bill dropped me off at a safe house in the centre of Beirut.

This safe house is one where I feel completely at ease because it's my own territory. The Americans have their own places in the city, but this one belongs to my agent in Beirut, a Lebanese of Iraqi extraction called Ibrahim Hussein. There is nothing military about this hideaway. It is an extremely luxurious villa, built on several levels, overlooking the bay – the kind of house that fitted the lifestyle of the old Beirut when it was the playground of the Middle East, before the warring factions shelled and mortared the city to pieces. So far the villa has escaped damage and it is a secure and comfortable place to hold briefings with Special Forces personnel.

Hussein, like many wealthy Lebanese traders, is a man with many faces. On one level, he is a successful international merchant and he keeps up the conventional front of a well-to-do Arab businessman. The house has a swimming pool, with a patio just above it and a terrace from which you can see most of the bay and the U.S. task force riding at anchor.

The hospitality is lavish. Hussein is a big, heavy-set man in his mid-forties and he plays the stylish host as he moves around the blue and white tropical furnishings he has collected from the better department stores of Italy, Switzerland and West Germany. He is also a brilliant intelligence agent. He and members of his family had already done the basic groundwork for this mission. He is also an arms dealer and acts as my own import agent for moving specialized military equipment into Beirut for the Americans. Most of the people in the villa, including the servants, are members of Hussein's family and it is very much his private domain, which the Americans can use only when I am there.

After a quick meal with Hussein, five Americans arrived for the mission briefing, including Tom Udall, who looked as he had on my previous visit, except that he was slightly more suntanned, and Bill Lundin. They arrived separately, wearing civilian clothes, mostly tropical suits or drill trousers and bomber jackets. They were all Special Forces soldiers, ranging in age from mid-twenties to late thirties, much older than the typical U.S. serviceman. Tom Udall would not be on this mission himself, but I knew all the rest of the team personally. They were all drawn from the Special Forces units in Fort Bragg and I had trained with them there, during spells as a contracted civilian instructor – another side to my career.

Rank is no big deal in Special Forces units, though oddly enough, the Americans make more of it than the British S.A.S. As usual, I would be in charge of the team, leading it without technically being in command of it. If I had not been there, the leader would have been Bill Lundin, with Mel Becklin as his second-in-command. Becklin looks much more like a professional soldier than Bill. His short dark hair looks almost cropped beside Bill's Scandinavian mane. He's a typical career army man, in his mid-thirties, married, with a couple of kids back in Virginia, but he is also a fluent Arabic speaker. I have never heard the third man called anything but Chuck, even though our paths have crossed several times in Vietnam and at Fort Bragg. He is another transferee to the Special Forces who started out in the Marines. The fourth guy was called Roger Moule and he was the youngest and the learner of the team – it was going to be his first taste of combat and it showed a bit, though he was handling it well.

The atmosphere of the briefing was very distinctive. It was like being in the innermost box of a nest of Chinese boxes. Somewhere out there in the

city was the official American presence in Beirut, technically a non-combat-
ant peace-keeping force, acting in moral and political support of President
Gemayel in his efforts to maintain a stable coalition government of Christ-
ians and Muslims in Lebanon. In here, the name of the game was survival.
We were not concerned with preserving peace in Lebanon, but with trying
to protect the American garrison and deal with the threats to it in the most
effective way possible.

Really, the Special Forces don't feel they are part of the U.S. garrison –
they even fly out separately to Cyprus and Germany for rest and recreation.
They don't make a big thing out of their superiority. They *are* better soldiers
and they know it, and they are often embarrassed by the shortcomings of the
Marines. The Special Forces people know that the Marines, like most regular
American troops, are too dependent on communication with home base and
on massive logistical support and that they're led by inexperienced general
service officers. Every man at the briefing knew damned well that the terrorist suicide attack which had killed over 200 Marines hardly two months
previously could have been prevented. The terrorists got through because of
lousy garrison intelligence, mickey-mouse security procedures, and too
rigid discipline. It is the kind of home truth that is better left unsaid, but this
team knew that to survive in the middle of a Lebanese civil war, you have to
be a lot sharper than that.

But it was when Tom Udall unfolded the mission that I really felt how far
away this was from the official U.S. role in Lebanon. Hussein's private intel-
ligence network – funded through me by the Americans – had located a
Druze headquarters on the western outskirts of the city where newly arrived
Syrian intelligence officers were operating. After analysing the situation, the
C.I.A. had decided it wanted one of the Syrians captured for interrogation,
and the Special Forces, who carry out most of the C.I.A.'s black operations in
Lebanon, had been tasked with carrying out a snatch raid.

Tom Udall had called me in Switzerland because snatch raids are one of
my specialities. I have done them in all kinds of places, from Vietnam to
Mozambique and Northern Ireland to Iran, and for all kinds of paymasters.
One of the things Tom Udall is buying when he calls me in is, quite simply,
experience. He is not too proud to admit it and he works for people who
understand the realities of covert warfare. His authorizations come from
Washington, not from the command structure in Lebanon, and most of the
top military brass in Beirut have absolutely no idea what the Special Forces
get up to. By most people's standards, Tom is a seasoned soldier but, really,
a couple of years in Korea and a couple in Vietnam don't add up to a helluva
lot of combat, especially as much of it had been in structured warfare. The
other Vietnam-trained men are also 'veterans', but they have had only one
tour each, as young soldiers, learning how to capture hearts and minds and

carry out R.F.I. (reconnaissance for intelligence missions) in Viet Cong territory.

All of them were glad to have me there. They respected my S.A.S. background and it didn't matter to them that I was a Brit and a civilian and that I was getting paid a lot more than they were for the mission. But that is strictly the Special Forces attitude. Officially my presence was not sanctioned at all. Throughout the whole of the seventeen months that the U.S. had troops in Lebanon, there was not even a hint of the use of civilian mercenaries, and if there had been, it is not difficult to imagine the outcry.

Suppose, for example, that this mission briefing had leaked out. Try to imagine the reporters asking questions about it at a press briefing and the questions being answered truthfully, with television cameras recording the exchange for all the world to see and hear.

'Major, is it true that U.S. Special Forces intend to carry out a raid into Druze territory to capture a Syrian intelligence officer, and murder others?'

'Yes. That's right.'

'And would you say this was consistent with the U.S. peace-keeping role in Lebanon?'

'Sure is. The Syrians are showing the militias how to use sophisticated optical and laser devices to target U.S., British and French positions here. They're also boosting the morale of the militias and helping them organize terrorist attacks. Our mission is to stop them, as best we can.'

'And this mission is to be led by a mercenary.'

'Yes. A very experienced S.A.S. guy who works for us a lot. We can use all the help we can get.'

'And this Syrian. He's to be arrested?'

'No. Not arrested. The Lebanese government has nothing to do with this. We just want to capture him and interrogate him. We need to know what the Syrians are up to in that section of the city.'

'And you believe the Syrian will tell you?'

'Yes, sir, I believe a night with a Special Forces interrogation team will take care of that.'

This kind of exchange is, of course, unthinkable. Assassinations, kidnaps, mercenaries, pre-emptive strikes, interrogations were all taboo words at press briefings, yet they were very much part of the real world in Lebanon. The so-called official briefings and statements were usually designed to dress up the fact that the United States was floundering in Lebanon. The Administration had no clear idea what to do, other than to try to mediate while remaining loyal to Israel and fulfil its commitments to America's Jewish community.

As the briefing continued, the contrast between the Americans and Hussein became particularly intriguing. Hussein sees the Lebanese situation with the cold, dispassionate eye of a realist. Beneath the courtesy of the host, he concealed a basic mistrust of American policy, because of its pro-Israeli bias. Hussein did not believe in mediation with Israel. As an Arab, his basic reaction to the Israelis is one of acute hatred. Mediation is just a political slogan. In this group, Hussein saw me as a kind of guarantee of objectivity. He needed the Americans and they needed him, but it was important to him to be able to filter his ideas and his intelligence data through someone like me who could take a neutral view of American or Israeli aims.

As Tom continued, I began to get the message that the Agency was very high on this particular snatch and that the Special Forces were equally keen to deliver. The target was a Syrian major, a senior intelligence officer who had been flown from Damascus specially – according to Hussein's information – to stiffen the Druze efforts in the sector. He was operating from a four-storey building which had been set up as a Druze command post. The mission profile was to infiltrate the command post, capture the major, kill as many others as possible, then lay explosive charges on exfiltration and do as much damage as possible to the building after we had left it.

Though I had some reservations, I had already decided to accept the mission. During a break in the briefing, I took Tom Udall aside to tell him so and to talk about money. The discussion was quick and amicable and we settled on a substantial fee in addition to the $75,000 retainer. Fees for a mission are determined by three factors: the duration, the number of personnel required and a professional assessment of the danger involved. In this case, I would be the only civilian operating with the Special Forces team and would take the whole fee, except for a commission to Hussein, but the figure is always high enough to allow for contingencies. I may decide on an assignment that I need private back-up; I may want to use local personnel without letting the Americans know, or I may want to use equipment that I don't want to end up as my employers' property. As a general rule it is prudent to have a few extra resources and not to let the principals know the full extent of your control over the mission. On this mission, no such extras were needed, but the fee allowed for the possibility.

One extra I don't allow, though, is insurance. On covert operations, I never bother to insure myself. I could do so, because if I were killed, the insurance company would never be allowed to find out how I died. No employer on this kind of mission is ever going to tell an insurance company that I was hurled off the roof of a Druze command post with a knife between my shoulder-blades. Officially, the most violent death I could ever meet would be a road accident in Beirut, but despite that, it is my personal choice not to take insurance, though I do insure people who work for me on multi-man missions.

When we had finished talking about money, I also let Tom know that I wasn't sure that it would be possible to get the Syrian major out alive.

'We'll get in and out and we'll get your man,' I said, 'but the exfiltration could be a problem.'

The plan was to enter the command post along a rope stretched from an adjacent building, going in from the roof and down to the third floor where the Syrians had been seen carrying out their planning sessions. Stage two was to isolate the major, seize him and drug him, kill anyone else we could, then get the major down through the building and out into the street, using confusion as cover.

'Have you added up how many people have been seen in that building?' I said to Tom.

'The Agency wants him bad,' Tom said. 'You've got to give it a go.'

'I always give it a go,' I said, 'you know that.'

I made sure that the tone of my answer was not a commitment and I made a mental note that once again one of my functions might well be to adapt the mission profile to the realities of the situation. Even men like Udall need some guidance from people like me. Tom is a superb soldier, tough, fearless, and skilled in the arts of special warfare, but mentally he is still a bit too rigid. In his private life, he is a very likeable, agreeable guy, a family man, religious, and a highly skilled pianist. But he is also bound by a rigid military code which makes it impossible for him to question his flag, his president—or an order. I survive by being a lot more flexible.

Of this team, Bill Lundin is the one most attuned to my own type of character. He is patriotic and loyal to the United States, but he's also able to step outside the rigid American viewpoint and he has acquired enough cynicism to make him a healthy Special Forces soldier. After Vietnam, most Americans went one of two ways. They either cried in their milk, or they became decent cynics. To get what I call a balanced view of life, you have to see betrayal and treachery, and there was plenty of that for everyone in Vietnam. If you haven't accepted that treachery operates on your own side as well, then you go into war wearing rose-coloured glasses, blindly following the flag, and in my book that makes you a menace.

A man like Bill Lundin can see all the problems of American policy in Lebanon, but he can still serve loyally.

Bill is what I would call an honourable cynic. It is a difficult concept to spell out, but I had better try as it defines my own attitude to warfare. Even though I am a mercenary, I believe in a soldier's honour, but I'm not a blind follower of causes. Even more clearly than Lundin, I see the total picture – all the deceits and compromises and the hidden levers that control military and political action. Despite that, I am quite comfortable in the Americans' service. I don't wave the Stars and Stripes but I believe in American society, even though I can see its flaws. I am a clear-headed mercenary and I won't serve just any paymaster.

One cause I do believe in, though, is counter-terrorism. I detest terrorists. I have never met a terrorist group yet that didn't end up being used by larger forces seeking to destabilize stable societies. Terrorists are just dangerous pawns. The Syrians' commitment to terrorism – and especially their links with the wellspring of so much of the world's terrorism, Libya – makes them, for me, a really worthwhile target.

Of course, working for the Americans in Lebanon also means that you are working indirectly for the Israelis. After all of my missions in Lebanon there was a joint C.I.A.-Israeli intelligence debriefing. I never took part; it was something I chose never to get involved in, but I was well aware of how closely they co-operated.

If I had ever had any doubts, they would have been cleared up for ever by one particular mission I did in Lebanon. It was a fast twenty-four-hour assignment to infiltrate Druze territory and target a building that was being used to direct fire onto American positions.

I went in with one other American, an expert in the use of the laser designator. That is a device which works by directing a laser beam on to the target from the ground, to provide a guide path for 'smart' bombs dropped from strike aircraft. The aircraft fly over, you switch on the laser, and the bomb-aiming computers do the rest. In open areas you can designate from a considerable distance, but this building was in a tightly enclosed urban environment and we had to get in close, and operate from a ruined building across a piece of waste ground. The mission had been tasked by the Americans, but when the strike was called in, it was flown by Israeli aircraft. The American with me was dumbfounded. Later, it was announced to the press as an entirely Israeli raid, with no mention of the fact that it had been set up by the Americans, based on Lebanese intelligence and with the target pinpointed by a British mercenary.

The Special Forces people quickly got used to this kind of co-operation but there were some aspects of Israeli activity that even they were not aware of.

Because I move in and out of situations and countries, I see links that are impossible to spot from within one situation. Just before this trip to Lebanon, I'd been in touch with some Arab intelligence contacts in London who had briefed me on the links between the Israelis and the fanatical Islamic terrorist organization, known under various splinter names including the Islamic Jihad Organization, which carried out the suicide bombing of the American Marine base in Beirut. It's a highly dangerous group which links Shi'ite Muslims worldwide in a kind of annex to the Iranian revolution. The Israelis talk to them because there are occasions when it can serve a particular Israeli purpose to create confusion by fostering Islamic fanaticism. But this Special Forces team was not ready for this kind of insight – it is a bit advanced even for Bill Lundin! Also, it is important not to distract a team when they are gearing up for a mission.

With all this talk about motivations, we mustn't lose sight of my basic one: once I accept an assignment, I make sure I do it right. I fight to win. There is no other way. It's like going into a tunnel. I'll do whatever the mission demands. The idea is to come out of the tunnel at the other end in one piece and get paid.

TWO

RAID ON DRUZE HEADQUARTERS

Infiltrating the denied areas of Beirut is surprisingly easy. There is so much confusion in the city, so many unoccupied and damaged buildings to provide hiding-places – and with so many people carrying weapons, a man doesn't lightly challenge another man on the streets.

I've tried various covers for these infiltrations. I got to one hit job against a Syrian observation team by posing as a Red Cross ambulanceman. Yes, I know it's against the Geneva Convention, but hell, I was there to save American lives! On another intelligence-gathering operation, I started out as a journalist, then went into hiding once I was up close to the target. Generally, though, I prefer to avoid role-playing. If you are challenged and questioned, it is difficult to be convincing.

For this mission, we simply walked into the area singly, using as little open ground as possible. Even as non-Arabs, we were not particularly conspicuous. The four Americans had let their stubble grow and looked pretty scruffy and unkempt; I was the only clean-shaven one on the team. We each carried some kind of bag which contained weapons, combat equipment and the satchel charges to mine the building at the end of the mission. Mine was a black canvas combat bag and I had on a three-quarter length canvas coat of the kind many Arabs wear, and a hat with flaps over the ears and neck that you see all over the place in Beirut. I also had a scarf round my neck, pulled up slightly around the throat, and I didn't really stand out in a city where much of the population wears some kind of military-style gear.

Not one of the five was challenged, and at intervals during the evening of the day after my arrival we entered the semi-ruined building that Hussein had spotted for us, right next to the Druze headquarters. The plan was to stay there for a complete day, to observe movements in the Druze building, then make the attack the following night. There could be only one hit and we had to be certain that our targets were in the building.

We set up our base in the cellars of the building and organized shifts to carry out the observation. Everyone was very relaxed and confident, except for Roger Moule who was showing a bit of tension. He wasn't scared, just a bit apprehensive about his first mission and it showed in the briskness of his speech and movements. I wasn't worried about him, though. I was sure he would fit in and I knew Tom Udall wouldn't have given me a weak link. During the day we talked very little. There was no chat, only a few words occasionally to deal with a particular problem. We ate lightly and spent a lot of time carefully preparing our weapons and changing into combat equipment. We had chosen MP5 submachine guns and 9mm pistols, both with silencers, as our basic armoury, and of course knives, which are always a crucial weapon on this kind of mission. We had all chosen the Marine SEAL knife, a nice, finely-balanced weapon, except for Chuck who had brought along a damned great Bowie-type blade. It wasn't any more efficient for killing, it was just his preference; personal weapons are very common in Special Forces units. The most fiddly job of the day was preparing the rappelling equipment we were going to use to cross between the buildings.

Basically, it was a simple black rope with a lightweight aluminium grappling hook on the end. There is a more sophisticated version with which you fire a bolt into the wall of the building you're trying to reach, but it was not necessary here because the gap was not too great for casting the grapple. The tricky part was to set up the harness attachments to carry the weapon load and the explosives across, but Lundin is an old hand and we did the job together.

The observation also went off well. There was a lot of movement around the Druze building but because it was, effectively, a military installation, there were no casual visitors. There was no obvious special security at the main entrance, apart from two rather bedraggled-looking guards, but the Druze and their allies kept a generally tight control over the whole district and anyone who went into the building obviously had business there.

As the preliminary intelligence reports had suggested, the key personnel seemed to gather on the upper floors, probably because they felt safer away from the street, and by afternoon we had established that at least two of the Syrians, including the major, were in the building. We caught only glimpses of them, but they were not difficult to spot. They had very much dressed the part as commanders, presumably to bolster their morale-boosting role. They wore camouflaged combat equipment and side-arms, with red berets and blue shoulder flashes, easily distinguishable from the green fatigues most of the Druze wore. The problem, though, was going to be to locate them within the building. There were four floors and at least a dozen rooms, virtually all of them in use, though most of the activity seemed to be concentrated on the third floor. By evening, we were satisfied that all three Syrian targets were in the building, and we decided to begin the raid just before midnight. At half past eleven, we progressed up to the roof of our own building and Bill Lundin and Chuck prepared the rappelling equipment.

The main problem with this kind of crossing is noise. The physical effort is routine; every member of the team had done it a hundred times on assault courses and on training exercises. We were well blacked up, there was very little moonlight and virtually no street-lighting in the area, so being seen in silhouette was not a big risk either. Noise is more difficult to avoid. First there is throwing the hook. If you don't get it right, even an aluminium grapple can make a nasty clatter against masonry. Then you have to keep the weapon loads quiet, as well as being careful of any noise your own physical exertions can make.

In the event, we made it smoothly. Bill Lundin hooked the grapple on to the roof parapet first time, and I led the team across with no hitches.

The roof of the Druze headquarters was flat, with a low parapet all round. The way down into the building was through a wooden door, set in a concrete fixture, and there was a big water tank taking up a lot of the open space. I led into the building with Mel Becklin behind me and Lundin bringing up the rear behind Chuck and Roger Moule. I had been right about Moule; he had complete control of his nerves. We moved down through the building, co-operating instinctively, covering fields of fire and staying completely silent.

On the floor immediately under the roof, there were two rooms, both with their doors closed. We paused, listened carefully for a moment, and realized that both contained sleeping men; there was no mistaking the smell and the noise of snoring. There was no sound of movement in either room, but we could not be sure there wasn't someone lying awake, so we moved on with great care, each covering one of the doors with our weapons as we went on down the shabby wooden staircase to the floor below.

There was no doubt that this was where the action would be. Our observation and the original intelligence reports made this, to all intents and purposes, the main floor of the headquarters. This was where the talking and planning were done and we could immediately detect signs of activity on both sides of the landing. On one side, the door of a room was ajar and we could make out the voices of three men. The room was full of smoke and we could hear a lively conversation and the clink of glasses being put down on a glass-topped table. As the Arabic speaker, Mel Becklin moved in closer to concentrate on the voices. Bill pressed himself against the wall on the other side to observe through the crack in the door. That left Chuck and Roger and me to cover them and the closed door on the opposite side of the landing where we could already make out many more than three voices.

After a moment, Mel indicated in sign language that there were two Druzes in the room and one of the Syrians, but not the major who was the kipnap target. Luckily, the major was easy to spot. He was much bigger than the two junior Syrians, and older, somewhere in his mid-forties, with a distinctive black moustache.

I made a decision instantly and signalled to Becklin to take out the three men in the open room. Mel didn't hesistate. With the rest of the team covering him from standing and crouching positions around the landing, he tapped smartly on the partly open door. A man in green fatigues answered the knock and as he pushed the door open, Mel shot him in the chest with his MP5. Before the Druze had even fallen, Mel forced his way past him and into the room and fired two more shots.

Inevitably, there were sounds of disturbance. When you shoot someone with a silenced weapon, that doesn't mean there isn't any noise. Three people may be shot quietly, but they don't necessarily die quietly. From the landing, you could hear the distinctive soft, muffled sound of the bullets hitting home; then one of the men must have fallen against the table, and though it did not break, it made a loud enough crack as it hit the floor.

We knew the noise would disturb the people in the other room, but at least Mel was quick about it. We heard him coming back to the door and, instinctively, Bill drew a bead on him, just in case it was the wrong man coming out. It wasn't needed. Becklin came out and indicated that all three were dead and we waited for the reaction from the room opposite. No one needed telling not to burst straight in; we didn't know how many men we would find inside. Better to wait for at least some of them to come out. That way we would catch at least one by surprise and have the door opened for us.

The wait was not long. Two men in olive fatigues came to the door. Both had weapons but they weren't drawn. They opened the door three-quarters of the way and one of them stepped out onto the landing. Mel had closed the room of the facing door again, and the man turned to look down the landing. I was crouching on his side of the doorframe, down low, hard against the wall, and the Druze walked right past me, his thigh almost brushing against my nose. If he had stopped there, I would have been the one to take him out, but he took one more step, into Chuck's range, before noticing something was wrong.

Chuck finished him with a classic knife attack. He grabbed the man's collar and twisted hard, dragging him downwards, choking, with his throat exposed. The movement almost drags the throat onto the knife, and Chuck sliced the windpipe and the main artery in a single cut. The second man never had time to work out what was happening. As he stepped out, Lundin came up off the floor and finished him just as neatly. It was a brilliant little piece of close-quarter combat but it had to have been seen from inside the room.

I was on the wrong side of the door to see exactly what was happening but Bill described it to me later. There was an armchair facing the door, with another Druze sitting in it, his leg dangling over the arm. When the second man at the door was knifed, the one in the chair saw him disappear from sight in the frame of the doorway. He swung his leg off the arm of the chair and stood up in a panic gesture that immediately started some confusion in the room. The Druze inside advanced towards the doorway, but all I could see at this point was Bill Lundin signalling to me, 'One coming. I will deal.' The Lebanese made Bill's job easy. He had a weapon but he came forward too uncertainly. The men in this room were all obviously commanders, not frontline militiamen hardened by constant street-fighting who would have reacted differently. The Lebanese was confused about what to expect on the landing. He had not seen the man killed, just his figure disappearing too quickly. Instead of coming out crisply, with his weapon aimed, and with someone else to give him back-up, he stepped out with a submachine gun loose in his hands and Bill shot him before he was over the threshold.

He fell, half blocking the doorway, and that was our signal for the final attack. No orders were given or needed; each man's task had been assigned in advance. Mel Becklin's job was to isolate the kidnap target and get him out of our field of fire. Ours was to kill everyone else, hesitating only long enough for Mel to deal with his Syrian.

I went in first, with Mel right behind me. There were seven people in the room, most of them on the right-hand side, grouped by a curious extra-long office-type sofa which ran the length of most of one wall, behind a low table.

The Syrian major was at the right-hand end. Becklin lunged for him, and smothered him in a flying tackle. I started to take care of the rest of the men along the sofa. The MP5 has a thirty-round magazine and I rippled it down the sofa, not in free fire, but in controlled bursts. picking up three Druze and the remaining Syrian lieutenant. I fred from a crouch and the force of the bullets threw the men bodily against the sofa. When you're hit by a burst of 9mm Teflon-coated ammunition, you don't stay still. The impact seemed to be sending them climbing up the back of the sofa, and with the force of Becklin's struggle with the Syrian at one end, the whole thing tipped over backwards.

Over to my right, the man who had been shot in the doorway was dying noisily. As I turned to make sure he was covered even in his death throes, I saw the last Druze die with a single shot between the eyes. I did not even know who fired it – Chuck or Roger Moule – but if the Druze had been more combat-ready, he could have been the one to cause us casualties. He was on his own, in a chair behind the door, with an AK-47 assault rifle beside him, but he had not even tried properly to reach for it. He died with his hands above him, in a feeble gesture that was half surrender, half horror at the sight of the five figures who had burst into the room. It is hard to convey the speed of the operation. Less time separated his death from the others than it takes to write a sentence; to say that one died after the other means that it happened only split seconds later.

That left the Syrian major. He was on the floor behind the overturned sofa with Becklin astride him, and though he was not fit and combat-tuned, he was putting up the kind of struggle you somehow manage when you know you are fighting for your life. When it was obvious that Becklin hadn't got full control of him, Bill Lundin went over the sofa after them and got a knife to the Syrian's throat. I could see them clearly from where I was standing now and it took only an exchange of glances between Bill and myself for him to know what to do. There was no way we were going to get the Syrian out alive. We could already hear people stirring below, obviously disturbed by the noise we had made, even though it had mostly been muted. All the gun-shots had been silent but the scuffling and the falling sofa were enough to raise the alarm. We could still try to fight our way downwards through the building, but it would be a very high-risk exfiltration, made even more messy by having the Syrian in tow. Whether we drugged him, as planned, or knocked him unconscious for a quicker result would make little differ-ence. He would still be too big a liability in the firefight that would break out below. So far, we had done a lot of very effective damage and taken no casualties; if we wanted to keep it that way, our only way out was back the way we had come, over the roof, and there was no way of taking the Syrian over the grappling line.

None of this was said, nor did it need to be. Bill Lundin and I think the same way. He gave me one glance to ask and I gave him one back to answer. Lundin seized the Syrian's head and cut his throat with a single sweep of the SEAL knife.

If we were to get out without a full-scale firefight, we had only seconds to get back to the roof, but there were a lot of tempting items on the table which we could not leave behind. We had obviously interrupted a planning ses-sion and there were maps and documents and files spread out over the table, and eight big black and white photographs, some of them of men in Lebanese army uniform. Bill scooped the whole lot up into a canvas case that was lying on the floor. The gesture took barely thirty seconds and we were off and moving, doubling back silently up towards the roof, with me leading and Chuck and Moule covering the stairs behind us.

There was more noise below now, but no one had started to come up the stairs yet and when we got to the landing under the roof, both the doors of the rooms where the men were sleeping were still closed. We thought we were clear, but there was a situation I had not anticipated when we got to the roof. I stopped to check that the whole team was moving up steadily, and Lundin went out onto the roof ahead of me. When I was satisfied everything was in good order, I went out after him, but suddenly he crouched down and waved me back into the doorway. In the darkness, at the far end of the parapet, mercifully well clear of our grappling rope, there were two men, chatting and smoking cigarettes. We had no idea where they had come from but they weren't guards and did not appear to have weapons. Despatching them looked straightforward enough but it had to be done quickly before real trouble came up from below.

Once again we went into a combat routine that needed no orders beyond a single signal from Bill Lundin. He moved forward quietly and crouched behind the water tank, the only cover between us and the two men. When he was in position he made a sign for someone to speak. That meant Becklin, our only Arabic speaker, and I motioned him forward. Mel assessed the situation, then stood up, leaving his weapon out of sight beside the doorframe. We could hear the noise below growing even louder and Mel pretended that we had come up to warn the men on the roof. He stepped out boldly, called to the men in Arabic, then made an urgent gesture for them to come quickly. The men hesitated. Mel gestured again and the two men started to hurry across the rooftop. Lundin's timing was perfect. He let the first man go past, then came out behind the second one, reached an arm round his throat and finished him with a knife as he dragged him down onto the surface of the roof. At almost the same moment, I had my knife into the front man. I literally charged at him from the shadow of the doorway and he ran into the blade.

The beautiful thing about a Special Forces team in action is that all the functions are carried out with each member assuming the others will cope with their particular task. During the time that Lundin and I were dealing with the men on the rooftop, Becklin was covering us, and Chuck and Roger Moule were ignoring us and getting on with their final task. They were laying explosive charges on the last section of the staircase and around the door to the roof. They just assumed that we would handle our problem, and when they looked out and saw that we had, they set timing devices for detonation in five minutes and we sprinted back to where the rope was still stretched over to our own building.

We were well over to the other side and down in the basement of our building when the charges went off, and from that moment on, as we had anticipated, chaos really broke loose.

When an explosion goes off in the upper part of a building in Beirut, everyone's first thought is that it is shellfire. That means that more shells are likely to fall in the same area and there is a massive scramble to get out of the vicinity. I knew it would not take long for enough confusion to develop to cover our exfiltration but I wanted to be certain that the figures in the street were confused and not a team of Druze militiamen coming out of the headquarters building in a state of combat readiness, looking for us.

As it turned out, there was more chaos than anyone had a right to hope for. The explosions on the roof of the headquarters had obviously woken the sleepers directly underneath them, and in a very short time shooting had broken out. God knows who was shooting at what. Maybe in the general panic the people on the top floor thought the militiamen rushing up from below were coming to attack them. We never found out and it didn't really matter. Soon the street was full of people and everyone was too busy trying to get out of the way of the shelling to worry about us. We went out singly, mingling with the running figures, and stopped when we were three blocks away. It was time for our last little trick.

During the day that we had spent observing the Druze headquarters we had placed explosive charges in the base of our own building, to be detonated not by a timing device, but by a remote radio signal. I had the transmitter myself and I have to admit that I felt a huge sense of relief as I detonated the final explosion. The size of the charge was a bit of overkill. It totally demolished the front and side of the building and left no one in any doubt that their area of the city was coming under heavy shellfire.

We watched the bang, then headed south, staying close to the cover of buildings, until we were well out of sight of the Druze headquarters. We regrouped in the doorway of a ruined building, took off our combat equipment, wiped our faces enough so as to look dirty without being obviously blackened up, put on our canvas anoraks and headed back to our base point – a pharmacist's shop in the centre of the city which the C.I.A. used for covert operations.

The aftermath of the operation revealed some interesting insights into the underside of the civil war in Lebanon. After a quick debriefing and some warm thanks from Tom Udall, I was shuttled out of Green Beach and was on a flight from Larnaca to Geneva within a few hours. It is always a sound move for a mercenary to get right away from the scene of a mission, just in case there is a security leak, but when I came back a few weeks later, I was given a full report of what we had achieved.

The C.I.A. people were disappointed at first that we did not get the Syrian major out alive, but as Tom Udall said to me drily on my return, 'They just had to be goddamn well satisfied with you taking out the whole Druze leadership in the area, and three top Syrians, as well as kicking shit out of their headquarters.'

The Agency got over its disappointment quickly when they analysed the material we had seized from the tabletop. What the Syrians had been planning was the defection of Druze officers in the Lebanese army when the militiamen made their final assault on President Gemayel's forces. The photographs were all of Druze officers in government units. The papers showed that they were all committed to defect, bringing their Druze men with them, and the photographs were to identify them to the militia to ensure the deal went off smoothly. The defection of the Druze in the army was the permanent nightmare of the Lebanese President and of the Americans; it was a move that would mean inevitable and certain defeat for the army.

The end for the Americans in Lebanon came less than three months later, but not before I had carried out one more special assignment for Tom Udall. In early December 1983, barely a month after the raid on the Druze headquarters, two American fighter aircraft were shot down over Lebanon. The way the story came out in the press was that they were striking at Syrian and Druze positions in the Shouf mountains as a reprisal for the October suicide bombing of the Marine garrison. World reaction was generally critical. Two planes lost in exchange for slight damage to the position did not seem a very efficient act of vengeance. What no journalist ever found out – and in fact most of the U.S. command in Lebanon never knew either – was that while the planes were in the air, U.S. Special Forces hit teams, two of them led by Bill Lundin and Mel Becklin, were carrying out much more efficient and devastating reprisal raids, using the air attack as a diversion.

Hussein's intelligence network had again been at work. The Marines in the garrison had been getting increasingly jittery at the accuracy of some of the shelling of their lines. Hussein had picked up word that the Syrians were helping the militias set up forward observation posts, which were using sophisticated Swiss and Swedish equipment to target the Americans. I was called back in, this time for a solo mission to pinpoint these forward observation posts. I located all eight of them and provided Udall with details of the positions, the manning strengths, and suggested routes for his men to attack by. I was out of Lebanon again before the attacks took place, but the Special Forces teams got seven out of the eight. How important they were was underlined soon afterwards when three Marines were killed by a mortar round targeted from the one O.P. they missed.

That one was a really worthwhile reprisal, but the military public relations people judged it prudent not to expose it. Special Forces raids of that kind – however effective – are just too sensitive to mention. In the crazy world of Middle East politics, Washington was happier to take the flak for a mickey-mouse air raid, rather than uncover the realities of Lebanese warfare!

After that, I had only one more call from Tom Udall. This time, it wasn't a summons, it was more of a call for reassurance. Speaking in the veiled language we had developed to a fine art form, Tom told me he was facing a serious dilemma. He had ordered an intelligence-gathering raid and it had gone wrong and he had lost three operators. That was bad enough but there was worse to come. They had not just been killed, they had been butchered, deliberately mutilated in the most obscene ways. Now, Lebanese intelligence had warned the Americans that the Druze were planning to expose them to the press to show the world what happened to American troops who penetrated Druze territory. The question was: should Tom risk more men to try to go in and get them? Because he knew I could tune in to his soldier's conscience, Tom wanted to talk it through with me, but I knew he had really made his decision to go already. Anyway, I agreed that there was no choice. 'You've got a day.' I said. 'Go in. Do it.' And he did. A team got the bodies out and in the process did some brutal revenge killing to show the Druze that not all Americans were naive. That kind of revenge makes sense to any professional fighting man. The message was clear: the Special Forces were not suitable targets for acts of personal savagery.

To me it was a sign that the Special Forces, at least, were learning properly the hard lesson of Middle East warfare. But it was all to no purpose in the end. There was no escaping from the fact that the American presence in Lebanon was both pointless and untenable and that Washington could not possibly shore up a Lebanese army which was as factionally split as the rest of the country.

When the Syrian-backed militias did launch their final attack on Beirut, one of the saddest and most ridiculous features of the final political writhing was the assurances coming out of Washington that the Druze in the army would remain loyal to President Gemayel, despite the appeals from the militias to throw down their arms, that Druze should not fight against Druze. As I listened to the radio reports in Geneva and London, I thought about the photographs we had taken out of the Druze headquarters three months earlier. The deal had already been struck then. The intelligence data we had gathered had been analysed and re-analysed, and checked with the Israelis. Everyone knew it was going to happen: the Lebanese knew and so did the Americans. But, to the end, the protestations continued – right up to the time in February 1984 when President Reagan formally announced, under mounting pressure from Congress, that the American involvement in Lebanon was over.

THREE

F-TROOP OF 21 S.A.S.

Though I really enjoy serving with the U.S. Special Forces, I am still most at ease with the Special Air Service. It is, after all, my own regiment, but that apart, I do believe they are the elite among Special Forces units and deserve their international reputation. I have always been too much of a loner to need the support of regimental structures and traditions, but, in military terms, the nearest I ever get to feeling that I am 'coming home' is when I walk into the Duke of York's barracks in Chelsea's fashionable King's Road, the London headquarters of the S.A.S.

The army word that sums up the atmosphere of an S.A.S. unit is that it is tight. There is a great feeling of strength and professionalism; I know of nowhere else where there is such a sense that every last man knows his business. The atmosphere of a typical American unit makes an interesting comparison. It is altogether looser, and friendly almost to the point of being chummy. The friendliness is fine, but people behave in the kind of extroverted, hearty way that makes you feel conspicuous when you have to join the unit for whatever reason – and there is no quicker way to make a Special Forces operative feel uneasy.

When I used to go into the American mess in Beirut, for example, I had to put a lot of effort just into keeping a low profile. As soon as I stepped up to the bar, there would be shouts of 'Hey, Gayle, how's it going? Great to see you. What are you drinking?' Often the greetings and the glad-handing would come from other Special Forces people, who should have known better. The Special Forces personnel were already held in awe by other members of the mess and when I was seen to be on such intimate terms with them, it just made people who didn't know me more curious, and they would immediately start speculating – or even asking – what I was doing there.

That sort of behaviour is inconceivable in an S.A.S. unit. When I walk into the mess at the Duke of York's barracks, the welcome is very different. The mess is on the first floor of the main building, overlooking the parade ground. It is quite simply furnished and decorated with photographs of the S.A.S. in the desert during the Second World War and pictures of the regiment's founding figures. At the bar, the steward will say, 'Good evening, Sir. What are you drinking tonight?' and his tone will be the same whether you were in the night before or whether he hasn't seen you for six months. If there is a group of people drinking at the bar, you don't interrupt them and they don't break off. If there is someone in the group you know well, he will probably come over, after a minute or two, for a quick exchange of greetings.

'Hello, Gayle. Good to see you. Everything fine?'

'Yes, fine.'

'Good. I'll talk to you later.'

Then he will go back to the group, leaving you to drink alone until he is ready to join you. It may sound colder than the American welcome, but in fact it gives you a feeling of being instantly part of the unit. The yelling down the bar in an American mess is well meant, but I am much more comfortable with the reserved atmosphere of the Duke of York's. It comes, more than anything, from the fact that there are no impressionable people in the S.A.S., and it is part of the regiment's ingrained professional style never to draw undue attention to your presence.

I first walked into the Duke of York's in 1975. After Vietnam, I lived in South Africa, building up my own aviation and air freight company and getting involved in covert activities in various parts of southern Africa, Europe and the Middle East – of which more later. Then, in 1975, I moved the headquarters of my businesses to Switzerland and started to operate out of London. Immediately, I was invited to enlist in the S.A.S. reserve, in F-troop of the 21st S.A.S. Regiment.

There are two types of reserve in the S.A.S. The Duke of York's barracks is the headquarters of the 21st S.A.S. Regiment. They are reservists, and although they are much more proficient and highly-trained than the kind of civilian amateurs who make up most conventional reserve units, they are still reservists, there primarily to be called to the colours in time of war, when the S.A.S. needs to be expanded rapidly. F-troop, though part of 21 S.A.S., is very different. It is made up of men who have served as regulars with 22 S.A.S. or, like me, with the Commonwealth S.A.S. There are few exceptionally gifted territorials who take their reserve service so seriously that they are prepared to adapt their civilian life completely to accommodate it. F-troop, however, is a kind of second string to the S.A.S. bow. It is used to absorb men with special expertise and to maintain a group of S.A.S. people who are circulating in civilian life. Some members of F-troop are in government; others are well placed in business and the professions and can be used for intelligence-gathering and to provide links with departments and organizations where the S.A.S. wants a private network of contacts to ensure efficient liaison. At the same time, they are kept tuned to S.A.S. standards, through the vehicle of 21 S.A.S., and can be integrated with regulars on special assignments even while still reservists.

I joined F-troop as a trooper, having held the rank of captain in regular service, but it is important to understand that the S.A.S.'s attitude to rank is
very different from the line regiments. Often the S.A.S. fight in small units
and an S.A.S. patrol which can operate for weeks or months on its own,
undertaking major tasks, may well have no officer with it. The unit commander on an operation is referred to as 'boss'; otherwise, people are called
simply 'mister' or their first name. Traditionally, the only person addressed
by his rank is the parade sergeant. He will call you 'Sir' on the parade
ground, but often in that special sarcastic and derogatory way normally
reserved for officer cadets.

I found that out very early during my time at the Duke of York's. I was due
to go on a weekend exercise in the Brecon Beacons, the mountains in Wales
close to the S.A.S. depot at Hereford, and I drove across London on Friday
evening to report. I arrived a bit late and I dashed into the barracks, put on
my kit, and raced down to the parade ground. The unit was already on the
square doing a parade march and I waited until they came to a halt, then
went over and took my place. You could have heard the sergeant's bellow in
Paris!

He yelled at the squad to double round the square and shouted, 'Rivers,
you come to me.' When I reached him, he put his nose a couple of inches
from my face and screamed, 'Just who do you think you are, Sir, joining a
parade without reporting to *me*?' I felt like saying, 'Look, you silly bastard,
I've just been sorting out a problem with a half-million-pound air freight
consignment to South America, and I got caught in a traffic jam and, anyway, I was only five minutes late.' But I said nothing, except, 'Yes,
Sergeant.' You take it, because it is the regimental protocol, and has a purpose.

The important difference between the S.A.S. and other units, though, is
that this kind of parade-ground bullshit does not carry over away from the
square. A few hours later that same night, I was climbing up into the back of
a truck in the mountains. I reached to grab the knotted rope and the same
sergeant offered me his hand instead. I just grinned and ignored it and said
something sharp about 'parade-ground idiots', and everyone laughed,
including the sergeant. In the S.A.S., you are judged by your competence
and fighting skills, not by notions of rank and class. As an officer, you are
apart on formal parades and in the mess. In action, you are completely integrated and social distinctions become meaningless.

The exercise in the Brecon Beacons was one of a series I went on – in
Wales, Scotland and once with N.A.T.O. troops in Denmark – partly to keep
me current with S.A.S. techniques and partly to fulfil my statutory reserve
obligation, but the reserve commitment was simply a way of getting me back
on the S.A.S. books. Like other members of F-troop, my skills were used to
the full and it wasn't long before I was involved in active operations in

Northern Ireland. I still drove across London at five o'clock on Friday afternoons but by midnight, instead of practising mountain warfare on some Welsh rockface, I would be buried under the turf of 'bandit country' in South Armagh, hunting I.R.A. terrorists in what they regarded as their safest stronghold. On several occasions, too, the S.A.S. had no inhibitions about linking up with my civilian activities when it suited their purpose.

The Special Forces world is a bit like a goldfish bowl. To outsiders it is completely closed and breaches of security are extremely rare, but insiders know each other's strengths and track records, and the regiment knew quite a lot about what I had been doing since Vietnam. They also knew that I was dealing in specialized military equipment and several times they became my customers. I would supply the equipment, brief S.A.S. personnel to use it and, sometimes, go on proving missions to demonstrate its use in active-service conditions.

Ironically, the only equipment-supply mission that gave me a real headache was one of the most routine ones. It began with an informal approach from Hereford for some equipment which the S.A.S wanted to purchase completely outside normal army channels. I agreed to supply it and deliver it clandestinely to Northern Ireland. As cover, it was arranged that I should make a routine delivery of a new car to a well-known showroom on the Falls Road in Belfast – with the equipment hidden, unknown to the dealership, in part of the boot.

It was to be a very simple exercise. To the dealers, I was just one of the band of casual drivers who delivered new vehicles from the mainland for a fee. I got the car into Belfast all right and into the showroom, after working hours, one Saturday evening.

Three S.A.S. operatives made contact to take delivery of the equipment, but unfortunately the I.R.A. was in a phase of hitting 'economic targets' and by pure coincidence they chose to hit the car dealership that night. A bomb blew out the whole of the front of the showroom, burying the car with its equipment under a mountain of rubble. Within minutes army Saracens were roaring up and down the Falls Road. Gangs of kids started pelting the armoured cars with stones. The army responded with tear gas, and before we knew where we were, we were caught in the middle of a full-scale riot. It wouldn't have looked too good if four S.A.S. characters had emerged from the ruins – especially as we were on a mission that had not been cleared by the army H.Q. anyway – so we went into deep hiding and spent the entire weekend holed up in the remains of the car showroom, waiting for the bomb disposal experts and police to finish cleaning up the area. Eventually, we got the equipment out and safely into the hands of an S.A.S. unit, but there are pleasanter ways of spending a weekend – even in Belfast!

Over the years, the S.A.S. has used me from time to time and in various ways. The regiment's great strength is its flexibility. It is not bound by conventional attitudes and army procedures. I have served them as a regular, as a reservist and, in effect, as a mercenary. In the S.A.S. I am never treated as a civilian, or as an outsider. There have been occasions – which I will come to later – when I have chosen for my own reasons to put myself outside the S.A.S.,and others when I have been temporarily frozen out, quite deliberately, to test the strength of my loyalty to the regiment. Those occasions apart, once you are S.A.S., you are always S.A.S. Also, not only have I been used by them as a civilian, I have actually used S.A.S. personnel on covert missions that I have undertaken as a mercenary – as long as the missions have had the tacit approval of the regiment and the British government.

The form is well established. The S.A.S. soldier is granted leave and takes the train home to Edinburgh or Lincoln, but somehow ends up in action in the Iranian desert. It goes without saying that if anything goes wrong on these missions the regiment is competely mystified as to why the operative isn't fly-fishing or playing with his children.

Ex-S.A.S. people are also infiltrated into Northern Ireland, and elsewhere, quite separately from the S.A.S. regulars who serve under cover during their colour service. Some of these agents may have left the S.A.S. years previously. In any event, they go into deep cover and are allowed to 'sleep' undisturbed for long periods, before being activated. They are completely disconnected from the regiment and often, in fact frequently, their existence is unknown to other branches of the intelligence community.

Sometimes, too, the S.A.S. maintains its links with former members of the regiment for other reasons. I know of cases where Hereford had decided to bring one of its men 'back in from the cold' for his own good and for the good of the regiment. One man in particular comes to mind. He left the S.A.S. after eleven years' service as a regular, but civilian life turned sour for him, his marriage broke up and he started drifting around the fringes of the Special Forces world, operating as a semi-mercenary and becoming involved in ventures that were definitely not approved of by the covert community. Pressure was put on him and he was put back on the S.A.S. payroll, through the medium of F-troop, and sent into Northern Ireland under cover. He was eventually killed there, but he died 'in the fold', doing something the S.A.S. considered worthwhile. For most former S.A.S. operatives, however, no such pressure is needed. Most will go to any lengths to retain the respect of the regiment and I have known men who would rather put a pistol in their mouths than be kicked out of the Hereford brotherhood.

In the past decade, though, Northern Ireland has created a lot of regimental disillusionment. These days, the public associates the S.A.S. with the Falklands and the storming of the Iranian embassy – both brilliant operations which have sealed the regiment's current glamorous image. But Northern Ireland is still the S.A.S.'s bread-and-butter war and, generally speaking, its members detest it. The S.A.S. doesn't hate Northern Ireland because it can't handle it, but because it feels it isn't being allowed to handle it. One word sums up the S.A.S.'s attitude to the fight against I.R.A. terrorism: frustration.

The S.A.S.'s troubles in Northern Ireland really started under the Labour Government between 1974 and 1976. It began by asking the S.A.S. to crack down hard on the I.R.A. The S.A.S. responded with enthusiasm. It put fighting patrols on the border with the Irish Republic, which the I.R.A. was crossing with impunity, using the South as a safe haven. The S.A.S. teams set up ultra-sophisticated infra-red and audio surveillance, and before long they were able to observe not only the gun-running across the border, but also active-service unit meetings in the border area, attended by leaders who slipped over from the South to give their orders, then retreated into the Republic again. The S.A.S. started identifying the leaders, as well as some of the principal assassins and bomb-makers; then they started going after them.

It was then, to put it bluntly, that the government panicked. The crackdown had been very hush-hush. The government wanted the credit without risking criticism from the liberal and civil rights lobbies. There were a couple of incidents in which S.A.S. patrols 'strayed' over the border into the Republic while pursuing an I.R.A. terror squad, and another in which an I.R.A. bomber was shot dead during an ambush. The civil rights lobby cried foul play.

The outcome was a complete reversal of official policy. Suddenly, the government would not even admit that the S.A.S. was in South Armagh. Operational directives were given that the S.A.S. was to be used only for intelligence-gathering; there were to be no ambushes or other active operations. If an S.A.S. patrol came into contact with an I.R.A. unit, they were not to engage them. They were to watch them, then call in whichever army unit was officially operating in the area at the time.

The results were chaotic. As often as not, the regular forces were green and inexperienced, on their first four-month tour of duty in Northern Ireland, on rotation from West Germany. The S.A.S. would locate a band of I.R.A. terrorists, watch it for a couple of days, then, to prevent them from slipping across the border, they would call in the Green Howards or the Grenadier Guards – whatever regular unit was serving in the area. Suddenly, a very effective operation would be in the hands of an inexperienced young subaltern who would bring in a heli-borne platoon too noisily and too late, and the terrorists would be away to safety in Southern Ireland with the S.A.S. watching helplessly from the sidelines.

For a while, the S.A.S. tried to go it alone. I went on one patrol personally – and I was aware of several others – where a cold decision was taken to carry out an ambush, and take no prisoners. Once I.R.A. terrorists were conclusively identified, they were engaged in a firefight and eliminated.

That phase did not last long and it was the regiment's high command who put a stop to it. That kind of activity is only a step away from 'freelancing' – that's the technical term for when a unit steps outside the protection of the government and operates on its own initiative. 'Let's get the bastard,' someone says, 'he's got away with too much for too long.' Freelancing can destroy a regiment, as the commanders well know. They cracked down internally, and word came down that patrols really were to be for intelligence-gathering only. The S.A.S. operatives on the ground complied, and it brought them right into the middle of one of the dirtiest private wars in Northern Ireland – the war between different factions of the intelligence community.

Intelligence is a world of egos and empires, and virtually every branch was active in Northern Ireland: MI5, MI6, the Intelligence Corps, the Royal Ulster Constabulary Special Branch, the military police, the intelligence officers of individual regiments, and countless small special units; the list is endless.

Intelligence-gathering is a self-perpetuating process. In collecting intelligence, you inevitably allow terrorist acts to happen that you could prevent – but only if you pull the agent out to safety first. But the intelligence bureaucracy is reluctant to pull out a good agent because, though it may prevent the I.R.A. operation and save some lives, its agent can't be put back, and someone else's empire will move into the ascendancy. So they always allow 'just one more operation' before turning off the tap. Also, S.A.S. intelligence-gathering was too efficient. It created jealousies and resentment, and when the information was fed into the general mill, it was dissipated and distorted and never resulted in decisive action.

The other problem with intelligence-gathering is that once it becomes really effective, the politicians are unable, or unwilling, to cope with the information, because it requires of them too much direct and controversial action. Most politicians are terrified of what Northern Ireland can do to their careers. They try as far as possible to ignore the information; they don't want to be told how really to get stuck into the problem of eliminating terrorism, Catholic and Protestant, in the Province, because they are afraid of the possible liberal electoral backlash to strong action.

By 1983, the I.R.A. should never have been in a position to place a bomb outside Harrods department store during the Christmas rush. In security terms, the cell structure which allowed that bombing to take place could have been destroyed long before, but the political will to grasp the nettle was never there.

Members of the S.A.S. never talk politics with outsiders, but inside the regiment you can fairly say that there is clear consensus that the I.R.A. could be destroyed in two weeks – if the S.A.S. were given a free hand. I do not mean that the S.A.S. are fascist killers who want to form death squads to eliminate people whose political views they disagree with. I mean simply that they need authority to make war on the I.R.A. on exactly the same basis as the I.R.A. makes war on the general public and the British army.

When you are operating with the S.A.S. on the ground in an area like South Armagh, you very quickly realize that you are fighting a war, not taking part in a police operation. Night after night, you lie in your hide, watching I.R.A. active-service units infiltrating from the safety of the South or moving around freely in areas they have made safe for themselves by murder, torture, knee-cappings and other intimidation. They are using sophisticated weapons, right up to heavy machine-guns, rocket launchers, landmines and massive quantities of explosives. Through studio surveillance, you listen to the planning sessions at which the orders are given for acts of sabotage that will involve indiscriminate civilian casualties.

Civilian police procedures cannot deal with this kind of threat. If you locate a team of men who are in the process of organizing an attack on a shopping centre with milk churns packed with high explosives and nails, you send a fighting patrol to attack it, you don't call the local bobby, any more than you would if you had located a Nazi commando unit in the Second World War, especially since none of the very accurate information produced by military surveillance techniques is admissible as evidence in a court of law.

Yet despite the thousands of acts of violence committed by both Catholic and Protestant sides, the S.A.S. has never enjoyed being put truly on a war footing, and as a result the level of frustration within the regiment has continued to rise.

I was a perfect barometer of the frustration level because my S.A.S. colleagues knew that I carried out mercenary operations and, to put it simply, the worse the situation in Northern Ireland seemed to them, the more often I was approached by people looking to buy themselves out and work as mercenaries. In one of the worst years, 1978, I was approached by the leader of a Pagoda squad, whose entire team wanted to quit the S.A.S. and offer themselves as a mercenary unit. A Pagoda squad is a team – of the type used to break the Iranian embassy siege – trained for selective shooting under duress, and it is so highly trained that its members fight, move and think, in fact virtually exist, as a single entity. This particular squad was so angry at the frustrations of Northern Ireland that they had asked their leader to sound me out to see if I could find them work guarding a sultan or doing security operations for a foreign government or an oil company.

At one stage, around September 1976, it looked as though the situation might improve. Roy Mason became Secretary of State for Northern Ireland, after having been Defence Secretary. He was popular with the forces and he promised a tough new line, in contrast to the inconclusive truce that had dragged on through most of 1975, handicapping the security forces without making any significant impact on the level of violence. Mason stepped up army undercover activity against the paramilitaries and officially 'permitted' the S.A.S. to operate throughout Northern Ireland, instead of only in South Armagh, responding to an upsurge in the number of sectarian killings and bomb attacks on civilian targets.

On the ground, though, the freedom was less impressive. In October 1976 I went on a special operation in Northern Ireland which could have ended up with the S.A.S. taking serious casualties because of a decision in London to tie its hands in mid-operation. It was an operation that tells the frustrations of the S.A.S. in Northern Ireland in one single, infuriating episode.

FOUR

A FOXHOLE IN SOUTH ARMAGH

The S.A.S.'s mission was to follow up on intelligence collected by a deep-cover in-country agent in Northern Ireland. He was a young doctor and, like most successful agents, he was of Irish descent. All the intelligence services search desperately for suitable men and women with family and, if possible, cross-border connections in Ireland since in areas like South Armagh and other I.R.A. strongholds, Britons arouse automatic suspicion.

The doctor had British nationality, but his father was Irish and their family had lived in South Armagh for generations. He had been selected for training in intelligence after his medical studies in England, and though he was not S.A.S. he had completed selection at Hereford. He had been back in South Armagh for almost two years, and was now a junior doctor in a big country practice that covered the sprawling farming area. For the first year he had been left to 'sleep'. Nothing had been required of him except to settle in the community, and he had managed to do this in a way that was possible only for a local man. Then, nine months before the operation, he had been activated and had begun to feed intelligence data about I.R.A. terrorist activities in the area – information that was priceless because this particular tightly-knit farming community had proved one of the most difficult to penetrate of all the I.R.A.'s home grounds.

About ten days before the operation he had warned London that an I.R.A. meeting was to take place, and the S.A.S. had been ordered to organize detailed surveillance. My role was to join the patrol as a 'guest', and provide some surveillance equipment of a kind that had never before been used in Northern Ireland. It was material that I was marketing outside Britain, and when the S.A.S. had learned about it, they had salivated politely and indicated that they would like to try it out unofficially. Using independent funds, they bought one set on an experimental basis and I agreed to help them put it to the test entirely unofficially, staying well outside army purchasing procedures to avoid possible security leaks and to enable them to get their hands on the kit quickly.

The equipment really was quite extraordinary; in the decade since, it has needed very little updating despite the amazing advances in electronic techniques. Stripped of the technical jargon, the equipment provides audio and visual surveillance over a distance of more than two kilometres. It can operate by day and by night, providing twenty-four-hour real-time surveillance, with images so sharp that it is like watching a T.V. programme, and with the facility to videotape anything that is wanted on record. The equipment is in two parts. One part consists of a camera, microphones, miniature transmitter and aerials which can be dispersed in the target area for better concealment. The operator's end consists of a keyboard with combined audio and visual controls, the videotape recording unit and a visual display unit (V.D.U.), all constructed to rugged military specifications and contained in one portable case.

It was decided that an S.A.S. patrol would move into the area to set up the camera and microphones three days before the I.R.A. meeting was due. I would join them later, bringing the more bulky keyboard, recording unit and V.D.U., and take overall charge of the surveillance end of the operation. The meeting was to be held at an old farmhouse in South Armagh, about fifteen kilometres from the border with the Irish Republic. I decided to go in through Southern Ireland, entering the Republic as a civilian businessman, then take the equipment across the border and join up with the patrol.

At the time, I was doing a lot of non-military business in Southern Ireland and one of my regular contacts was the managing director of an electronics firm who operated what amounted to a research laboratory at his large country home not far from Longford, just south of the border. The country house was almost a castle and the owner was a private flying enthusiast who had made his own airstrip in the castle grounds. I flew over regularly, using a Rockwell Turbo-Commander executive aircraft and I decided to fly to the castle, do a little business, then take a fishing trip which would allow me to stray over the border.

Put like that, it sounds almost pleasant, but infiltration in that area is not easy. Border-crossing was one of the most sensitive political issues of the period, with the Irish government constantly being accused of laxity in controlling the activities of I.R.A. terrorists. Infiltrating successfully meant running the gauntlet of special patrols by the Garda, the Irish police, on the south side, and of the I.R.A. and random British patrols to the north. Even being caught by the British would have been a serious failure as it would have drawn very unwelcome attention to an S.A.S. operation, not to mention the possibility of damaging publicity to a very secret side of anti-terrorist activities in the area.

The S.A.S. briefed me well on routes but the one they selected for me meant a ten-kilometre night march, most of it in very hostile country with a great many potential watching eyes. Also, there was the weather. Operations in Northern Ireland always seem to be carried out when it is wet, very wet, or wet enough to drown in, and conditions when I left my rented car on the southern side of the border were somewhere on a scale between rotten and disgusting, with rain drifting over the fields and the ground underfoot sodden and thick with mud in many places. The first part of the infiltration, at least, had gone very smoothly; the castle owner was out of the country on business but there had been no objection to my using the airstrip and I had even managed a useful chat with his deputy about a possible contract before setting off on my supposed few days' holiday.

My rendezvous with the S.A.S. patrol was to be made at a map reference in open country, with almost no landmarks, well away from any habitation or commonly-used transport routes. Because of the weather and the need for silent movement, the crossing took much of the night, but though I reached the rendezvous point in darkness, well before dawn, as I had anticipated, no one made contact. I knew the patrol would be there, watching me through infra-red, image-intensifying glasses. I just hunkered down, burying myself in the sodden turf, and waited. The patrol waited also – in fact they left me alone for the next day, watching me throughout to make sure I had been neither followed nor spotted by I.R.A. observers. Unlike less experienced units, the S.A.S. never forgets that South Armagh is the I.R.A.'s true home turf. They own it, they know every inch of it, and their intelligence – based on the loyalty of some locals and the intimidation of others – is superb.

After more than twelve hours, contact was judged to be safe and I was met by two members of the four-man fighting patrol who were carrying out the operation. They took me to join the patrol commander, a young warrant officer I had never worked with personally before, and the fourth man, a sergeant I did know from Hereford.

Immediately, we moved on to the farm to set up the equipment. The meeting was due in two days but it was standard I.R.A. procedure to infiltrate cell members in ones and twos, sometimes well in advance.

The group was to meet, according to the doctor, in a tractor shed behind the main farm buildings, and the patrol had already scouted the area and set up the camera and audio bugs. It had not been possible to conceal the camera inside the shed, but bugs had been placed to give full audio surveillance of the conversations, and the camera and transmitter were positioned within sight of the entrance to the shed, to give clear pictures of the movements in and out.

I set up my end of the equipment just below the cloud line of a hill overlooking the farm. The weather conditions were still vile, with mist collecting in pockets around the low-lying farm buildings, but we managed to get near-perfect pictures, which impressed even the singularly unimpressionable patrol commander.

We established our own positions in individual foxholes, spaced out over the hilltop in such a way that we could change places under reasonable cover, and operate the surveillance keyboard in shifts. During the first twenty-four hours of the surveillance there were no serious snags, but we did have our first surprise of the mission; the meeting looked like being a much larger one than had been anticipated. The doctor's intelligence report had led us to expect two key I.R.A. figures at the meeting, including one coming in from over the border, but before long we had clocked ten arrivals at the farmhouse, including three I.R.A. commanders and three known bomb experts.

There was one man in the group whose presence would have surprised me even more had I known at the time who he was, but the S.A.S. operates on a strictly need-to-know basis and the patrol commander did not even hint that one of the other four men was a British traitor. I was told about him only months later; at the time, he just seemed to be another young I.R.A. terrorist, a slender, fair-haired youth in jeans and a leather jacket who could have been a farm worker or a mechanic. In fact, he was a British soldier, a corporal serving with a unit at Colchester in Essex, who was supposed to be in London on leave at the time. Eight months later, he was dishonourably discharged after being sentenced to three years on a criminal charge which had nothing to do with his I.R.A. activities. He went to gaol never even knowing that he had been spotted several times in Northern Ireland.

The surveillance was also to yield a far bigger shock that no one, including the patrol commander, had anticipated. When the meeting actually started on the second day of the surveillance, one of the first items on the agenda was a discussion of whether our doctor was a British spy! Once again, I would never have known who our agent was if his name had not come up at the cell meetings. At the beginning of the mission, his identity was known only to the patrol commander and one other soldier, but once the I.R.A. started to talk about him, the whole situation changed.

At first, the doctor appeared to be under only passing suspicion, but soon the discussion turned to him in detail and it became obvious that he was close to being totally blown. Two weeks previously, an I.R.A. operation had been routed by the police and two people were being held for questioning. The I.R.A. had suspected an informer, and the doctor – it now appeared – was being exposed by nothing more sophisticated than farm gossip. By chat and cross-chat between I.R.A. members, I.R.A. sympathizers and ordinary locals, they had pieced together a list of people who might have known about the movements of the people on the aborted operation. The list grew shorter and shorter, and after an hour of argument in the tractor shed, it had been virtually narrowed down to the doctor. Once that happened, other suspicions were aired and the mood became more and more hostile.

The cell had no proof, but we knew that would not take long. 'It's time to pull the fucker in and have a few words with him,' was the verdict of the unit leader, and there was little chance the doctor would survive the kind of harsh interrogation that was the I.R.A.'s style.

The patrol commander than briefed us fully on the background, revealing to three of us for the first time that the doctor under discussion was our own man. Even as we talked, the man wearing the surveillance headphones reported that the gang was deciding how to pick up the doctor. He was to be summoned to a farm about eight kilometres away by an I.R.A. sympathizer who was ill, and two members of the meeting were going over to take him.

The patrol commander made an immediate decision. 'We're getting him out,' he said, 'and I'm going to ask for permission to destroy the cell.' In the security climate of the times, it was a decision that the patrol commander could not take alone, even though, in military terms, it was the right and obvious one. Fortunately, communications with Hereford were superb and, using standard codes, the commander put the request to the S.A.S. depot, using burst-transmission radio equipment. The contact with Hereford was completed in a few minutes but there was – as we knew there would be – a further delay to allow for a phone call from Hereford to London. Twenty minutes later, the coded answer came back: 'Extract the man. Leave the cell alone.'

It is not hard to imagine the effect the answer had on the morale of the patrol. When fighting men are trained to the pitch of the S.A.S., it is essential that they should have the satisfaction of what is known as 'mission closure'. They need to achieve a target, and they were being told yet again to walk away. Pulling out an agent is demoralizing enough, but the order amounted to being told as well to let ten I.R.A. hardliners, including six known killers, get on with their terrorist activities in peace. You could almost taste the disappointment. The patrol commander had nine years' service in the S.A.S.; for two of them he had been in and out of Northern Ireland and, like his men, he was heartsick of watching the same people going backwards and forwards on their terrorist missions and being ordered right from the top to leave them alone. Someone, almost certainly in London, not Hereford, clearly did not want the political responsibility of taking out a group of I.R.A. hardliners. I took no part in the decision – if I had been in charge of the mission as a mercenary, the outcome would have been very different, I can tell you – and the patrol commander, for all his disillusionment, was too loyal to regimental discipline to disobey. He did decide, though, to try to save something of the situation. We knew from the surveillance that two of the ten men in the shed had come across the border from the South and would probably be returning by the same route. The patrol commander decided to alert Hereford and try to arrange for them to be ambushed by another S.A.S. patrol operating in that area.

The immediate problem was how to get our hands on the doctor. The two

I.R.A. men detailed to seize him were already leaving. We had no vehicles and did not know the exact location of the farm the doctor was being summoned to. There was no way we could steal a vehicle and get there ahead of them; the only solution was to let the I.R.A. men pick up the doctor and then ambush their car on the only road leading back towards the farm where the cell was meeting.

A still bigger problem was our own exfiltration, which had been seriously compromised by the London decision. If the surveillance mission had gone according to plan I would have gone south alone, and the four members of the patrol would have exfiltrated slowly northwards over the next two days, making their way to a safe area where they could be picked up by helicopter.

When we grabbed the doctor, there would probably be a firefight and, whatever happened, both the I.R.A. men and the doctor would go missing. Within hours at the very most, every I.R.A. gunman in the district would be combing the fields and it was a very long way northwards to anything approaching a safe area.

The surest way was for the patrol to come out southwards with me, but crossing the border was an absolute taboo at that time. However, politicians who make these taboos don't have their lives at risk and I said to the patrol commander that if he were willing to cross the border, I would fly the whole patrol to Cardiff, as long as he could sort things out with the authorities once we got to Wales.

The decision did not take long to reach. Two members of the patrol would ambush the car and get the doctor, then we would all move south, get over the border as fast as possible and use my aircraft to get the hell out of the Republic.

The period that followed was tense both for us and for the I.R.A. Eerily, through the surveillance equipment, we listened to the members of the unit phoning around to see whether the doctor had responded to the summons. They called the surgery but the woman who answered did not seem to know where the doctor was. Eventually, they did get confirmation that he had arrived at the other farm, which meant we had to assume he would be picked up and brought back under escort very soon. It was time to set the ambush.

Setting an ambush in South Armagh is no easy thing. It is violent country and the kind of I.R.A. hard men who had been sent for the doctor cannot be halted just by stepping out into the road and waving an arm. We feared the ambush could be messy and that was how it turned out to be. One S.A.S. man tried to block the road, but the car did not slow down, and the second S.A.S. man opened fire from the roadside. It meant taking the risk of killing the doctor, but fortunately he kept his head well enough to follow his training, and as soon as the firing started, he managed to get the car door open and roll free of the vehicle. The car swerved, crashed through a hedge and ended up axle-deep in mud in a ploughed field. One of the I.R.A. gunmen was killed instantly, but the other managed to get out of the car and fired off two shots with a 9mm Browning automatic. The S.A.S. weapons were silenced, but the Browning was not and we could hear the shots clearly from the hilltop. We could also hear them through the surveillance equipment, but not very distinctly, and the I.R.A. men at the meeting – if they heard the noise – did not recognize it as gunfire. But they were getting very tense at the non-arrival of the doctor and were starting another round of phone calls. We had to get away quickly, but first we had to deal with the emotional state of the doctor.

When he arrived with the two S.A.S. men who had ambushed the car, he was beside himself with anger. He had believed at first that he had been caught accidentally in a routine ambush, but when he was told he was being pulled out deliberately, he thought he was the victim of a clumsy error. The two S.A.S. men had not had time to explain and they had virtually force-marched him up the hillside, in real hard-nosed S.A.S. style, to keep the momentum of the ambush moving. When he reached the hilltop, the doctor recognized the patrol commander. That calmed him a little, and when the situation was explained to him and he was allowed to listen to some of the I.R.A. conversation on the surveillance equipment, his anger subsided. Despite that, he was still a problem.

For an agent, the moment of being pulled out is psychologically devastating. The doctor had made a complete life in Northern Ireland; he had a girlfriend and a home and a medical practice, all built up in parallel with his intelligence activities, and it was now all totally in ruins. In this kind of situation, the emotional let-down dazes a man completely and for at least twelve hours after being pulled out, the agent is to all intents and purposes useless. During the exfiltration, for all his training, the doctor was going to be a passenger, but I had other concerns.

My prime task on the mission was the surveillance and it was my job to see that the equipment did not fall into I.R.A. hands. When the camera and transmitter were put in position, explosive charges had been laid around them so that they could be destroyed if necessary. But the signal for the detonation had to be transmitted in line of sight. That would have given us two kilometres' start at most – not enough in the fraught circumstances of the exfiltration. My solution was to go down and put a timing device on the explosives which could give us three hours' start. There was a risk of civilians being in the vicinity when the charge went off but it was very slight and it was a necessary risk in the situation. I knew the route down to the camera – I had crawled down once early in the mission to check the remote detonation device because I had not been sure it was working efficiently – and I was confident I could slip down again, plant a timed detonator and catch up with the patrol later.

The patrol commander wanted the timing device placed but he had some doubts about letting me do it. He didn't doubt my competence openly – that isn't the fighting man's way – but we got into an oblique discussion about how current I was; in other words, could I be trusted not to make a shambles of the exfiltration by stumbling around clumsily close to the tractor shed.

Ironically, even as we were talking, the surveillance equipment was providing us with some really worthwhile intelligence, something we had almost given up hope of, including some planning involving the British soldier from Colchester. But we were also picking up growing signs of their agitation about the doctor, and the patrol commander came to a decision quickly: he would let me plant the timing device.

What I did not know until later was that he also hedged his bets and detailed another member of the patrol to stay close to me and cover me in case anything went wrong. I am sure he knew instinctively that I wasn't clumsy, but he had not seen me in operation before, even though he knew my reputation, and S.A.S. operatives do not take unnecessary chances.

I did get down all right and spent a little time fiddling around with the device. I didn't arouse the attention of any of the people scurrying around the tractor shed, but it would have been comforting to know that there was an S.A.S. marksman with a nightsight covering me throughout the exercise.

Meanwhile, the three other members of the patrol, plus the doctor, were heading south, on a route that would not take them near where the two I.R.A. men were expected to cross. I caught up with them two hours later and as I closed in on them, the man who had been watching my back came in too. He said nothing and just grinned. This is how the S.A.S. operates.

We crossed the border without problems and reached my car under cover of darkness. Luckily, I had rented one that was big enough to take six people without appearing too obviously cramped and we arranged everyone's kit so that we looked fairly civilian, except on close examination. The car journey went off smoothly but it was fully daylight by the time we reached the castle grounds and I had to find a way of getting the team on board the aircraft without alerting the house. I wasn't sure whether my host would be back or not, and neither he nor any of his staff knew anything about my S.A.S. activities; the scandal of a story getting out about a team of fully-armed S.A.S. men boarding a plane in the Irish Republic was too horrendous to contemplate. No cover story could possibly explain them. Through a speeding car window, they looked just about ordinary enough to pass, but close up, there was no concealing the fact that they were in full combat gear, with weapons, communications equipment and other military kit.

My business contact employed at least a dozen people in his laboratory and there was also a small office and accounts staff, maybe twenty or thirty people in all, any one of whom might see the take-off from the windows of the castle. Fortunately, the geography of the airstrip gave me some small advantage. Even for a private airstrip, it was a bit primitive. It was all grass and pretty bumpy and you normally landed up a slight slope. You could take off in only one direction, whatever the wind conditions, and luckily that was towards the house which meant that you carried out the pre-flight routines some distance away.

I dropped the S.A.S. team and the doctor in the trees at the far end of the runway, trusting them to conceal themselves totally while I went to the house to make my departure noises. I readjusted my dress so that I looked as though I had been on a fishing trip, made up a few stories about the frustrations of the bad weather and the 'ones that got away', and said goodbye to the chief accountant who was running the place as the managing director was not back. Having the boss away was easier in some ways, but the chief accountant was also a flying buff and at one point he was all set to come down to the airstrip to see me off, and take a closer look at the Rockwell Commander. I excused myself, explaining that I was in a tearing hurry, and managed to persuade him not to bother coming down.

The plane was parked in front of the house and I taxied slowly down the U-shaped grass track which led towards the far end of the runway, aware that there could be many eyes on me. I went as far as I could from the house, then taxied very slowly into position, preparing to give the signal to the patrol commander and his men in the trees. Fortunately, the Rockwell Commander is a high-winged monoplane and, being an executive aircraft, it has a door designed for easy access. If the S.A.S. team had had to scramble over the wing to get on board, they could well have been spotted. As it was, I barely needed to pause longer than normal to rev the engines to take-off speed before they were out of the trees and into the aircraft.

It was a smooth, discreet departure, but our problems were not yet over. I dared not contact Hereford during the flight – the danger of the signal being picked up by air traffic control was too great – so I touched down at Cardiff, with the authorities unaware of my passenger load, and parked in one corner of the airport apron.

The patrol commander briefed me on procedures and I decided to go at the problem of Customs and Immigration head-on. I went straight to the chief Customs officer and, without giving details, I said I had some special individuals on board and if he wanted to make a Customs inspection he had better make a call first to his security liaison number. He could have been awkward but he wasn't, and he allowed me to make my own phone call to a number provided by the patrol commander. I left the airport with the S.A.S. team still on board the plane and deliberately did not return until early evening. When I came back, the plane was empty and the chief Customs officer just nodded and grinned and cleared me for departure for England.

Later, in London, I had a debriefing on the use of the surveillance equipment, and in what was about the only positive aspect of the mission, I tied up a very satisfactory sales contract. I learned at the same time that the patrol commander had also had his consolation – another S.A.S. patrol had ambushed and killed the two I.R.A. men on their journey back to the Republic. That made four I.R.A. dead on the operation, but only one of them was a leader and six others – including badly wanted assassins and bombers – had walked away free. Apart from the sales contract, I was paid no money for the operation, beyond my reservist's pay, which probably paid for enough petrol to get me to the end of the runway on the outward flight. Months later, however, though I had never asked for any compensation, my accountant told me that a fee had been paid by an organization he had never heard of for a charter he had no record of. It was a typically low-key way of someone saying thank you for something.

FIVE

TERRORIST INTERNATIONAL

However the situation develops on the ground in Northern Ireland, one of the surest ways of crippling I.R.A. terrorism is to break its links with the United States. The American connection is essential to the I.R.A.'s survival. It provides a veneer of political respectability, credibility in the international terrorist community, money and, above all, arms.

The idea that the I.R.A. has a prominent place in the international terrorist community at all upsets many Irish-Americans. When they put their five-dollar bills in the collecting glass on Dooley's Bar in response to an emtional appeal from an Irish Northern Aid Committee – NORAID – fund-raiser, they prefer to feel they are simply answering a call for contributions to the victims of British colonial oppression in Northern Ireland. They do not want to be told that the I.R.A. has direct links with Palestinian terrorism, the Spanish Basque separatist movement E.T.A., Bader-Meinhof and the Red Brigades. Nor do they want to believe that their contributions to NORAID may well rebound on them directly by helping to make easier an attack on American servicemen in West Germany or the infiltration of a bomb expert into the United States to aid a Hispanic liberation group.

Sadly, Irish-Americans try to dismiss such concepts as right-wing paranoia, akin to finding a Red under every bed. The reality is, in fact, very simple and straightforward. For the past two decades, terrorist organizations have been co-operating closely, even when they have no ideological common ground. They train together and exchange instructors; they help each other smuggle key personnel across frontiers and provide safe houses for them; and they collaborate in buying and smuggling weapons. To help one terrorist organization is to help them all. The co-operation also extends to mutual help in laundering funds. If a bank is held up in Belfast, the proceeds are unlikely to be used to fund directly an I.R.A. arms purchase – the connection would be too easy to trace. Instead, the money will pass through a dummy company in Switzerland or Greece and be used to buy arms for Spanish separatists. In return, the Spanish may well use I.R.A. funds collected in the United States to buy weapons from Middle Eastern suppliers and do a joint smuggling run – dropping off part of the consignment in Spain, the rest in Northern Ireland.

One of the main purposes of NORAID is to ensure that this kind of truth is not allowed to trouble the Irish-American patriot while he is in the process of being separated from his dollars. NORAID has learned how to manipulate powerful emotive symbols to stir the hearts of the sixteen million Americans who claim some Irish ancestry and to convince them – quite wrongly – that the root problem in Northern Ireland is that Britain is using force of arms to hold on to a colony. The little old ladies doing their grieving grandmother act outside Bloomingdale's during British trade weeks, handing out photographs of children allegedly maimed by plastic bullets fired by the security forces, the nuns at the charity bazaars selling harps carved by prisoners 'rotting in British concentration camps' all serve this purpose brilliantly.

Irish-American patriots are even told they now being given the chance to repay the service given by Irishmen in the American war of independence two hundred years ago! NORAID has had plenty of time to refine its act since it was founded in 1970 by three Irish-Americans claiming bitter memories of British discrimination against the Roman Catholic minority in Northern Ireland. The emotional appeal of Irish patriotism is such that a blind eye is easily turned to the fact that one of them, Michael Flannery, is one of the most notorious of the I.R.A.'s gun-runners. In accordance with the Foreign Agents Registration Act, NORAID has had a registered office in Belfast since 1971. Despite the arrest and conviction of numerous NORAID associates, the organization maintains vigorously that it is a charity whose sole purpose is to provide help for the victims of British terrorism in Northern Ireland. In the words of NORAID's chief propagandist, Martin Galvin, in February 1984, 'Not one single penny of NORAID money has ever been spent on armaments'. The organization, he said, gave only 'moral support' to the I.R.A.

In 1981 the U.S. Department of Justice won a court order to force NORAID to register as propagandist, apologist and collection agent for the I.R.A., but three years later, in 1984, NORAID was still successfully stalling – thanks to Irish-American voting power which has appeals stronger than common sense.

In fact, most of the estimated 10,000 Americans who make substantial regular contributions to NORAID are perfectly well aware that their money is going to buy arms – but they believe that the I.R.A. is a dedicated army fighting for Irish freedom. From within the counter-terrorist world, the I.R.A. is seen in very different focus, as a key element in international terrorism. I.R.A. men, like I.R.A. money, turn up everywhere – all over Europe and the Middle East. Terrorist International was the name given to the original mechanism of co-operation in which Libyan-funded training camps for Palestinian terrorists took in members of other terrorist groups, including the I.R.A., Bader-Meinhof and the Red Brigades. Now, international terrorist co-operation is firmly established and some of its fruits would shock even the most tough-minded contributor at a NORAID fund-raising dance.

I have seen, for example, evidence collected by various American security agencies in conjunction with Italian intelligence, which satisfies them and me, that it was an I.R.A. bomb-maker who constructed the device which a right-wing neo-fascist group placed in Bologna railway station in 1980, killing more than eighty people. The man is an Irish-American, with E.O.D. (explosive ordnance device) experience, going back to Vietnam, in both bomb-making and sabotage techniques. He is committed to the Republican cause but the I.R.A. uses his services for trade in the world terrorist community. Many of the senior Irish cadres originally trained in the Libyan-backed Palestinian camps have gone on to become extremely successful urban terrorists. They work internationally – and the knowledge that American funds effectively keep the I.R.A. alive has no corresponding emotional appeal to prevent them from working against U.S. targets, in Europe and on U.S. territory.

Later in this book, I look very closely at the I.R.A.'s links with Spanish and Hispanic-American terrorism and the threat it presents to America's soft underbelly: the oil heartlands of Texas and Louisiana. For the moment, it is enough to say that the connections between NORAID's fund-raising and worldwide efforts to destabilize stable societies are so obvious that NORAID's protestations of fund-raising innocence have to be dismissed as one of the more outrageous forms of Irish blarney. NORAID officially admits to collecting – for charity – about half a million dollars a year. Quite apart from the fact that these sums are disposed of under the direct orders of the I.R.A. leadership in Belfast, they are anyway only the tip of the iceberg.

The NORAID style, as the U.S. Department of Justice has proved on several occasions, is to channel off funds into countless obscure companies – some of them set up for just one arms purchase and closed down immediately afterwards. More than one of my own companies dealing in military hardware has been approached by I.R.A. front men with American funds to spend on weapons. I have always turned them down; one of the basic survival skills of my profession is to know who is fronting for what – it saves a lot of nasty shocks later. But when you are in among the arms traffic, the flow of NORAID funds is too obvious to ignore. Money collected in NORAID's seventy-odd chapters is used to buy arms both in the United States itself and in Europe. In the States, the traffic is greatly helped by the high proportion of Irish-Americans in American law-enforcement agencies – witness the strong contingents of New York's finest in every St Patrick's Day parade – and by the Irish-American strength among dockers.

In Europe, the I.R.A.'s international connections give it a flexibility which worries security agencies well outside Britain. One of them – the West German Bundeskriminalamt, the Federal Criminal Investigation Department – employed me in the spring of 1978 to catch a team of I.R.A. gun-runners who were operating in conjunction with the P.L.O. in Western Europe. The story should make a useful antidote to the NORAID propaganda dished up in places like Dooley's Bar.

The assignment began with another phone call to Switzerland, this time from the Bundeskriminal office in Wiesbaden. They found me at a friend's house, overlooking Lake Geneva, where I was having an evening drink and enjoying the view of the lake. That may well be my last view on earth, incidentally, because there is a compact among myself and some friends over there that if ever the politicians' craziness leads to a nuclear war we won't go down into the fall-out shelters the Swiss insist on putting in every apartment building, but will have a party on this balcony instead and watch the lake boil!

Anyway, I had been half expecting the call from Wiesbaden as I had been having some discussions with the West German federal police about the problem of I.R.A. and Palestinian gun-running and I had been asked if I would be available to help them outside their own borders. I had already agreed in principle, but I had not anticipated how quickly they would want me to move into action.

The Bundeskriminal had been tracking for some time the movements of a team of I.R.A. gun-runners who were operating out of Italy. They were based in Turin and their route was to cross the border into West Germany and collect consignments of weapons and explosives from a Palestinian safe house near Munich. The weapons were normally taken by car from the house, than transferred to a truck, ready for the long-distance journey across Europe. Twice previously an I.R.A. team had taken this route, which went from Munich to Antwerp in Belgium and then across to Northern Ireland. This time, the federal police had intended to seize them but they had been thrown by an unexpected change of itinerary. The police had observed the transfer of the weapons from the car to the truck close to Freiburg in the Black Forest, but then, instead of turning north towards Frankfurt to take the Belgian route, the truck had, for the first time, gone straight over the border into France at Mulhouse. The Bundeskriminal were in a dilemma. They were not sure whether the route had been changed because the I.R.A. knew they were being watched; more significantly, they were not sure they could count on the kind of co-operation they wanted from the French authorities.

The investigators wanted the I.R.A. team back in West Germany and they were by no means certain they could count on the French to make the arrest and push through extradition. My Bundeskriminal contact, who had been running the investigation for months, foresaw the prospect of losing them altogether – either because the French police failed to make the arrest or because the Irishmen would slide away through a tangle of legal niceties. I was asked in direct terms whether I could go immediately into France, intercept the I.R.A. gun-runners and somehow get them back into West German jurisdiction.

The West German detectives trailing them reported that they seemed to be bedding down for the night in a truck park not far from Colmar, just inside the French border. They would, undoubtedly, make an early start and in the heavy French motorway traffic they could easily be lost, especially as the West Germans had no idea whether the truck would make its way towards Calais or Bologne or head westwards towards Brittany and cross the Channel from Le Havre or St Malo.

I said yes, immediately. I had already established a good understanding with the Bundeskriminal. I knew there would be no problem about fees and I knew also I could count on their skilful co-operation if I could get the Irishmen back to the border. I said I would need back-up and this was accepted. I put down the phone and began straightaway to make my arrangements.

I chose as back-up a French mercenary called Yves Kergal, an ex-paratrooper I had worked with several times before. He has underworld connections in both Paris and Marseilles, and if he was available, he would also provide weapons which would mean I need not run any risks with Customs when I crossed the border out of Switzerland.

I phoned him in Paris. He was available and enthusiastic and we agreed a rendezvous point not far from Colmar.

It was an exhilarating high-speed drive. The night was cold and clear and in the warmth and comfort of the Porsche it was easy to think and plan as I sped through the light traffic up from Geneva towards the border and the Black Forest.

We rendezvoused on schedule and after a quick exchange of greetings, transferred to Kergal's Peugeot 505, in which he had concealed two Uzi sub-machine guns and two automatic pistols. Kergal is a real hard man who loves this kind of work, but he also knows how to keep a cool head and, despite his links with the criminal milieu, he goes about his missions very much as a trained military man, not a gangster.

At the truck park the assignment lost some of its romantic edge because of the weather. Once we were outside the car and, crouching under other trucks, observing the Irish vehicle, we became acutely aware of the bitter cold. It was 3 a.m. by the time we were properly in place, and the temperature was well below freezing, the ground was frosted and the wooded areas surrounding the truck park were dank and chill.

The Irish truck was a huge tractor-trailer of juggernaut dimensions; British built, but left-hand drive and registered in West Germany. It was painted with the logo of a food company and appeared, from the locks and seals, to be bonded for international border crossing. We could see no one in the veh-

icle and we assumed that the team were in the transport café at the far end of
the truck part. The West Germans had deliberately made no contact with us
– a way of politely indicating that if anything went wrong, they were not
keen to get into a tangle with the French authorities. But they had reported
that the team appeared to consist of a driver and one mate.

I decided, after consultations with Kergal, that we had better immobilize
the vehicle. That would give us a chance to observe the situation better when
the Irishmen returned, and we could then decide whether a snatch inside
the park was feasible. I had been warned in the initial phone call that we
were dealing with an experienced team of terrorists, not ordinary truckers
working on contract.

I took care of the immobilization of the vehicle myself. I used a fairly standard procedure, attaching two powerful bulldog clips at different points on
the hydraulic fuel line. This sealed the line between the tractor unit and the
trailer and locked on the anti-skid dead-man's brake so that the vehicle could
not be moved. Then we settled down to wait.

We were neither of us in the brightest of moods. It was bitterly cold; we
were both sleepy and we kept awake drinking from a flask of coffee and
alternating between spells inside the Peugeot checking weapons and spells
outside watching for the return of the Irishmen.

Just before six o'clock, we saw two men return to the vehicle. They were
both wearing dark blue donkey jackets, the type you see the merchant navy
wear, but one was slight and young, probably in his early twenties, with
dark hair and almost gipsy colouring, while the other was a man in his forties who looked as though he had been driving trucks all his life and seemed
definitely to be in charge. They did their paperwork at the small office in the
corner of the truck park and moved over to the juggernaut. There were not
too many other vehicles in the park and we considered briefly moving in on
them there and then, but the idea did not last long because when they
started to prepare the vehicle for departure, a third man appeared from
inside the vehicle. He had obviously been sleeping in the back of the cab and
one look at him was enough to tell that he was the bodyguard, the real heavy
of the team. He was a massive man with carrot-red hair sticking out from
under a woollen tea-cosy hat. He had huge broad shoulders and the gnarled
face of a real street-fighter – an axe-handle man if ever I saw one.

With him on their team, there was no possibility of seizing them in the
truck park without a major disturbance and we switched immediately to our
first fall-back plan, an ambush on a stretch of road suggested by Kergal about
ten kilometres from the park. There was not much doubt they would take
that road – it was the obvious heavy-vehicle route to take them towards the
motorway heading south of Paris, which they would want to join whichever
port they had chosen for the Channel crossing. The immediate question,
though, was what they would do when they discovered they had problems
with the hydraulics.

We watched from the edge of the truck park as they settled three abreast in the cab. The older man took the wheel and started to pull out of their parking bay until he felt the juddering motion which told him the trailer wheels were locked. He stopped and got out, looking angry and frustrated at having to leave the warmth of the cab. As an experienced driver, it was obvious to him where to look for the fault but it still took him a few minutes to find the cause of the blockage. When he did, he showed immediate signs of panic. He ran back to the cab and began talking agitatedly to the other two, obviously telling them that the bulldog clips could not have got there by accident. All three men began to look around the vehicle and the park. From the red-haired man's gestures, I could see that he had a pistol under his jacket. The driver went back under the truck to check the line again and the red-haired man started shouting at him to hurry up. It was obvious he had decided it was safest to get out as quickly as possible. I had placed the second clip right at the end of the line and it took the driver several minutes to locate it. When he had, he checked again and a third time to make sure there was no damage to the braking system, then they all got into the cab and the truck began to pull out of the park.

We could see straightaway that the ambush we had planned was not going to be easy. They did take the right road – they could hardly have taken any other apart from heading back towards the German border – but they were now alerted by the clips that someone was interested in them and the driver was piling on speed as soon as they hit the road.

The ambush had to take place before they reached the autoroute, which was less than fifteen kilometres away. Before the main highway, they would pass through a heavily-wooded, hilly stretch of road. Kergal, who knew the road better than I did, reckoned there were at least two suitable ambush points along it, but we had to have some luck with the traffic and not have many other vehicles around at the points where the steepness of the incline would force the truck to slow down.

We let them get out of sight of the park, then followed swiftly in the Peugeot, overtaking them without even looking across at their cab, and sped on beyond them, checking only briefly through the rear-view mirror that they were all in line abreast in the cab.

Kergal is an old hand at the moving ambush and we decided on a technique that both of us had used before. Kergal really put his foot down, putting the Peugeot at least two kilometres ahead of the Irish truck, before dropping me on a rising slope, near a left-hand bend, at a point where the trees came practically down to the road.

Swiftly, Kergal did a U-turn and raced back towards the truck, then turned again, putting himself just ahead of them as they began the ascent up the long, steady incline.

It was Kergal's plan to carry out a manoeuvre guaranteed to send any other driver crazy.

He slowed down until he was only a few metres in front of the truck, then slowed still more, driving jerkily as though he was trying to climb the hill in the wrong gear. The driver of the juggernaut, afraid he would lose all momentum and be forced to go right down to his lowest gear, hooted his horn and tried to intimidate Kergal by practically riding on his back fender.

Kergal ignored them, pretending still to be in difficulties. Predictably, the truck driver pulled out, angrily determined to pass this fool, blocking the road. At that stage, the Irishmen showed no sign of believing there was any threat. The driver of the Peugeot – which had Parisian licence plates – apparently looked to them like a tourist who happened to be a lousy driver or was having mechanical difficulty and didn't have the sense to pull over.

The truck pulled out and as it drew level to overtake, Kergal speeded up, forcing the truck driver to stay in the left-hand lane. Kergal's timing was masterful. There were no other vehicles in sight and unless the Irishman lost his temper altogether and tried to run the Peugeot off the road, he would still be in the left-hand lane when he reached the point at the crest of the hill where I was waiting. More importantly, all three men in the cab were completely wrapped up in the Peugeot's antics. They were staring down out of the cab at the roof of the saloon car, cursing and swearing so loudly I could hear them above the engine noise. All their eyes were fixed to the right and the truck driver was accelerating as hard as he could up the incline to try and get ahead. Kergal just went on driving them wild, holding his rear wheels exactly in line so the juggernaut was dangerously blocked in the left-hand lane.

As it drew abreast of me, it was doing only about twenty miles an hour and the leap up to the cab was not too difficult. There was no running board, only a kind of step for the driver. Fortunately, the driver's window was open and I didn't have to hammer in the glass. I hit the step with my left foot, grabbed the door column with my left hand and stuck the nose of the Uzi in against the driver's head.

I yelled at the driver to sound his horn – that was my signal for Kergal that I was in control. The driver was all set to obey but the red-haired heavy who was furthest away from me decided to go for his weapon. It happened very fast but I still had time to yell at him not to. I might as well have saved my breath; he was proud, stupid and determined, and he went ahead anyway.

As he leaned forward to get a pistol free from under his jacket I fired three shots past the gipsy-looking youngster and hit the red-haired man twice, one round in the neck and another in the shoulder, close to the collar bone, which put the big man out of action, without killing him. I put the muzzle of the Uzi back right up close to the chin of the driver and yelled at him again to slow down and sound his horn. There was a wide verge along the side of the road and the driver slowed down and pulled in, with the Peugeot drawing in ahead of him.

The red-haired heavy was cursing and shouting and bleeding all over the place and was also having trouble staying upright. Kergal jumped out of the Peugeot and I shouted to him to go to the passenger side of the vehicle. Holding his Uzi in one hand, Kergal opened the nearside door of the cab and the red-haired man immediately began to fall out. The cab was a good height off the ground. Kergal, who had no way of knowing how badly hurt and out of action he was, stood back to cover him, and let him fall.

It was the right move, but as he saw Kergal retreating, almost out of sight, the young gipsy kid decided to try to be a hero. With Kergal out of vision below the level of the cab and me preoccupied keeping the driver covered, the kid went for a weapon in the footwell of the vehicle, directly below the steering column. He managed to get his hand to it and I saw it was a Czech-made Scorpion submachine gun – a light, deadly weapon which has a very rapid rate of fire. Because I was blocked from view, the kid came up pointing the weapon through the open door towards Kergal but he never got his finger to the trigger. I yelled at Kergal that the kid was having a go and the Frenchman came back into view and gave him a burst with the Uzi, killing him instantly. It was a very noisy and messy situation – dangerous in the circumstances – but the young guy's heroics had left us no choice.

We now had to move really fast. I still had control of the driver who wasn't going to make any moves but we had the kid slumped, dead in the cab, and the red-haired man on the ground beside the truck, bleeding badly and struggling half-heartedly to get himself upright. It was a measure of their professional level as an I.R.A. team that both of them were managing to control their fear. They were scared but they weren't scared enough. We needed information from them quickly and there was no time for a prolonged interrogation. We needed to know where the arms shipment was located on the vehicle, where the documentation was, what other weapons were concealed, and whether they had any back-up.

I got the driver down from the cab, frisked him, then made him lie face down behind the truck with his left hand palm down behind the rear wheels. Kergal made sure the red-haired man was out of action, then climbed back up into the cab. I started to ask the driver the questions we wanted answering. He was panicking badly now but he still didn't believe we would do it. It was his mistake. When you are in that much of a hurry, there isn't time to keep on threatening and I signalled Kergal to let the truck roll backwards over his hand. It travelled only a few inches but it was enough to crush the fingers and the driver screamed in agony. I let him scream, then Kergal moved the vehicle forward again and I made it clear to the driver that I wasn't going to argue with him. He had just a few seconds to decide whether he wanted the same treatment on his right hand.

The driver talked straightaway and he gave us everything. He described the exact position of the weapons consignment in the base of the vehicle inside the bonded section. He told us where to find two more weapons, a handgun and a submachine gun, and two grenades in a compartment in the cab. He also told us where to find the Customs documents which they had hidden in another compartment in the sleeping area of the vehicle.

By this time, the red-haired man was beginning to come to and we put him side by side with the driver against the truck and told them in hard-nosed terms what would happen to them if they didn't co-operate.

I kept them covered while Kergal got the body of the young kid into the trunk of the Peugeot, then we staunched the bleeding of the red-haired man's neck and shoulder wounds as best we could, tied his hands behind his back and put him back in the truck, on the sleeping bunk. We told them it was a hijack and we intended to have the weapons. We said we were in the arms business and were working for someone who knew about the consignment and wanted it. We also told them we didn't give a damn about them and we would as soon leave them dead by the roadside – if that was how it had to be.

The driver's hand was pretty badly damaged but he could still drive and I decided that was the best way to keep him out of trouble. I had to give him some help with the gear changes but he was very experienced behind the wheel and far too scared now not to make the effort.

The first problem was to find a telephone. We had to contact the Bundeskriminal and there are not many places where you can park a juggernaut. Heading back towards the West German border, we could find nowhere more suitable than the truck park, so I told the driver to pull into the short-term area. There was a lot of mess inside the cab because of the fight but nothing you could see from road level, and we got in without arousing suspicion. Kergal put the Peugeot in a nearby parking area and came across to watch the truck, still without anyone noticing anything unusual. Using my weapon to cover them, he stayed in the truck cab, while I went to find a callbox to contact Wiesbaden.

When I made the call, the Bundeskriminal immediately took the situation under control. There are a lot of jokes made about German efficiency, but the fact is, they are efficient, and they had made detailed preparations for getting the vehicle back over the border if we did manage to apprehend it.

Speaking in veiled, almost casual terms, my Bundeskriminal contact gave me precise instructions. We were to bring the truck to a point he designated, a parking area on the French side of the border at Mulhouse, just within sight of the Customs post. All we had to do there was to simulate a breakdown; they would take care of the rest.

I wasn't sure what they had in mind but I had had enough dealings with the Bundeskriminal in other situations to trust their competence. I hurried back to the truck, gave Kergal a quick briefing, then put the Irishman back at the wheel.

The red-haired man was doing a lot of swearing and cursing at this point but he was too weak to do anything. The driver had long since got the message that we meant business and I think they both believed that we only wanted the weapons and they could hope to end up dumped with the vehicle once we had arranged the transfer of the consignment.

Kergal went back to the Peugeot and followed at a discreet distance as the Irishman pulled out of the truck park and turned onto the main road back towards Mulhouse. It was eight o'clock by now and fully daylight but from ground level there was nothing to see. Inside the cab it was a very different story. There was blood everywhere and there was very little we could do to clean it up. The truck was bonded so we could not put the red-haired man anywhere else but the bunk; he would be too conspicuous if we transferred him to the Peugeot. The next stage clearly depended on the West Germans and they really proved their professional efficiency in high style.

When we got to the area they had designated, about two hundred metres from the Customs post, I ordered the Irish driver to dump hydraulic fluid on the road so that everyone could see we were in trouble. I had given the Bundeskriminal an estimate of our arrival time at the border, and though we were a bit late, they were still ready for us. I left the driver in the truck and made another phone call to a number I had been given by Wiesbaden, to let them know we were in position. Then I made a show of looking around the vehicle, got back into the cab and sat as though waiting for help.

The French Customs service is one of the most touchy organizations in the world and the Bundeskriminal people did not put a foot wrong.

They arrived in a Volkswagen panel van – painted in the same colours as the truck and with the same logo of the food company, something they must have prepared overnight since observing the original transfer of the weapons shipment. Positioning their vehicle carefully to give the maximum cover, they transferred the body of the Irish kid into the back of the panel van. Then they untied the red-haired man and put him in the front of the van, guarded by one of the three West Germans who were all in mechanics' overalls.

Kergal and I were left with the Peugeot – the leader of the West German team said that if any comment was made about us, we would be referred to as people from the food firm who had been summoned to help the truck once it started getting into difficulties. They simulated doing some work in the cab of the vehicle which gave them an excuse for draping a white sheet over the blood-stained seat, of the kind garages use to stop the upholstery from getting dirty while they are carrying out repairs.

Then they were ready for the border crossing. Their story – which was completely plausible thanks to the preparations they had made in advance – was that the truck had developed mechanical trouble on its way across France and had been forced to come back to be checked by company mechanics. The mechanics had discovered a major fault so the truck would have to be brought back into West Germany for repairs. Kergal and I watched admiringly as they crossed the frontier, going through Customs procedures without a hitch. The French, who had seen the Volkswagen pass through only half an hour previously and had watched the supposed mechanics working around the truck, did not even bother to look inside the panel van. The truck also cleared Customs again, its container section still bonded and unopened as the cargo was shown on the documents as being of West German origin and was now returning to West German territory. It was all breathtakingly smooth.

Kergal and I watched them cross, then he drove me back to where I had originally left my Porsche. We shook hands and went our separate ways. The West Germans paid a fee of £55,000 plus expenses for the mission, which reached my Swiss bank account promptly two weeks later. They were delighted with our performance and I was satisfied, too, at having worked with a law-enforcement agency that knows what can be done when you tackle terrorists on their own terms.

SIX

AMERICAN VULNERABILITY

Outbreaks of terrorism on foreign soil often seem very remote to Americans. Even the I.R.A., operating in a country which has cultural and emotional links to many Americans, seems to be safely distant, yet it is quite wrong to believe that foreign terrorism does not have any direct bearing on the security of the United States.

In the world of terrorism there are no islands and no safe havens that are immune from the threats of violence. In my view, one of the most serious law-enforcement problems facing the United States today is the American public's inability to recognize the international links forged between terrorist organizations and the impotence of the authorities to come to grips with the threat they pose to American domestic order.

There is no shortage of warnings, many of them coming from highly placed individuals within U.S. security organizations. Numerous people, spread across police forces and intelligence organizations, try constantly to bring the attention of their superiors to the extent of the threat, but the leadership refuses to recognize that it is necessary to take effective action.

In recent times there have been some truly dramatic examples of international terrorism impinging on American daily life – and some major disasters have been very narrowly averted. One terrorist scare in 1982 which never reached the American newspapers could have resulted in the destruction of a large part of Manhattan. It remained a scare and never became a reality only because of an international investigation which began with an arrest made by Scotland Yard's anti-terrorist squad in London.

As a result of information acquired during an interrogation, the squad had been combing London searching for weapons caches established by Libyans in a series of luxury apartments in the fashionable districts of the city. The British had been concerned about the activities of the Libyans both because they were active in fostering international terrorism by supplying both money and arms, and because feuds in Britain between supporters and opponents of the Libyan leader, Colonel Qaddafi, had destroyed property and injured British citizens.

The anti-terrorist squad found several large stores of weapons and made a number of arrests. They also found evidence that some of the Libyans were working in close conjunction with other Qaddafi agents in West Germany.

The British consulted the C.I.A. office in Frankfurt, which had been investigating rumours that Libya was trying to put together a large-scale international terrorist operation directed at the United States.

Libya has shown through its support of the I.R.A. and E.T.A. that it is capable of boosting a terrorist organization to prominence, and the rumours suggested that for the American operation, Tripoli was planning to use several organizations simultaneously.

The C.I.A. organized an operation which involved the use of foreign mercenaries as well as their own agents to abduct Libyans from Britain, Spain and France and bring them to West Germany to try to piece together the conspiracy which had been partially glimpsed during the London investigations.

The result was the uncovering of a plot which shook even hardened American security experts.

The Libyan plan was to collect together a massive quantity of explosives on a subway train in New York City. The explosives were to be assembled by several different terrorist organizations, each of which believed it was working alone and for its own purposes. The Libyans had contacts with, among others, the Rastafarians, composed mainly of Puerto Rican fanatics who had formed a splinter group from the Jamaican 'Rastas', the Jewish Defence League, the Black Liberation Army, and the extreme Muslim fanatics, the Islamic League. Each group was to infiltrate a relatively small quantity of explosives into the New York subway system.

The concentration was to be assembled finally on one train and detonated at a point in mid-town Manhattan where there is a land fault. It had been calculated that an explosion there would cause widespread subsidence and the collapse of a huge section of the city, as well as destroying underground water installations, affecting sanitation and the pressure of water in hydrants, which would hamper fire-fighting operations.

The idea was based on a plan originally conceived by E.T.A. for use in Madrid. That concept was to hijack one of the trainloads of explosives which regularly passed through the Spanish capital, then detonate it in one of the tunnels under the city.

The New York plan was worked out in separate segments. Different Libyan representatives had contacts with the various terrorist groups and the pages of the plan were to be kept separate and brought together only on an agreed date.

Disaster was averted by making it known in the terrorist community that the plan had been uncovered and preparations made to prevent it from being carried out, but the police and the security specialists lived through some very nasty moments until the plot was unravelled.

Nor was this Libyan-sponsored scheme an isolated example. When successive American presidents have publicly accused Colonel Qaddafi of fostering terrorism and plotting anti-American acts, it has not been simply political rhetoric. The evidence exists to back up the accusations and the I.R.A. is nearly always prominent.

In the subway plan, the I.R.A. had no active role – though it knew of the plan. Despite its so-called concern for New York's thousands of Irish-Americans, the I.R.A. was quite prepared to let the operation go ahead; its own ties with Libya and other terrorist organizations were far too valuable not to.

Not long afterwards there was another Tripoli-sponsored operation in New York, and this time it was to be carried out by the I.R.A.

The aim was to infiltrate the New York City Police Department's bomb squad and to collect as much data as possible on its bomb-disposal methods. By collating all the information on bomb-making which it had assembled itself and which it had received from other police forces in the United States and abroad, the idea was to enable terrorists to construct bombs which could defeat the efforts of explosive ordnance disposal teams in several countries, as well as in the United States. The infiltration was foiled only because of information acquired during an interrogation of an I.R.A. suspect in London, which was passed on to the U.S. authorities.

Terrorism has no frontiers. Palestinian and other Arab terrorists infiltrate the United States, both to buy weapons and to plan operations on American soil; the American Jewish Defence League has reversed the process by sending hit teams to Europe to counter the violence of the fanatical Islamic League. The Jewish teams were in part a response to the bombing of synagogues in Paris but their overall purpose was to retaliate, by counter-assassinations, for any killing of Jews in Europe. Their tactics were like those of any other terrorist group. They won the support of several prominent members of British Jewry, for instance, by promising no violence in London. Thus they were able to have a safe haven in London, while planning terror in Paris.

Such threads can be followed in many different directions. During one series of intensive operations in Spain, which resulted in the arrest and interrogation of dozens of E.T.A. militants, two of its leading members managed to get out of the country. Their escape route was to Mexico where they found refuge in the Hispanic-American terrorist community.

There they became involved with a group of Mexican dissidents who were engaged in filtrating trained terrorists into the southern United States aided by the I.R.A. The two E.T.A. men came to the attention of Pemex, the Mexican state-controlled petroleum corporation, whose security division is headed by Colonel Carlos Medaya, a former army officer who has strong personal links with the Mexican government and police security services. Medaya passed on the word to Mexico City; Mexico City warned various

U.S. law-enforcement agencies, but the warning came to nothing because it ended up on the desk of an Irish-born police officer who had several good reasons for not drawing attention to the Irish-Hispanic link in his area.

The example illustrates not only the co-operation between E.T.A. and the I.R.A., but also one of the problems which the United States faces in dealing with the threat: the infiltration of law-enforcement agencies by both I.R.A. and Hispanic sympathizers. In fact, infiltration is the wrong word. The I.R.A. and Hispanic groups do not need to infiltrate people, the people are there already and there is a whole structure within American ethnic political life which provides an umbrella for their activities.

Both the Hispanic groups and the Irish groups have their special strengths. The Hispanics have a solid base in Mexico where poverty, injustice and social inequality provide a rich seedbed for anti-government discontent. They have ties with Hispanic politicians and police across the border in the United States and have, up to now, concentrated on developing the infiltration of 'wetback' cheap labour into the U.S. and on drug-smuggling and distribution.

The I.R.A.'s strength is its ties to the powerful Irish-American community and the vast array of politicians, police and other law-enforcement officers who are of Irish descent.

To maintain its hold on Irish-American communities, the I.R.A. uses subtle but effective forms of intimidation, playing strongly on local sentiment and emotion. An Irish-American is quite naturally afraid to be out of touch with the community spirit. The I.R.A. manages to 'hijack' that spirit and create the impression that if Irish-Americans do not support NORAID then they are likely to be cut off from their roots in Ireland – and despised by their Irish-American neighbours who know where their loyalty lies.

It is no less than straightforward blackmail and a great many Irish-Americans who do not actively condone violence in Northern Ireland give in to the pressure and contribute to NORAID in order not to be ostracized. It is cheaper and simpler to play the I.R.A.'s game than risk becoming an outcast in the community – a threat very skilfully implied by the I.R.A. fund-raisers.

The late Mayor Daley of Chicago used the social blackmail approach to raise hundreds of thousands of dollars for the I.R.A. – with the support of the Roman Catholic Church in the city.

Now, on an ever-increasing scale, the I.R.A. and E.T.A. are joining forces. One result is that Irish law-enforcement officers are aiding the infiltration of Hispanic terrorists into the United States.

They do not always do it with positive action. Usually, the aid comes in the form of turning a blind eye to the activities of certain individuals who are known to have Irish political connections. For the dishonourable policeman, the mechanism is simple. He goes on the payroll of an Irish-American politician – or of a businessman supporting that politician – who has a powerful vested interest in furthering causes like the I.R.A. which are viewed by many voters as patriotic. If the policeman is not corrupt and insists on becoming active in investigations which are leading to people who have protection, he is seen as 'unpatriotic' to Irish causes and finds a brick wall blocking his efforts.

The situation can create some strange ironies. I remember once going into an Irish bar in Chicago with an officer who was a key figure in Illinois anti-terrorist operations. The man had been born in New York of Irish descent and as he listened to the Irish songs belted out by the woman in the green dress with the NORAID collecting box I could see his heart warming to the occasion. As was intended, the whole evening was stirring his sense of nostalgia for an Irish homeland he had never known. Yet I have sat with the same man in seminars in which he was being briefed on data from the Scotland Yard anti-terrorist unit on I.R.A. devices planted in London, along with other explosive devices planted by terrorist groups throughout Europe.

One day, the same man may well be called on to defuse a bomb in Chicago which has its origins with the I.R.A. – and the irony will have very serious practical implications for the American man in the street.

Sometimes the links of corruption and patronage between politicians and law-enforcement officers of the same ethnic group can have other negative results.

In the Hispanic community, in particular, there are examples of officers who react strongly against the help which some of their Hispanic colleagues give to militant groups. They go the other way and, in an attempt to redress the balance, deal harshly with their own people and create added fear of the police in the Hispanic community.

But the terrorist links are not limited to E.T.A. and the I.R.A. Terrorism is as truly international as multi-national corporations, and links between terrorist groups are frequently purely pragmatic, rather than ideological.

In recent times, black militant groups have been relatively inactive in the United States, but they too have been very busy, away from the public eye. Current counter-terrorist intelligence briefings contains reports that the Black Liberation Army and the Black Panthers, aided by the remnants of the Weathermen, a violent anti-establishment group of the 1960s, are constructing a network of safe houses, weapons caches and hot cars in preparation for a massive terrorist offensive.

One common misconception in the United States, however, is that all terrorist groups are left wing. One of the most dangerous at the moment is the Posse Comitatus, an ultra-right-wing organization which grew out of white agrarian tax resistance in Montana and has now spread and become active in several states. The terrorists of Posse Comitatus are true hand-on-heart, flag-waving Americans, and one of their bomb experts may also run the local general store. Yet despite the fact that they are anti-black, anti-Puerto Rican and anti-Jewish, they have been drawn into co-operating with non-white, left-wing terrorist organizations. This co-operation is necessary for survival, and survival always transcends ideology.

It is because of the shallowness of the cause which motivates most terrorist organizations that they are easily used, and those which are struggling for survival are especially vulnerable.

The Ku Klux Klan is on the wane as a force in American society but it still poses a security threat because it is being used by various left-wing extremist groups, acting as a large anti-Klan element at a relatively small Klan march, to create disorder. At many recent Klan rallies there has been serious rioting and each time it has been started by left-wing extremists who see the chance to create social disorder on someone else's back. The police note the same faces before each riot and have pinned them down to a variety of extremist splinter groups which run under the vague leftist banner.

I have attended enough security and intelligence briefings in the United States over the past few years to be convinced that before very long the country is liable to be blown apart by a massive upsurge in terrorist violence unless Americans rid themselves of their present blinkered and parochial views on terrorism.

The United States is ripe for a terrorist explosion. Europe has got its counter-terrorism machinery into good order – it has had to because of the persistent upheavals of the last decade. The United States is now the vulnerable zone. European police forces have learned just how strong the ties are between world terrorist groups but it is, sadly, a lesson still to be learned in the United States.

If there is one lesson to be drawn from this book, it is that terrorists move as smoothly from country to country while carrying out covert operations as I have done while trying to combat them, and that terrorist groups help each other for their own protection and survival and to maintain the momentum they must have in order to survive.

The American public has to come to this realization quickly for its own survival because at the moment its law-enforcement agencies are working under a serious handicap in their struggle against terrorism. The constitution of the United States prevents the most efficient anti-terrorist units – those related to the armed services – from being used domestically, and to complicate the issue further the constitution creates jurisdictional problems which paralyse those agencies which do have a domestic role.

When the Iranian embassy in London was seized by terrorists, it took a few direct phone calls to the Prime Minister's office to advise of the danger and a few more from the Prime Minister to bring the S.A.S. into action.

Such a simple and direct approach is completely impossible within the United States. The president is highly restricted in his ability to call in the military on U.S. soil. Either constitutional change or radical overhaul of the structure of domestic counter-terrorism forces is going to be necessary if major threats are to be dealt with swiftly and effectively.

To achieve either change, the American public's level of awareness of terrorist matters will have to be raised.

SEVEN

TARGET: GULF OF MEXICO OIL TERMINAL

Law-enforcement agencies and American business, as well as the American public, need to be educated in the terrorist threat.

Within these institutions there are always aware individuals but the institutions themselves need a hard jolt before they begin to take the issue seriously, and I have at various times had a hand in trying to provide it.

During 1981, I became involved in a series of discussions among American counter-terrorist experts about the growing terrorist threat in the United States and the jurisdictional problems that have to be faced in dealing with it.

We were looking mainly at the problem in the southern United States, especially Texas and Louisiana which are coming more and more to be regarded as the soft underbelly of the United States. Its long coastlines, the richness of its commercial infrastructures and its proximity to Mexico make it a perfect target for terrorist attack.

Commercial targets are particularly tempting. Assassinate the President of the United States and the process of political renewal swings automatically into action, despite the nationwide shock and mourning; but destroy a vital commercial installation and the disruption can be incalculable.

The scope of modern terror is such that an attack on, say, a dam anywhere in the United States is conceivable, but we had in mind something which would be smaller in scope but just as disruptive.

What, we wondered, would happen, for example, if terrorists using Mexico as a jumping-off ground seized an oil platform in the Gulf of Mexico off Louisiana? Or suppose they went one better and took one of the capping platforms which collects crude from the rigs and pipes it either ashore or out to a terminal for collection by tankers? If three such platforms were knocked out, about one-third of the whole U.S. domestic oil supply would be affected. It would be easy to do and extremely difficult to deal with effectively, given the rivalries and jurisdictional divisions between the multiple agencies which would become involved.

The discussions at that stage were informal. Special Forces people from

Fort Bragg took part, as did representatives of the Louisiana Police Department, the C.I.A. and other agencies, but the talks were limited strictly to a group of specialists who were genuinely concerned about the problem and understood that such a threat was not just idle talk.

During this period, I was doing work with the United States Navy SEAL teams, the waterborne special warfare units based at Norfolk, Virginia.

I was advising them on underwater demolition and the use of new technology in marine environments and it was suggested that I should write a scenario for a training exercise in which a SEAL team would simulate the capture of an oil platform by an international terrorist organization.

As weapons-carrying swimmers, SEALS were ideal for the role and I devised an attack scenario which would lead to the complete takeover of a Gulf of Mexico oil-collection terminal by as few as ten men.

To the group who were looking at the problem of protecting the oil installations, it was obvious that if the scenario succeeded, it would result in a security nightmare, but up to that point no one outside this small group had taken the problem seriously.

The security companies advising the oil companies were generally apathetic. They had instituted routine security procedures and in general comforted themselves with the illusion that if there were a terrorist threat, the U.S. government agencies would be competent to deal with it. Most of the law-enforcement agencies, including some represented unofficially in our private group, simply did not want to recognize officially that the Gulf coast area was that vulnerable, and it was out of this realization as much as anything else that the idea grew of putting the scenario into actual operation.

Why not, it was argued, shame the oil companies into admitting that they were vulnerable? Why not show up the extent of the jurisdictional problems and the impotence which would result?

The idea won solid support, but those in the group were all senior members of military and police agencies, they had careers to protect. Using U.S. military forces to seize the property of a major oil company without authorization is not the way to win promotion and ensure your pension rights! What was lacking was the appropriate authorization from Washington and this was supplied through the channels of the Central Intelligence Agency.

With Washington's approval – albeit given covertly – everything else fell into place and thus began one of the most significant counter-terrorist exercises ever carried out in the United States.

The first that the oil company knew about it was when they received a radiotelephone call at 6 a.m. one morning about a month later advising them that a 'foreign terrorist organization' had taken over one of their collection platforms in the Gulf of Mexico, offshore from the port of Morgan City, Louisiana. Further communication would be made at 11 a.m.

The call to the oil company came minutes after a similar one to the Louisiana State Police. At that stage, only a handful of individuals knew that the terrorists were not genuine. Louisiana police had no idea, even though one of its senior people had formed part of our planning group. No other agency knew officially and even the command structure of the U.S. Navy was not aware that some of their SEALS constituted the 'foreign terrorist organization'.

The attack had begun three hours earlier at 3 a.m. when the shrimping fleet from Morgan City had set sail. The shrimp boats left harbour trailed by two five-man SEAL teams in rubber boats who boarded and seized them an hour later. The shrimp fishermen were captured and were not told that their captors were not the terrorists they purported to be, and their boats were steered towards the platform.

Working unobtrusively, under the guise of carrying on normal fishing activities, the SEALS put out lobster pots, with the lines stretched between the shrimpers – and an electronically detonated mine put in each pot – to constitute a defensive perimeter. Then the SEALS swam silently to the platform, scaled it and overpowered the crew.

Scaling a rig is no easy task. It is a hard, exhausting climb up the metal stanchions which are slippery, and offer no footholds. The SEALS climbed using ropes and suction clamps and a device known as an 'ascender' in which one foot is held in a loop as the climber is drawn up by the use of hand-operated clamps.

After the climb, the crew did not give in easily; they believed they were fighting off real terrorists. Some heroes had to be dealt with rather severely and later there was some awkwardness about lawsuits as two of the crewmen threatened to sue the Navy for assault!

The rig was a large platform with a multiplicity of pipelines radiating out from it both above and below the water. On the platform were some accommodation units and a helipad which was the first objective secured by the SEALS. Once in control, the SEALS radioed their shore units and a command structure was flown out by helicopter to open negotiations.

It all went off very smoothly, but it had taken many weeks of preparation to bring about. I had trained the SEAL teams myself at Norfolk, Virginia, but that was, on balance, the easiest part. The hardest was to ensure secrecy while the training exercises were being carried out as constitutional problems could arise in the use of the military to practise such an exercise even in its own training areas.

When the rig was secured and the calls to the Louisiana State Police and the oil company were made, a period of barely describable chaos and confusion followed.

A number of steps were taken, but it would be quite wrong to set them out as though they were taken in logical sequence. The oil company called the

F.B.I. and it took five hours for an F.B.I. team to reach Shreveport where the operational base had been established. The Louisiana State Police office called the private security company which was responsible for rig security and they tried for a while to contain the crisis within their own jurisdiction and work it out 'within the family' without calling on federal agencies.

Some members of the press found out and pushed into the building where a tactical headquarters room – a TAC room – had been set up. American journalists cannot be given the kind of brush-off that the press would have been given in similar circumstances in Europe and a desk was set up to provide occasional briefings for the reporters – even though there were as yet no developments. U.S. police departments are quite neurotic about public relations and no one had the authority or the will to tell the journalists to go to hell and not to start complicating the problem.

Finally, the F.B.I. sent another team from Washington which did not acknowledge the authority of their own people from the regional office who were already in place.

The first gathering of the agencies produced one memorable confrontation which set the tone of the whole scene. The senior F.B.I. agent, attempting to take control of the situation, said loudly: 'Well, who have we got out there, so we can get profiles on the bastards?' which drew the dry reply from the senior Louisiana police officer present, 'No one has been out to fucking well ask them, asshole.'

Despite the lack of encouragement, the F.B.I. did its best to keep control of the situation. It set up a team in the TAC room which interviewed the representatives of the numerous agencies who had been called in – from Special Force Delta in Fort Bragg to the U.S. Coastguard.

The simple fact was, however, that the F.B.I. could not handle the task. The F.B.I. has changed a great deal from its so-called legendary G-man days. It has become a bureaucratic data-collection agency. Gradually, throughout the day, it became evident, as had been predicted in the scenario, that no one had the skills, the training and at the same time the constitutional authority to deal with the situation, or provide the co-ordinated and contained response necessary.

At one stage, a military raid on the platform was contemplated, as negotiations with the 'terrorists' continued to drag on. The idea petered out when the 'terrorist' negotiator disclosed – as had not been done before – that the shrimp boats lying round the rig had been transformed into a floating minefield.

The confusion and disarray went on all day. I observed them from the sidelines, attaching myself by turns to the explosives ordnance disposal team, with which I had worked on several occasions, and with the sole representative of the Louisiana State Police who knew what was really going on.

The 'terrorists', for their part, made various demands for money and for communiques to be read out. One of them was an I.R.A. propaganda screen and I was disturbed to note that the initial reaction of one senior police officer present was, 'Hell, if that's all they want, why not do it? It's only about Ireland.'

Eventually, in the early hours of the following morning, the news was broken that it was, after all, only a training exercise.

The hour was chosen because the frustration and fatigue levels of the people in the TAC room were reaching the point where there was a risk that someone might make a serious mistake – like trying to call in the military unconstitutionally – and enough was judged to be enough.

The first reaction of most of those who had been caught napping was straight fury – much of it directed at me as I was revealed as the planner of the scenario, acting in my familiar role as a 'deniable' person, a 'civilian'.

The oil company's anger was tempered slightly with relief, but they were still livid at having been made fools of as well as at the lost production caused by the interruption in pumping on the platform.

The next stage was also predictable. After the initial bouts of abuse and anger, most of the agencies went into huddles to try to discover who, within their own organizations, had been 'in the know' from the beginning. They were less concerned with the security of the oil installations and the national interest than with protecting their own necks – and an essential part of that was to evaluate whether it was 'cool' to denounce the exercise.

Meanwhile, throughout it all, a representative of the Senate Anti-terrorist Committee was preparing a special report.

Once the dust had settled, there were a number of interesting results from the exercise. I was commissioned by the oil company, who had not realized the extent of their vulnerability, to do a counter-scenario to demonstrate how to retake a platform that had been captured. That was carried out six months later and though it succeeded – with the use of a HALO (high altitude low opening) parachute drop, done while helicopters and various vessels carried out decoying manoeuvres – the conclusion that everyone correctly drew from the counter-scenario was that it would be better not to let the rigs be quite so vulnerable, as it is a helluva lot easier to capture one than to retake it.

On the law-enforcement side, there were a number of interesting consequences. The F.B.I. laid more emphasis on its active role and speeded up the creation of a fifty-strong force of agents who later began training and equipping for rapid response and assault technique at the Quantico Marine base.

Another conclusion was that an agency needed to be found which could cut across the jurisdictional maze. One suggestion which emerged was that it could be the U.S. Marshal's Services, a body which can cross state lines to arrest and seize felons.

Overall, the platform-taking exercise demonstrated very clearly the vulnerability of a key commercial installation to well-organized internationally trained terrorists. Many lessons were learned, but the political sensitivities surrounding the issue are such that by no means all of the right conclusions have yet been drawn.

EIGHT

MI6 ASSIGNMENT TO ASSASSINATE

British Intelligence officials are very hesitant about commissioning assassinations. They don't like to order them, and when they do they don't like to pay for them; they prefer to cling to the myth that killing is more honourable when it's done purely for Queen and country. The British can be ruthless – just as ruthless, in fact, as the intelligence services of any other nation – but they go through quite senseless contortions about employing mercenaries, even when they clearly recognize the need for them. It is a very strange mentality and peculiar to the British. The French have no inhibitions about that kind of clandestine contract – they might as well be emptying out a mattress full of used bills in front of you; with the Americans it's done almost like signing a credit card slip; the Spanish do it with dignity – the money is cleared through a ministerial department and you are accorded stature as the recipient of such an important payment. With the British, the transaction is always made to appear grubby, as though they are keeping the money tucked inside frayed cuffs and don't actually want to part with it.

Still, there are occasions when the British recognize that they need to keep their hands clean. They need a deniable person and that is what I am paid to be. Among the operations I have carried out for British Intelligence, there were two assassination assignments – one in Spain and one in Greece – both directed at I.R.A. gun-runners. With both of them, my relations with MI6, which was running the operations, were almost as complicated as the operations themselves.

The Spanish mission was the easier of the two; in fact, it was really very straightforward. The complications came from the delicate relations between British and Spanish Intelligence.

My own connection with Spain goes well back in my career. While I was operating my aviation interests out of South Africa, I acquired a contract to fly supplies to the military garrison in the Spanish Sahara. Out of that grew a second contract to advise them on handling explosives and on special anti-guerrilla techniques. Gradually, I built up a relationship with the Spanish Special Security Operations Group – later given the official name of G.E.O.S. (*Grupo Especiale para las Operaciones de Securidad*) – their equivalent of the

S.A.S., which is part of the Policia Naçional, not the army, and with the paramilitary Guardia Civil. I was supplying equipment to both organizations and advising on training and tactics.

These contacts led, eventually, to my major assignment for the Spanish government – operations against Basque separatist terrorists in their hideouts on the French side of the Pyrenees, which I shall come to shortly – but by the mid-1970s, I was already deeply involved with the Spanish security services and, among other contracts, I was helping them gather intelligence on gun-running to the Basque separatist movement, E.T.A.

Then, as now, there was very close co-operation between E.T.A. and the I.R.A. and joint arms shipments were common. The weapons were purchased in the Middle East and shipped to various European ports, with part of the consignment dropped off in Spain for E.T.A., the rest passed onwards towards Northern Ireland. These joint shipments were extremely difficult to track. One of the 'security *pro formas*' handed to me during a briefing in Madrid in 1975 shows just how complex the wheeling and dealing was. The *pro forma* was an order to put under observation a cargo ship, sailing under a Panamanian flag, which British Intelligence had warned was suspected of carrying weapons to Spain and Northern Ireland. The vessel was an ancient rust-bucket of about 2,000 tons, which had already been sold for scrap and was due to make its last voyage very shortly. The Spanish had established: that it was soon to ply from an unspecified port in Greece; that it would carry a dual cargo of coal and scrap iron; that the coal would be unloaded at an unspecified Spanish port; the iron would be delivered in Northern Ireland; the ship itself would then proceed to another unspecified destination to be broken up.

Spanish Intelligence had also ascertained that a Southern Irish broker had purchased the ship from a Greek company and that three Irishmen were going to travel on board for the trip, along with a crew composed mainly of Greeks and Cypriots. They had also learned that the same Irish broker had chartered two lorries from a French company and these were presumably going to be used to move the weapons, but it wasn't known at which stage in the journey the arms would be disembarked and how much of the journey was to be made by road. A further complication was that the gun-running operation was extremely sophisticated and several runs without weapons on board had been deliberately made on highly suspect vessels, chartered through the same Greek company; a very expensive but very effective way of confusing the security service.

Both the Spanish and the British were investigating this arms smuggling route from the Middle East but their liaison was poor – and that was mostly the fault of the British.

My contacts in the Spanish Interior Ministry complained to me many times that the British were making poor use of intelligence data on the I.R.A.

being passed from Madrid, and I knew why from the reactions to the Spanish that I was picking up in London.

British Intelligence had a curiously disdainful attitude to the Spanish police and to their security and intelligence services in general. The British seemed to classify them as Latins, and therefore disorganized. A shambles really; a bit of a joke. From my neutral standpoint, I would have backed the Spanish against the British both in intelligence skills – general finesse, experience of undercover operations – and in their ability to take tough action without dithering about. Under the years of Franco's rule, the Spanish had developed a highly sophisticated and competent police force and their intelligence-gathering throughout Europe – working through the various Spanish communities – was excellent. British Intelligence has many more problems. It is curious that while the British have managed to create the Special Air Service, which is a model for special forces throughout the world, they have never been able to create an intelligence organization of comparable stature.

The rivalries between MI5, which is supposed to operate only domestically, and MI6, whose sphere is outside the United Kingdom, are well known. But beyond the rivalries and jealousies, there is a deeper problem, which I have always attributed to the level at which the British intelligence services recruit. They don't choose from a wide enough range of candidate and many of their senior people are astonishingly immature, lacking what the Americans call street wisdom and even simple worldly common sense. Spanish Intelligence, by contrast, seems to contain many more men with the stature and personal substance needed for the rough work that has to be done. Yet I have heard them written off in London as 'an inexperienced bunch of dagos' by men who would not even be hireable in the intelligence community in Madrid.

The British suspected the depth of my involvement with the Spanish and they liked even less the fact that I did not automatically pass on any information I gathered to London. At the time, I was spending part of the year in Spain. I had an office in Madrid, run by a retired Spanish army colonel, and I owned a home in Marbella. There were good times to be had in Marbella in the early and mid-1970s. There were fewer tourists than there are now and many more adventurous people, including a good sprinkling of mercenaries, as well as film stars, sportsmen and wealthy members of the international yachting and golfing communities.

I had a plane based at Malaga and between assignments and business dealings in Madrid, London and elsewhere, I enjoyed short but intense spells of Mediterranean beach life. Water sports are among my great passions and the sea provides many of my favourite ways of relaxing. In those days, windsurfing, which is one of my favourite sports now, had hardly started, but there was water-skiing, sailing, swimming and scuba-diving. I also enjoyed the discos in Marbella and the surrounding ports. In London, discos are of less interest, but in Marbella, the expensive discos attract a full cross-section of a very lively and interesting community and are a perfect place to combine two of my favourite recreations – beautiful women and music – and generally let my hair down.

At the time, I had done very little work for the Spanish in Marbella itself. Their own intelligence network was well established there – though it was set up more to monitor the extensive drug trafficking that went with the wealthy Marbella beach life, rather than the arms trade – and I had reported for them more on the Greek and Cypriot end of E.T.A.'s arms-smuggling operations.

The first proposal for some enquiries in Marbella itself came from the British, very obliquely, during one of my visits to London. The approach was made by Colonel Leo Newby, a tough old bird who presents a very deceptive face around Whitehall and St James's. On the surface, he is a retired colonel who works as a Ministry of Defence civilian expert, doing technical evaluations of equipment offered for purchase, and handling liaison with commercial companies like mine who deal with the Ministry. He is, in fact, a full-blooded S.A.S. reserve colonel who can be seen most Friday nights chatting in the Special Forces club or in the mess at the Duke of York's. He is one of the most respected early members of the regiment, a Second World War sabotage expert with a reputation since then as a really hard-nosed operator in intelligence matters.

Leo called me up one day when I had flown in from Madrid. We met, and over lunch he told me about some people in Marbella that MI6 was interested in.

It was typical of MI6 to make their approach through Leo, a man they knew I got on well with because we could talk straight to each other. On numerous occasions, his people had tried approaching me direct, mostly to attempt to gather intelligence on the cheap by trying to debrief me on missions carried out for other people. They had always got the same rough answer from me: 'You weren't paying so it's none of your damned business.' In fact, I had passed on a great deal of information to the British through my S.A.S. contacts; I have far more British patriotic sense than MI6 has ever given me credit for; it is simply that I don't much like the way they go about their business.

On this occasion, though, the assignment, which eventually turned into an assassination, began with a routine query.

Would I take a look at three people in Marbella and see what I thought they were up to? I was immediately cautious. Reading between the lines, what MI6 was really asking was would I find out what the Spanish thought they were up to. I said I would sniff around, but made no firm promises. Leo left it at that and I flew back to Marbella.

The three names I was given were not hard to locate. They formed a little group that always went about together and the main reason our paths hadn't crossed before was that part of their life was centred on golf which is not a sport I'm interested in. The oldest member of the group – and its presumed leader – was a wealthy Englishman called Robin Maitland. He was about forty, with an easy, outgoing manner, quite good-looking, and I discovered that he owned a converted M.T.B. (motor torpedo boat) – the *Methuselah* – which I'd already seen a few times in Marbella harbour. The second person in the group was his girlfriend, a woman called Shirley Brandon. She was in her mid-twenties; quite pretty, especially with a Marbella suntan, and a British accent that I always call mid-county, which is my way of saying I don't know enough about British accents to place it. She wasn't a Londoner and she didn't have one of those strong northern accents that I can recognize. It turned out that she came from Luton, but she had spent the last year with Maitland, living in his flat on the edge of Marbella. If MI6 hadn't been interested in her, I would have said she was a typical fun-loving hanger-on; the kind of girl who comes to Marbella for a good time and usually attaches herself to an older man with enough money to pay the bills. The third person in the group was the give-away, however, a rough hard-bitten Irishman in his late twenties called Colin McGrath. He seemed to look after the boat, but he wasn't an employee. I gather he played golf also, but I never could imagine him on a golf course. In fact, he didn't fit the Marbella scene at all.

I wasn't ready to move close in on them yet; I wanted to know more about what MI6 wanted of me, but I decided to fish gently among my Spanish contacts to see if there was any interest there. To ensure maximum discretion, I decided to put the question to Colonel Juan Alvarez, my closest contact in Madrid. Alvarez was once one of General Franco's personal bodyguards and was at this time in charge of a police intelligence unit specializing in Basque affairs. Alvarez is a highly intelligent and subtle man, with a dry sense of humour and the kind of detachment and long-sightedness that I always like to find in those I work with. I dropped the names of Maitland and McGrath to him and he grinned and said, 'You mean the ones that the swimmer was interested in.' I said I didn't understand and made sure Alvarez knew that I wasn't lying. Alvarez grinned again. 'There was a British swimmer. Very energetic man, in Marbella last month, while you were away. He asked about McGrath, Maitland and the girl. You might say he asked some of the right questions in the wrong places.'

We went to lunch and Alvarez told me the whole story. About a month previously, a short, stocky, tough-looking Englishman had arrived in Marbella, apparently a tourist, and had drawn the attention of the Spanish police by his curious swimming habits. Two or three times a week, he would go down to the beach, carefully fold his clothes, and swim straight out to sea. Each time, he was gone for nearly two hours and sometimes longer – which made him a powerful swimmer by any standards – and very conspicuous in a resort where swimming usually means a few quick splashes between sips of white wine. Alvarez told me that the police had assumed that he was swimming out to make contact with vessels offshore, but they had not been able to identify them. They had become even more interested when he had started asking questions about McGrath, Maitland and Shirley Brandon, in one of the bars of the port. It was obvious to me by now that the man had some connection with British Intelligence and it was typical that he had apparently gone about his enquiries quite clumsily, never thinking that the bar where he was asking was run by Spanish police intelligence. To him, I am sure, it had been just another bar run by a fat, jovial Spaniard and his busty, noisy wife, not – as Alvarez pointed out with a grin – two of the best police specialists in drugs intelligence-gathering in the area.

Soon afterwards, the Englishman had left Marbella and the Spanish had taken a look at the trio. 'They use their boat a lot. Deep-sea fishing mostly,' Alvarez said. 'We assumed they might be mixed up in smuggling drugs, but they don't mix with the drug crowd.'

Unlike the British, Alvarez was too subtle to ask outright what London thought they were doing. He knew that I had asked him a favour and would return it, but he knew also that I went to a lot of trouble not to get my paymasters mixed up.

A week later, I was back in London. I called Newby, suggested a drink and told him the very superficial information I had gathered about the group's lifestyle. 'That's a bit thin,' Newby said.

'You can put it together with what your own people collected down there. Then when you level with me about what the hell you really want, maybe I'll do something about it.'

Newby didn't like my tone but he got the message clearly. I wasn't playing any games in Marbella unless I was properly briefed – and if there was to be a mission involved, properly paid.

Newby came back to me two days later, and over lunch at the Athenaeum Club he told me what MI6 were really after. As I had assumed, the English swimmer was one of their people – an operative from the Royal Marine Special Boat Service – the S.B.S. – on attachment for the mission. He had been swimming out to make contact with a small British submarine – one of two that Naval Intelligence had been using in a major operation to track cargo vessels suspected of carrying I.R.A. arms shipments.

I didn't say what I thought about the swimming escapades. I didn't need to. Newby is a pro who didn't need to be told that it was real boy scout stuff to make yourself that conspicuous when it would have been much more professional for the sub to have sent signals to Portsmouth and for the S.B.S. man to have their contents relayed in veiled terms in a telephone call from London.

However, people have an unfortunate habit of doing what they are trained to do best.

Anyway, S.I.S. (the Security and Intelligence Service) had also had people in Marbella and they were interested in Maitland because they believed his boat was being used to make radio contact with the cargo vessels going through the Strait of Gibraltar, passing on instructions about where to drop the weapons shipments and identifying which of the ships were the carriers and which were the dummy-runs.

'McGrath is a real bastard,' Newby said. 'He's running the operation. It's not his usual game. He's a bomb man mostly. The Provos shoved him down to Spain because things were getting too hot for him in Belfast. He's on the most wanted list. Maitland's doing it for the excitement and the I.R.A. is letting him use his money to pay for their operation. The girl's even more of a thrill-seeker. But she's in very deep. She owns a house in Luton. She's let it to I.R.A. people and they're using it as a safe house. We have tapes of calls in and out. They have already helped one shipment to get through. A big one.'

'So what do you want from me?' I said.

'Nothing much,' Newby said. 'We want you to have a look at the boat. No one has managed to get on board. You live there. You're part of the scene. It shouldn't be too difficult.'

'And after that?' I said.

'We'll see,' Newby said. 'Maybe an assignment, maybe not. The Spaniards are paying the freight for you down there anyway, aren't they?'

The same old undertone was there, as always. This resentment of my working for the Spanish would not go away.

'All right, I'll take a look for you,' I said. 'Just make sure your friends in Six know they're having a favour done for them.'

I have to admit, I wasn't really prepared to put myself out to investigate the boat. I didn't like the way they were handling me even now and I especially didn't like the way they had let me use up a favour with a Spanish contact to find out information they already had from their own people.

In the event, investigating the boat turned out to be so easy that I had the information I wanted within a weekend.

I don't know what kind of efforts S.I.S. had made to examine the M.T.B., but no one had done the obvious and chartered it.

Maybe they hadn't thought of it, but Maitland did take out private parties and I took a girlfriend and a couple of flying pals and paid for us all to have a day's deep-sea fishing. During the trip, making friends with Maitland was no problem; he was a natural extrovert, gregarious and a bit of a show-off who loved to talk about his golfing – and his boat. McGrath had a much deeper professional reserve; he simply didn't care if guests on the boat found him taciturn and unhelpful. He would never have shown me the boat in the way Maitland did, but the Englishman wasn't trained to be suspicious and I showed enough technical interest for him to really open up.

I established two things about the M.T.B. that went a long way to confirming MI6's suspicions that they were doing a lot more than taking fishing trips. First, the boat had a special long-range fuel tank fitted behind the bilge pump, an extra that was quite unnecessary for leisure use as the M.T.B. is perfectly well equipped for normal cruising. Secondly, there was far too much wireless equipment. In fact, they had a unit on board that would not have shamed a service vessel.

I didn't feed the information back to London immediately. I was more interested now than I had been and I spent some time cultivating their friendship. I didn't get involved in their golfing but we started to have a regular evening drink at a little bar in the port in Marbella where I am well known. A week later, I took Maitland and the girl for a flight in my plane, a Rockwell Aero-Commander. I took some aerial photos of Marbella as a cover, and the following week they invited me back for another day's fishing, this time for free.

If I had been McGrath, I would have worried about Maitland. He was too open ever to have made a professional, but presumably the I.R.A. thought it was worth the risk as there could not have been many boats in the area that could have been subverted so easily for their purposes.

I let Juan Alvarez know that I was making a few enquiries for the British but gave him no details at that stage; I was sure he would have his own people watching the trio now anyway. I said nothing about the British use of submarines in trying to track gun-running vessels or about the special equipment on board the M.T.B. Alvarez didn't ask; but he was sharp enough to know that if I did agree to do anything for the British in Marbella, it would be something that the Spanish would also consider to be in their interests.

When I was next in London about a week later, the British did ask me to work for them – but I didn't like what they wanted or how they asked. Colonel Newby carried the message once again and he put it to me in harsh, direct terms.

In London's view, I was getting in too deep with the Spanish. I wasn't co-operating enough with the British. It was time I showed my patriotism. Intelligence wanted Maitland, McGrath and the woman brought back onto British territory; they were counting on me to find a way of doing it.

Equally bluntly, I told Newby to shove it. I wasn't interested and what they wanted wasn't practical anyway. I was resisting for two different sets of reasons. In purely professional terms, an abduction was too complicated to bring off without enormous expense and preparation. The Spanish were watching the group too closely and they would not stand for a messy, complex snatch job which could have done serious damage to Anglo-Spanish diplomatic relations if it had gone wrong. Also, I was sure that the I.R.A. team had more protection in Marbella than MI6 had probably discovered. There were certain to be other I.R.A. people in the area who had no social contact with the group at all, but who would be available as back-up if I moved in on Maitland and McGrath. Alvarez would probably know but Newby was insisting that London didn't want any Spanish involvement.

I was resisting also because I didn't like being pressurized by MI6 about my so-called lack of patriotism. I had nothing to prove to them about my loyalty to Britain and I didn't like that kind of phoney emotional appeal being used to try to get my services as a mercenary on the cheap.

When these kinds of confrontation take place, though, there are always many more nuances and levels of meaning than are at first apparent. MI6 use people like Newby to deal with me because they know he can talk tough to me, in a way that they could never do themselves.

Newby doesn't bother with Civil Service niceties. We talk to each other like soldiers and on this occasion he said simply: 'You have to get the fuckers out, Gayle, or they're going to do you. They'll find a way.'

It is the kind of threat that someone in my profession has to take seriously. I need favours from British Intelligence if I'm going to work within the British spheres of influence. Many of my mercenary activities involve flying, often on the borderline of legality or over it; Intelligence can turn nasty when I'm trying to move sensitive cargoes into areas of the world where there is a strong British presence; I can suddenly find I have licensing problems with my aircraft and they won't stop short of even rougher tactics if necessary.

Favours can be withheld and they can also be offered, and they often are as part-payment for work I've done for them. The British like the trade-off system; it helps preserve the fiction that they aren't really hiring me as a mercenary or that they are not involved in such activities.

This time, what they were asking was too complicated, so I decided to cut through the nonsense.

'If I've got to get involved to get you lot off my back, I'll do a closure job for you. We'll hit the three of them. You tell your people to send the man and the kit.'

Leo went on talking rough and tough but I sensed that it was what he had expected and I had the feeling also that it was what he wanted.

It is important to understand that Newby is not a messenger boy. In these waters, he is a shark. Among the civil servants who often play at intelligence, he is a hard-nosed realist who has long since discovered how to manipulate the whole system to his advantage. As we talked some more, I was convinced that he wanted McGrath dead. Maybe the Irishman had killed a friend of Newby's in Northern Ireland; maybe someone else in the regiment had it in for him. That's the way Intelligence works. It is very personal. And a man like Newby has the leeway to exercise his own killing instincts because his ability to deal with people like me gives him a unique power in Whitehall, among men who don't have the skills to really handle agents in the field. I could easily imagine Newby's report to MI6: 'If you want to use Rivers, he'll get the three of them. But that's all you'll get him to do. You won't get him to fuck around with abductions.'

He would make it sound as though he had failed to arrange the abduction – but he would really be the one doing the manipulating.

'How much are we supposed to increase your fortune by for this one, Gayle?' Newby said finally.

'Ten thousand pounds,' I said.

'Each?'

'No. For the three. Plus everyone gets off my back. I guess it's favours time for all.'

'I'll arrange it,' Newby said.

Within a week of the conversation with Newby, Maitland, McGrath and Shirley Brandon were all dead.

There is no point in trying to dress up the operation; it was not difficult. When I got back to Marbella, I called Maitland and suggested a drink. I told him I'd been commissioned to take some more aerial photos of the area around Marbella and I wanted to feature his boat. I offered him a substantial fee, with £200 up front for advance expenses and petrol, if he would cruise offshore and let me use the boat as a focus for some sea-scapes in the bay. Maitland was flattered and the fee was generous; we settled on the following Wednesday. On the Tuesday night, I went on board the *Methuselah* and planted plastic explosives under the long-range fuel tank, connected to a device for radio detonation which I concealed among the wireless equipment on the bridge. There were a couple of tense moments. The bilge hatch refused to open and I spent twenty minutes ferreting around for a screwdriver; and I had to undo several difficult screws and replace them without leaving signs that they had been tampered with. When it was time to leave, my exit was blocked by passers-by admiring the boat and I had to cross the bow ropes to the boat alongside, force a window and steal a jersey to enable me to slip ashore, passing as a crew member.

The next day, it was all over in two hours. It was a beautifully fine, clear morning. I drove to Malaga airport and collected the man from the London flight – the usual taciturn, nondescript technician. We drove to where I hangared the Aero-Commander and filed a flight plan for Tangiers V.F.R. (Visual Flight Rules), which would take me directly over the point I had asked Maitland to position the M.T.B., about three miles offshore.

Maitland kept the rendezvous exactly as agreed. They had even cleaned up the boat for the photography session and I like to think that it was McGrath who had done the washing and polishing. They were expecting me to come in low and circle the boat but, instead, I flew on a constant heading, passing over the boat to beyond where I would have to report the explosion or be close enough to be linked to it in any way, just in case anyone happened to be watching through glasses.

I let the M.T.B. slide out of sight beneath me and carried on, almost to the limit of the range of the radio detonation signal, then our technician activated the transmission. As he did so, I thought of the girl. What a bloody waste! Silly bitch! I found myself willing her to fall overboard. This was too high a price for 'good times, bad company'.

There was no need for detailed verification. I had packed enough plastic round the fuel tank to reduce the boat to matchwood. There was no chance any of them could have survived. I simply flew straight on, landed at Tangiers, and spent the night there before flying back alone the next day to hear the news of the tragedy.

There was never any enquiry into the explosion. Four weeks earlier there had been a similar blast and an enquiry had established the cause as a spark igniting gas from a faulty fuel feed unit. Local gossip wrote off this explosion as similar – another faulty fuel tank which had mysteriously blown up – and the Spanish authorities did not press for an enquiry, with the approval, no doubt, of Juan Alvarez who did not even mention it to me.

It was a clean hit, with no aftermath, because it was in everyone's interests, but it led directly to a second assassination assignment for the British which involved a game of deadly stalking through Greece and southern Italy. The death of the I.R.A. trio had done serious damage to the gun-running operation, but the next decision taken was to go after the Greek organizer himself.

NINE

A BRITISH OPERATION

It was the Spanish who first identified Nikos Gavrades conclusively as the principal organizer of the arms-smuggling shipments from the eastern Mediterranean to the Basque separatists, E.T.A., and the I.R.A.

It was his company, which he ran out of Athens, that chartered the vessels and arranged the 'innocent' cargoes of coal, scrap iron and chemicals which were interspersed with the arms shipments to confuse the Spanish and British and Irish authorities. When Colonel Alvarez briefed me in Madrid, he did not disclose directly what the Spanish wanted to do about Gavrades. Others actually travelled with some of the shipments and often passed 'within reach' of Spanish Intelligence. They were concerned with Nikos Gavrades who took no active part in any of the arms-smuggling operations—though he was responsible for most of them—and never came close to Spanish jurisdiction.

Alvarez asked me if I would go to Athens on the way back from one of my regular trips to the Middle East and take a look at the Gavrades company—'from a commercial point of view', as he put it. It was to be strictly a routine check, no real undercover work was involved; just a day or so in Athens at Spanish expense, looking at the way Gavrades operated.

I knew what was in the back of Alvarez' mind but he obviously had no mandate to talk to me about it yet and I didn't press him. I accepted the assignment and flew to Athens two weeks later, on my way back from a business trip to Baghdad.

Gavrades was not there at the time; he was working from his other office in Brindisi in southern Italy, and I did a straight commercial scouting job, asking questions which, even if reported back to Gavrades, would not type me as anything more than a potential customer. Superficially, Gavrades ran an operation similar to a dozen other shipbrokers and freight-handling agencies in Athens. Their offices were in the newer section of the port of Piraeus, around the area known as the Lagoon. They occupied two three-storey buildings on the waterfront, with a large clearing warehouse next to them. One give-away to the illegal side of their operations was their use, for additional storage, of two vessels berthed near the warehouse. One of the classic methods of handling illicit shipments is to keep them in a berthed vessel, then moor another ship alongside and make the transfer between the vessels so that no handling takes place on the quay itself.

I asked about Nikos Gavrades' lifestyle and learned that it was opulent without being too ostentatious. He owned a luxurious villa south-east of Athens; he travelled everywhere by top-of-the-line Mercedes cars or by one of two Italian-built high-speed motor launches; the only curiosity was his security team which included both Greeks and Turks. That is a really unusual combination, since the two nationalities do not mix easily, though the Gavrades family had strong links with Cyprus. Gavrades was known to have two Turkish bodyguards as well as one Greek. The word around the docks was that the Turks, especially, were light-hearted lads but real professional heavies; blindly loyal to Gavrades, it was said, because he had some kind of hold over their families on Cyprus.

There wasn't a lot of information to report but I was beginning to get a feel for the way Gavrades operated, which is usually more important for my purposes than collecting bare facts. When I was back in Madrid, I reported personally to Colonel Alvarez. He thanked me, but his reaction was guarded. He showed me some more ship *pro formas*—profiles of cargo vessels which the Spanish suspected Gavrades was using for weapons shipments, with details of the crews and some rather sketchy intelligence reports on their intended itineraries over the coming months. Alvarez hinted that they had been passed to the British and, without saying so outright, he let me know that he was not happy with the state of co-operation between London and Madrid.

At the end of the conversation, it wasn't difficult to guess what Alvarez was working towards. Spanish Intelligence needed to know more about exactly when the arms vessels would pass through Spanish waters and they wanted to know who was working inside Spain to arrange the paperwork and licences for the cargoes – illicit and innocent – to be offloaded. But most of all they wanted to get Nikos Gavrades into their jurisdiction, and I sensed that Alvarez was planning to try to use me as a front man to set up a deal which would make Gavrades hungry enough to risk coming onto Spanish soil.

Obviously, though, Madrid wasn't ready and it was the British who made the first real move about a month later.

The approach was made by Mike Porter, one of MI6's Middle East operatives, a man I've dealt with several times before. Porter is like me in some ways; he works for the British regularly, on a contract basis, but he chooses not to be an insider. Porter ran agents for British Intelligence in Cyprus during the E.O.K.A. terrorist period before independence; a clumsy move by the British administration exposed two of them – nineteen-year-old Greek boys – and they were murdered. Porter went on working for MI6, but mentally he keeps his distance. He goes on because it's a job, it's what he's good at; they keep him on because they need his field experience and his contacts on the ground.

Mike knows that I'm very familiar with the way the Intelligence mind works and he didn't bother dressing up the warning he'd been asked to give me. 'They won't let you get away with working just for the Spanish on the Gavrades thing,' he said. 'They want to be in on this one.' To make the point that I was being watched, he produced copies of some coded telexes I had sent from London to Madrid dealing indirectly with the I.R.A. and E.T.A. arms shipments.

I gave him the answer he must have been expecting: 'The Brits aren't paying, so it's none of their business.' We both knew it was not as clear-cut as that; it was what trade unionists call 'an opening statement' to kick off the negotiations, but Mike had no brief to negotiate.

We sparred for a bit, then he said again: 'They won't let you go ahead with this one just for the Spanish. They want to be in on this.'

'Mike,' I said, 'I didn't say I wasn't available; I just said I'm not interested.'

Mike left it at that. I knew MI6 were serious when they came back to me via a different route, this time through Alexander 'Sandy' Haldane, a man they know I have a great respect for. If a film director were casting someone to embody what the public likes to think of as the best traditions of the British army, he would pick someone like Sandy Haldane. He is a former Royal Green Jackets major who has served with distinction in the regiment. He's good-looking, athletic, well educated, and impeccably turned out whether he is in uniform or in one of his superbly-cut civilian suits. Most of all, his bearing is dignified even when he is under pressure; he is, in short, the prototype aristocratic officer and gentleman. Beneath the image, he is also a hard man – a ruthless, dedicated soldier and, in his patrician way, as much of a straight talker as men like Mike Porter.

In civilian life, Sandy is director of a large defence company with which I do business quite often, and he called me up to suggest a meeting to discuss a possible supply sub-contract. I invited him to lunch at my club. Once the pleasantries were out of the way, he came to the point about Gavrades. The Greek had become an MI6 target for several reasons: the rhythm of the flow of arms from the Middle East was quickening and – as there nearly always is in intelligence matters – there was also a personal angle. In the past six weeks, Gavrades' Turkish bodyguards had been involved in two killings. One, in Paris, had no obvious connection with the arms shipments, but in the second an Englishman had been shot dead in an Athens waterfront bar,

apparently a tourist who had got out of his depth and become involved in a
drunken argument.

'London doesn't like losing its people like that,' Sandy said quietly.
'They've decided they want Gavrades brought in close.'

The phrase has two meanings in the intelligence world. It can mean that
someone is to be killed, or it can mean that the security services have decided
to close in on him and use their full resources, legal and illegal, to get evidence against him.

Sandy quickly made it clear that it was the second option London had
in mind. They wanted to set up Gavrades by using one of my companies
to run a shipment of weapons through Gavrades' system, with me
collecting the evidence along the way.

'We'll give you every support,' Sandy said. 'We'll provide the arms consignment, you won't have to buy on the open market.'

'And the Spanish?' I asked.

'They won't be involved,' Sandy said. 'It will be to their advantage, of
course, but it will be a British operation.'

I said I would tackle it in the same way as I tackle most of my major assignments – in stages, with payment for each stage as I examine the situation and
decide on the feasibility of the next step. Sandy knew that was how I operated and didn't argue. We talked money and agreed, without any quibbling,
on an initial fee to cover the first approach to Gavrades to see what the pros-
pects were of his doing business with me.

For this stage, I sought no support from Sandy. I rang Gavrades' London
office, made an appointment, then went in 'cold', with no introduction, and
announced that I wanted a cargo taken out of Beirut to San Sebastian, for
onward shipment by road into France. I told the agent I was acting for a
French diving company which had been carrying out repairs on vessels in
Beirut harbour and I had been contracted to return some heavy underwater lifting gear to home base. I was deliberately vague about who owned
the equipment but I dropped the names of a couple of specialist
companies—including one of the larger French operators—who were
actively involved in this kind of work in the Lebanon, and I said I wanted to
discuss the shipment with his principals in Athens.

The London agent sent a preliminary telex and I flew to Athens three days
later to meet Nikos Gavrades. I remember it as a very conventional introductory business meeting except that I had trouble suppressing an impolite fas-
cination with Gavrades' hairstyle.

I have never seen one like it on any other man, and for the opening part of
the conversation it was distinctly distracting. Gavrades was in his late forties, rather thick-set for a Greek and a bit overweight, but in most respects
very average-looking except for the haircut which was a one-off special. It

was a military-style crewcut at the front, but at the sides he had let the hair grow longer than normal length, and slicked it hard back, like a 1950s teenager. To complete the mixture, there was a bald spot the size of a large coin right in the centre which gave him an almost clown-like appearance from certain angles.

But in business matters, Gavrades was certainly no clown. Within minutes of our getting down to serious conversation, he had picked up my deliberate mistake. I described my imaginary consignment of lifting gear, mentioning that it might also include a small diving bell, and then specified that I wanted a certain type of 3·5-ton vessel – a type that Gavrades was known to have used at least once for arms shipments.

'The access on such a vessel is not large enough for the goods you are describing, Mr Rivers,' Gavrades said. 'You are in need of a much larger vessel.'

I refused to listen, and insisted again that I wanted exactly that type of vessel. Gavrades just shrugged. 'Very well, Mr Rivers, as you wish,' he said. 'When my men inspect the cargo, we will be able to sort out any difficulties.'

I said I wanted no such inspection. I would take responsibility for the contents of the shipment.

Gavrades smiled. 'Let us be direct,' he said. 'Are we talking of weapons here, or drugs?'

'I'll be direct too,' I said. 'I don't know the exact nature of the consignment. I have been told the kind of vessel required and the route to be taken. Officially, it is diving gear. All I need to know is whether you can make a vessel available.'

'Of course, of course,' Gavrades said blandly. 'The content of the shipment is, as you say, your responsibility, but there are special rates for hazardous cargoes. There will have to be further discussions.'

That evening, he invited me to his villa outside Athens, a house of almost dream-like luxury, which Gavrades appeared to have decorated with fine-looking women, in the way lesser men use plants and flowers. There seemed to be beautiful women planted all over the villa – on the terraces, in alcoves, beside the pool – in little tableaux. There were no men with them, and Gavrades made a point of letting me know that they were available – to me, and to anyone Gavrades should choose.

During dinner, on a terrace looking out towards the islands, he quizzed me again, this time concentrating on the final destination of the merchandise. If the cargo was bound for France, why was it to be unloaded in a Spanish port? I said I had not been told. My freight company had been charged with getting it to San Sebastian; after that, the owners would be responsible.

We were, of course, only playing word games. We had each other's measure by now. Gavrades knew that I would never move a consignment without knowing what it was. I knew that none of his vessels would be chartered until Gavrades knew the exact nature of the shipment, who my principals were, how it would be handled at all stages, and until a precise rate had been haggled over and agreed – within his scale of charges for 'hazardous cargo'.

This was just the preliminary stage, but I felt that he was ready to go further with me, and the situation could now start to develop very quickly. It was time to fly back to London and discuss with Sandy the details of the actual shipment.

I briefed Sandy on my meeting with Gavrades over lunch in a quiet restaurant favoured by Ministry of Defence officials and their suppliers to help preserve the fiction that we were talking about a defence sub-contract – which, in a way, was quite an apt description!

I said I felt Gavrades would deal with me, but I had gone as far as I could, talking in abstract terms; at the next meeting with Gavrades we would have to get down to specifics.

'I'll get onto it this afternoon,' Sandy said. 'I'll call you around six o'clock. Try to keep the evening free.'

He called promptly at six. 'Good news and bad news,' he said. 'Looks as though everything will go ahead as you want, but you aren't going to like the contact.'

'Do I know him?' I asked.

'Oh yes,' Sandy said lightly, trying to pass it off as a joke. 'He shuffles a lot, or so you say. We'll meet you at the Hoop and Grapes at seven o'clock.'

The Hoop is a pub near Harley Street, the centre of fashionable medical practices in London. From choice of meeting place and the reference to shuffling, I knew the contact had to be Ron Baxendale, and I wasn't surprised that Sandy put the phone down before I could yell something rude to him.

I hadn't seen Baxendale for more than a year, but when I saw him with Sandy at the snug bar of the Hoop and Grapes that evening, he had barely changed at all except that his clothes seemed to have grown even more scruffy and threadbare.

Baxendale is an experienced MI6 operative who would be reporting directly to a controller, but he has the look of a failed family doctor who can't think how he is going to meet his month-end bills. Baxendale also has a haunted look about him, the look of a man who is sure someone is bedding his wife and behaves as though it's probably you! Agents like Baxendale come on very strong, but they feel inferior in your presence; they try to counter that by intimidating you, and when that doesn't work, it worries them even more. In his appearance and manners, Baxendale is a very seedy, mediocre character. Even while he's agreeing to fees of hundreds of thousands of pounds, you have the feeling he's planning how he can duck his round of drinks and still put it on his expense account.

Yet it's very important not to underestimate men like Baxendale. A layman could easily write him off as ineffectual, a bit of a twit, but he has too much power to be written off like that. Because of what he does, he's a deadly son of a bitch. He can put you behind bars; he can arrange to have you dealt with in all kinds of ways. He may not really be up to his job, but he's the one doing it and he has the ear of people who can cause you a lot of grief.

I dislike talking in pubs. They're not the place for a serious briefing. You have to use too much veiled language, which is fine when the conversation is between people who are on the same wavelength and can tune in easily to each other's thought processes. With Baxendale, it was a strain and it took more than half an hour of hints and allusions to establish that his boss was prepared to provide an arms shipment, and that they wanted taped evidence of my dealings with Gavrades over it. We also discussed, in the same roundabout terms, the possibility of a closure in killing Gavrades. When I raised it, Baxendale typically took it as a chance to get something done on the cheap. 'If that became necessary for you,' he said, 'I'm sure we wouldn't have any objections.'

'Ron, that's not the way it works,' I said. 'If it becomes necessary, it's something you will authorize and pay for.'

Baxendale didn't like being cornered as directly as that and he used the defence mechanism that always seems to come most readily to that kind of operative: he called a taxi and left. I sometimes think people like Baxendale live in taxis; they seem to be always coming and going in them. I'm sure they change their clothes in them. Maybe they even sleep in them.

When he had gone, I had a final drink with Sandy who could see I wasn't happy, even though Baxendale had – astonishingly – given his authorization for everything I had asked for concerning the weapons consignment and for two further payments for the next stages of the mission. I would have preferred to deal throughout with Sandy personally, but that is not their way. They will use someone who is a known face to you for the running liaison on the mission, then send in someone like Baxendale for a quick in-and-out, unsettling the whole process. However, I decided to go on, cautiously, to the next stage.

I phoned Athens and learned that Gavrades was in his Brindisi office. I wanted to get things moving so I arranged a meeting with him, flew to Rome and drove down to Brindisi in a rented car. This time, I was much more open. I admitted to Gavrades that we were talking about weapons and ammunition, and I said my principals had authorized me to come into the open as they had satisfied themselves through third parties that Gavrades ran a reliable operation. The reason for my frankness was that I was wired for sound, using an extremely sophisticated miniature recorder, made in two parts, located in my shoe heel and belt buckle. It is a beautiful little instrument which escaped expert frisking by one of the Turkish body-guards, but it has the serious drawback that its playing time is only ten minutes. You activate the microphone by running your fingertip along the top of the waistband of your trousers – a gesture that normally attracts no attention – but you have to choose your moment carefully, because once the recorder in the heel is running, it cannot be switched off.

I wanted Gavrades on tape agreeing to handle a weapons shipment but he was far too cautious to make that kind of commitment. Instead, he made general encouraging noises and asked me to give him the name of someone he knew who could vouch for my principals. I wasn't surprised; I had set the tape running only on the off-chance that he would commit himself. I asked for twenty-four hours to get the 'name'.

At this point, I improvised, going right outside my mandate from Sandy, and called Madrid instead of London. Though Sandy himself is a great improviser in a fighting situation, he is far too British in upbringing and training to have approved of my call to Colonel Alvarez. It was a call that made good sense to me – within the framework of a mercenary's logic. For a mercenary, it is always prudent to stay a little bit further down the path than your paymasters think you are – that way they can't chop you so easily with-out warning.

I didn't know how much Alvarez knew, through liaison with the British, about my assignment, but I had sensed that he was happy with my move-ments between London and Athens and he had stopped hinting about bringing Gavrades onto Spanish soil. I knew Alvarez would grant me the favour I asked, knowing that an operation against Gavrades, which the Spanish government did not have to pay for, could only be to their advan-tage. I called Alvarez from a pay-phone in Brindisi and asked him to arrange the arrest of a Spaniard who was being watched by Spanish Intelligence and who was known to have played a part in a joint E.T.A.-I.R.A. arms ship-ment on one of Gavrades' vessels. Sandy could have found me a name equally well, but he would not have moved as quickly as Alvarez, and any-way in my profession it pays never to be predictable.

Alvarez didn't hesitate and the next morning I made a second call to Mad-rid and received confirmation that the arms middleman, Juan Ortega, had been picked up for questioning.

Within an hour, I had given Ortega's name to Gavrades. The Greek knew Ortega well – that much had been established months previously in the early investigations into the arms-smuggling route. The question now was whether Gavrades would deal with me, once he discovered that the

Spaniard had been arrested and couldn't be reached for confirmation of my bona fides.

It would probably be at least another day or so before I knew the answer, but in the meantime I had another problem, a phone call from my own London office hinting that there were no signs of even the earliest preparations for the promised arms shipments out of Beirut.

I took the decision immediately to fly to London. It would get me out of Gavrades' way and save awkward questions about Ortega, and it would also give me a chance to check at first hand the most important aspect of the whole deal – whether there was any chance I might be pushed out onto a very precarious limb by the powers that be and left with no weapons to back up my presentation to Gavrades.

In London, I deliberately avoided calling Sandy. I arrived at Heathrow at ten o'clock in the evening and went straight to a small flat in the part of London known traditionally as 'behind Harrods'. It belonged to a man called Nigel Redpath who ran a shipping agency which British Intelligence used for a number of its freight-handling operations. Baxendale had indicated at the meeting at the Hoop and Grapes that Redpath would be dealing with the arms shipment. With no preliminary phone call, I went to the flat and found Redpath. I admit I was in a very irritable mood; I don't like being messed about over something as important as my dealings with the Greek, and when Redpath tried to stall, I literally put him up against the wall with my elbow across his throat. Redpath is not one of nature's heroes and straightaway he confirmed that he had received no instructions. 'There's been some talk about a shipment but I've had nothing firm yet,' he said, adding almost in a whine, 'Look, I just do what they tell me to do. It's not my fault.'

I didn't stay to argue with Redpath. It was already past midnight and I went straight over to St James's to Sandy's flat and pressed the buzzer on the entryphone at the main entrance.

'Sandy, it's Gayle,' I said, when he answered. 'I think you'd better come down and talk to me.'

Sandy came downstairs immediately and we went for a walk along an almost deserted Pall Mall, towards Buckingham Palace, then turned into one of the paths leading across St James's Park. Apart from a few lovers and home-going revellers, there was hardly anyone about and I told Sandy bluntly what had just happened at Redpath's flat.

When Intelligence falls down like that, it can either be deliberate or a fuck-up. I had already decided that this was probably the latter – there is certainly no shortage of those within Intelligence – but that was no consolation.

I came to the point in a clearing beside the Mall, leaning on some crowd-barriers that were being stored under the trees ready for a parade the next day.

'Sandy, I'm going to hit the Greek,' I said.

Sandy was appalled. 'You can't,' he said. 'It's too early for that. We haven't got a quarter of the intelligence we want. I'm sure the shipment is coming through.'

'Maybe it is,' I said; 'but that's no longer good enough. I'm out front and vulnerable. If I press ahead with Gavrades and no weapons appear, I am fully exposed. That's not an acceptable risk. You tell the powers that be in the morning that I'm going to hit the Greek and I expect them to pay for it.'

Angrily, I gave him the details of what I wanted done to repair the situation. I knew that now I had taken this stand, no weapons would ever appear, but at least some documentation could be provided to improve my cover in the short term.

Sandy hated every minute of the conversation. He knew he was having to defend an indefensible position and he does not like situations where friends become openly aggressive. He is an urbane man who likes to sort things out smoothly, but I deliberately let him see that I was at the point where I had to be listened to. When you do the work I do, it is essential for people to be a bit afraid of you. They have to understand that if they let you down, there are going to be consequences – for them. Otherwise, you can too easily be treated as a pawn in the permanent games played by the intelligence bureaucracies. I wasn't threatening Sandy. I was conveying through him my anger at the contractors in a way that would leave no doubt that they had to do what I wanted.

The next morning I called Athens and left a message for Gavrades that I would be arriving and was ready to inspect the vessel. Then I called Marseilles and asked my old mercenary friend, Yves Kergal, to join me for a little job in Greece.

TEN

THE FINAL RUN

It amazes even me sometimes how quickly a man like Kergal can organize some weapons. Within half an hour of my briefing him in a little café near Athens airport the next day, he had arranged for us to collect two 9mm Browning pistols from a contact in the city. I have my own weapons caches in various places, but when possible I prefer to keep them in reserve and make use of Kergal's underworld connections which give him instant access to a network of untraceable weapons.

When we had collected them, I called Gavrades at his villa and told him that my consignment manager had arrived and we were ready to inspect the ship as soon as possible. Gavrades wasn't too pleased at being called that early in the morning, but he invited us to lunch at the villa and said he would arrange for us all to go out straight afterwards to the cargo vessel he had in mind for us.

The lunch was tense, despite the relaxed setting and the constant attentions of Gavrades' little knots of beautiful women. The problem was the Spanish contact, Ortega. Gavrades had made several calls to Madrid and Ortega was still being held by the Spanish authorities. I pretended that this news made me jumpy too and wondered to Gavrades whether there was any connection between the arrest and the shipment I was handling. The Greek wasn't happy at all, but he agreed to take us out to the ship, with no further commitment beyond that, until he had been in touch with Ortega.

We went out to the ship in one of Gavrades' Italian launches – a really beautiful job, fast and sleek, all engine, with just enough room under the canopy to make a few passengers comfortable.

There were five of us on board during the swift exhilarating ride out to the berthage area: Kergal and myself, Gavrades and two Turkish bodyguards, both built in the wrestler mould with thick necks and sloping shoulders and differing only in that one was in the middleweight division, the other a heavyweight. I was not yet sure how soon I wanted to try for the hit, but I had agreed in advance with Kergal that we should look for the first opportunity to improve the odds against us by taking out one of the Turks. Kergal is brilliant at arranging 'accidents' – it is his house speciality, as it were – and

I had told him that if he saw any chance from this point on, he should not waste it.

The vessel was a typical Greek coaster, battered but still serviceable, and the only thing that struck me as odd about it was that again there was a mixed crew of Greeks and Turks, under a Greek skipper.

The captain greeted us effusively and took us for drinks to his tatty, smoke-stained cabin. We sat in the cramped quarters, chatting affably in an assortment of broken languages; the only sour note was a feeling I had that Gavrades was still suspicious of Kergal.

The difficulty was that Kergal did not know enough about the situation to back up my verbal manoeuvring about Ortega and the cargo and was leaving the talking to me. I emphasized as best I could that Kergal was only a technician; as my consignment manager, his job was to inspect the vessel to make sure that my freight company stood to make money out of the deal and would not encounter any costly loading or shipment difficulties. Fortunately, Kergal is very knowledgeable about ships. He comes from a Breton family, though he is married to a mainland Corsican woman and is far more at home in the Marseilles-Corsican milieu than in Brittany. He was able to ask searching questions about the vessel and his knowledge also gave him a chance to have a go at one of the Turks.

The stuffiness of the Master's cabin gave me a good excuse to suggest that we go up on deck, and while the Master and Gavrades took me forward to look at the view, Kergal went aft with one of the Turks and a seaman to check on the hold. The 'accident' came minutes later. There was scarcely any noise, only some cursing and a shout from Kergal that the Turk had slipped while trying to follow the seaman along the edge of the hold and appeared to be dead.

It was a tricky moment. Neither Kergal nor I was armed; our weapons were in the rental car back at Gavrades' villa. If anyone were suspicious of the Turk's fall, it would mean some nasty, unarmed infighting, but Kergal managed to be completely convincing. He described the fall, but allowed the seaman to show us the place, a narrow, slippery passage between some winding gear at the corner of the hold. The Turk had fallen more than twenty feet onto a metal surface and his neck had broken cleanly; death had been immediate and there were no worries about the possibility of a dying man's accusations, but even though Kergal was not blamed, the death caused immediate panic in our party.

Foul play or not, there was now a body on board and Gavrades and the Greek Captain disagreed sharply over what to do about it. They started arguing agitatedly in Greek which I could not understand so I asked Gavrades what was happening. He said that he was in favour of dumping the Turk in the bay, but the Master was insisting on reporting the death to the authorities as he was sure his crew would talk once they were on shore.

Eventually, the Master won the argument but Gavrades himself had no intention of being on board the ship when the police arrived. He hustled Kergal and me back down into the launch with the other Turk and we set off shorewards. We could not take the direct route into the harbour for fear of being seen by the police launch which would soon be on its way to the ship, so we headed southwards along the shoreline.

I was concerned now that too much time was slipping by. Once we were away from the ship, Gavrades began to relax and he was quite happy to cruise about, killing time until the police had done their investigation and returned to shore. To avoid that, I suggested that we should go ashore up the coast somewhere and have a drink. Gavrades liked the idea. He knew the coast well and always enjoyed playing host, so he ordered the helmsman to turn into a small fishing port-cum-holiday resort about five or six miles from the berthage area. We drank on the terrace of a tiny café right on the jetty, reclining in white steamer chairs under brilliant orange parasols. It was one of those moments when you really are struck by the incongruity of the contrast between the events you are living and what is going on around you. Apart from the bar owner and a couple of fishermen who recognized Gavrades and came to pay their respects, everyone on the terrace was a tourist. Most of them were British and though, mercifully, they were subdued by the afternoon heat, they still chattered happily, glancing frequently at us and at our launch which had docked with something of a flourish as Gavrades was a man who liked to make an impression.

For these tourists we were the centrepiece of the picturesque local setting. They had no way of knowing that they were looking at two mercenary assassins, an international arms dealer who was on British Intelligence's most wanted list and was nearing the hour of his death, and a Turkish killer. Probably no one on the quay had ever been closer to people like us than in a seat at a James Bond movie and I am sure they could not have mentally accepted that such a situation had suddenly become part of their real lives.

We stayed on the quayside for about half an hour. I was growing more and more impatient and, as Gavrades seemed to know the locals well, I asked him if there was anywhere he could hire or borrow a car so we could return to Athens by road. The trip in itself would not create the opportunity for the hit, but I wanted to get the whole situation in motion again. Gavrades was getting a bit restless too; there was no more to be had from this village in his role as wealthy visiting patriarch and a Mercedes was quickly found for us.

At this point, Gavrades was not at all suspicious of me and he accepted quite happily my suggestion that he and I should take the car, leaving Kergal and the other Turk to go back in the launch. Kergal would have to arrive in Piraeus with the other Turk intact – he had got away with one accident, but a second one would blow our cover wide open. Also, our own hire car, with our weapons in it, was still at Gavrades' villa and we could not get back inside the well-guarded perimeter walls without Gavrades. But at least we were moving again. Gavrades drove the Mercedes along the coast road and we stopped only once for a brief patriarchal performance at another small village.

On the journey, Gavrades tried to persuade me to stay overnight. He offered me hospitality at the villa and the companionship of my choice of his women, but I insisted that I must get away that night. We went back to his office at the Piraeus docks, met up with Kergal and the Turk who arrived soon afterwards in the speedboat, then Gavrades and I settled down to another negotiating session.

Once again, there was a risk we would lose momentum. Gavrades was quite happy to while away the evening in a chat. He wasn't ready anyway to close any deal until he had spoken to Ortega who was still in gaol in Madrid, and I think he was quite enjoying my company, or at least enjoying having a foreigner to show off to, and was quite ready to let the evening pass the point when I would have no choice but to stay.

The Turkish bodyguard left, presumably at the end of his stint of duty, and was replaced by an equally burly Greek Cypriot guard, who was extremely suspicious both of me and of Kergal. The evening dragged on, with an interlude for an early supper at a fish restaurant near the office because Gavrades was hungry again. At the end of the meal, I said that I must leave, come what may, to catch one of the late flights out of Athens. At the same time, I signalled to Kergal that it was time to try to create an opportunity for the final run.

Kergal took my cue and announced that he had lost his cigarette lighter and thought he had left it in the launch.

Gavrades, seeing he was not able to persuade me to stay, reluctantly offered to drive me to the airport – this time in his personal Mercedes – and on the way we were to stop off at the marina to look for Kergal's lighter. The Cypriot bodyguard drove and, on Gavrades' instructions, parked on a small promontory overlooking the main harbour. It was lit up now in the deepening dusk, and Gavrades, ever playing the host, wanted to show me the view while Kergal went for the lighter. To allay any suspicions, Kergal insisted on going alone, but I did not need to be told what the plan was. During the break in the discussions at the office, Kergal had told me that on the way back in the launch, the Turk had boasted about the weapons that were kept on board and had even shown the Frenchman the secret arms compartment in the cockpit of the boat!

As I expected, Kergal vanished into the crowd of people strolling along the edge of the marina and did not return. After a while, Gavrades became mildly agitated and sent the Cypriot bodyguard down to see what was happening.

The marina was quite silent. The small crowd watching the boats had moved on, leaving us with the rhythmic sound of water lapping against the hulls. As we waited, it subconsciously registered that the water was becoming more disturbed, and I instinctively realized that it was due to the activity on Gavrades' launch.

There was a delay of about twenty minutes then, very quietly, Kergal opened the rear door of the Mercedes, on Gavrades' side, slid in beside him, and thrust the muzzle of a small Czech machine pistol hard into his ribs.

Gavrades' face drained of all colour. Kergal's move was a total shock. The Greek had not anticipated it at all and he was too scared to form even basic words. Kergal said nothing. He didn't need to. He told me later what had happened on the launch.

He had gone down supposedly to look for the lighter and had concealed himself in the aft well. Kergal knew he would have to deal quickly with whoever came down, as although the launch was moored at Gavrades' private landing stage, well away from the passing strollers on the quay, there was still a chance that a commotion would be heard or seen. When the Greek Cypriot bodyguard had come down, Kergal had tackled him low in the legs, dragging him down out of sight, and aimed what was supposed to be a death blow at the base of his neck. Kergal punches like a man who can make holes in a tree trunk, but he had managed only to stun the bodyguard and he had been forced into a vicious and messy struggle which had ended only when he had managed to crush the man's skull by banging it against one of the metal mooring rings protruding from the quay just above the side rail of the launch. Kergal had hidden the body under a tarpaulin in the stern of the boat, forced open the weapons compartment and brought back the Czech machine pistol he was now pressing against Gavrades' side, and a small Beretta which he handed to me.

I got out of the car and motioned to Gavrades to get into the driving seat. He was too petrified to argue and I got into the front passenger seat beside him, leaving Kergal in the back seat, with the muzzle of the machine pistol stuck into Gavrades' neck. I told Gavrades to drive us back up to the villa. He tried to stall, saying he would do a deal, but a quick prod from Kergal urged him into action.

My immediate task was to calm Gavrades down. We could not kill him until we had retrieved the hire car and our own weapons, which meant making sure the Greek's nerve held long enough to get us in through the villa gates and out again.

The conversation that took place on the drive to the villa was too incoherent to reconstruct in detail. Part of it consisted of crisp orders from Kergal to stop Gavrades from driving too fast. He wasn't trying any particular tricks, but fear was making him put his foot down too hard on the accelerator and we were also weaving conspicuously on corners in a car that was already well known in the area.

Gavrades wanted to know if we were with Intelligence. I said no. This was a business problem; we represented a dissatisfied customer. As I had intended, this calmed him a bit. I deliberately spoke quite matter-of-factly, in the kind of voice that told him a deal was definitely going to be possible. Gradually, Gavrades regained control of himself and he began to talk rapidly, almost non-stop, as though he could somehow contain the situation by smothering it with words.

He began to blabber about his customers, reeling off name after name as he tried to establish which one we were working for. He was too terrified to be prudent and he gave us an unexpected intelligence bonus which I later divided up judiciously between my British and Spanish paymasters. I played him along, refusing to say who had sent us – though I can't pretend any skill was needed. By now, Gavrades was simply pouring names out in terror.

'Just tell me what it will cost me,' he kept saying between bursts of anger at the contacts he thought had paid for his death. 'I am a businessman. I'll pay. I know how to settle these things.'

When we got to the villa, it was quite dark, but we could see plenty of movement inside the walls. The grounds of the villa were not large on the road side of the house. There were tall iron gates, with an entryphone speaker on one pillar, and the gates opened onto a drive not much more than a hundred yards long, leading up to the villa. The garden and a tennis court at the side were in darkness, but there was movement and activity in the cluster of lights around the main door and we could make out at least two people close to where Kergal had parked our rented Citroen.

Kergal is always exceptionally cool in these circumstances. He slid the machine pistol over to me, then got out of the car and nonchalantly walked over to the speaker on the gate. He said in French that he was with Mr. Gavrades and we had come to collect the Citroen. A voice answered in Greek.

'Flash your lights,' I said. Gavrades did so, and after a few seconds' pause, the gates began to swing open. Kergal got back in, and Gavrades drove slowly into the grounds. As soon as we were in, the gates began to close again and I saw the beginnings of a smile forming on Gavrades' face.

'Stop. Stop, right now,' I said sharply. Kergal got out and I said to Gavrades, 'Flash your lights again.'

Gavrades hesitated. I could see he was beginning to feel secure for the first time since the marina, with the villa gates closed behind him and his men not much more than fifty yards away.

It was time to get Gavrades' full attention. I pushed the muzzle of the Beretta pistol hard into his mouth, cracking two side teeth and making him cry out with pain and fear. Gavrades could not flash his lights fast enough, then he sat, his hands on the steering wheel, whimpering quietly, his whole body rigid with fear.

Immediately the gates began to open again. By now, Kergal had reached the Citroen and I ordered Gavrades to back up. He reversed the Mercedes back through the gates and Kergal followed in the Citroen, at an almost leisurely pace, waving to two men on the steps of the villa entrance as he did so. When we were outside, I made Gavrades use a small side road to do a three-point turn. We let Kergal go past, then set off after him, at a fast pace, heading for the airport.

On this final stage of the journey, Gavrades became frantic. Names poured out again as he begged me to do a deal. I mostly kept quiet, pressing the Beretta into his ribs whenever he made a wrong driving move and allowed him to keep up the flow of what had become serious and valuable intelligence data.

As we neared the airport, he started to curse, harder and harder, then turned to whining again.

'Why do you want to kill me?' he moaned. 'I work for everybody. Who cares if a few lousy Spaniards get blown up. The Spanish government doesn't care. They do business with me. I have contacts in Britain. Everybody wants weapons. I cheat nobody.'

Interspersed with all of this, his figures for buying me off went on escalating as he became more and more distraught. We were up to a million dollars as the price of his life as we drove into the airport parking zone.

It was almost 10.30 and time to finish the job. I told Gavrades to stop the Mercedes; Kergal parked beside us and transferred our two unused Brownings from the Citroen to the rear door pocket in the Mercedes. I handed Kergal my passport and he drove the Citroen over to the European lot, depositing the keys, then took out our hand luggage and went into the departure terminal building.

As he disappeared through the glass doors, I said to Gavrades, 'All right, let's talk serious money.' But he was too scared now to do more than repeat his wild figures.

Kergal came back without the hand luggage and he signalled to me that our departure was arranged. He got into the back of the Mercedes, retrieved the machine pistol, and we drove slowly along the perimeter fence. It was fully dark now and there were only a handful of planes drawn up, ready for the final departures of the night.

Gavrades was struggling to regain some kind of calm. I could sense that part of him simply would not believe that we were prepared to kill him. He was thinking like a merchant. What was the point? What was the profit for us? Who could possibly turn down offers of money so infinitely greater than what must surely be our fees as assassins?

At Athens airport there is a main terminal, then a general aviation park reserved for small private aircraft. I made Gavrades stop the Mercedes about two hundred yards down the perimeter fence, well away from the activity of the arrival area. Most of the movement around the terminal consisted of groups of tourists, who had come in on the last off-peak flights, boarding coaches lined up and marked with placards bearing the names of hotels and tour operators. In our part of the parking zone, there were only a handful of cars.

When the Mercedes came to a stop, Kergal got out, leaving the machine pistol on the floor of the Mercedes. I got out too, walked a short distance away and stood, to act as a look-out, with my arms stretched up on the wire fence, apparently gazing at the small aircraft on the tarmac and enjoying the view across to the low hills on the far side of the field which were studded with the lights of isolated houses and the occasional moving vehicle.

Gavrades thought he had won some kind of reprieve. Then, very quietly, Kergal ordered him to crouch down, with his head below the level of the steering wheel. He still could not bring himself to believe what was about to happen, and even with his face contorted from the discomfort of his position, he went on hissing figures and begging me to make a deal.

Kergal shot him once, in the back of the head, right at the base of the skull. The Beretta was not silenced but it made scarcely any noise. Kergal had positioned himself outside the car so there was no risk of being splashed with blood or tissue and he had measured the angle carefully to avoid any risk of breaking glass.

As Kergal walked away from the car, there was no trace of violence. Gavrades' body had slumped forward onto the floor of the car. To anyone passing on the perimeter road, it was just an empty, luxurious Mercedes, legally parked, waiting, perhaps, for the owner to pick it up after flying in on his private jet.

Kergal caught up with me and we walked casually down the perimeter road towards the main terminal. Shielding my hand from view behind Kergal's back, I took the Beretta, wiped it clean and held it wrapped palmed in my hand. As we approached the terminal, there was a pile of baggage belonging to some incoming tourists who were busy competing for good seats on a waiting coach. Several of the bags were open-topped. I picked a half-empty duty-free carrier bag and slipped the Beretta in as we passed.

That would take care of the disposal. No one who finds a gun abroad – at least, no one with any sense – reports it to the police. I was sure that some anguished tourist would do my disposal job for me, hurling the Beretta out to sea somewhere.

Though late now, it was still a warm evening. We had a few minutes to wait and Kergal bought me a beer at the little bar in the departure lounge. Neither of us said very much. Then we caught the last flight to Geneva.

ELEVEN

BASQUE SEPARATISTS: SPAIN AUTHORIZES SECRET WAR

The Spanish government gave its final approval for the secret war against Basque terrorists in France at a meeting in a restaurant in Madrid at the end of 1979. There I was authorized to begin a series of operations to assassinate or kidnap and bring back into Spain a number of leaders of the Basque separatist movement E.T.A. – operations which would eventually cost the Spanish authorities almost a quarter of a million pounds sterling in contract fees and cause the deaths of more than a dozen key E.T.A. figures.

No details were discussed in the restaurant; the groundwork had been laid over many weeks of negotiations, figures had been agreed and methods discussed. The purpose of this meeting was to bring me face to face with the senior official of the Ministry of the Interior who would be personally responsible for using foreign mercenaries for the first time against the Basques who were hitting hard against targets in Spain, then retreating to sanctuaries on the other side of the Pyrenees in the French Basque region.

The restaurant, el Botin, was one of the most romantic in old Madrid, situated in the calle Cuchilleros in the picturesque warren of alleys close to the central Plaza Major. On the ground floor, ornate glass doors open straight onto the foot of a narrow staircase which leads up to the first-floor restaurant. As I walked in, I was greeted warmly by Colonel Juan Alvarez. The police and the Interior Ministry use this restaurant regularly, and their private security routines are well practised. Everything was worked out for the protection of the man I was to meet. At the top of the staircase, waiting to welcome me, was José-Martin Bolivar, the security services' chief interpreter. He is a round-shouldered man, balding, though probably only in his thirties. He looked an almost shrunken figure beside Alvarez who, though well into his sixties with grizzled hair and a deeply lined face, still retains the powerful block-like physique which made him a figure of awe during his years as one of General Franco's personal bodyguards. Other guests entering the restaurant were discreetly held back so that I was the only person on the staircase, covered by Alvarez from below and Bolivar from above.

The restaurant is extremely fashionable. The walls are covered with elegant blue and white tiles and decorated with scenes of old Andalucia; even Madrid's leading families have trouble getting reservations, but I did not need to look around to know that at least two other strategically placed tables would be occupied by police marksmen.

Somewhat incongruously, the Interior Ministry official, as a gesture of courtesy towards my English-speaking background, had been given the code-name Richard. As I approached the table, I couldn't help thinking that it was hard to imagine a less suitable name for someone so typically Spanish-looking. He was in his mid-forties, short, stocky, with swarthy skin and tight black curly hair. He sat like a man who is used to being active, and though dressed like a senior civil servant in a tan blazer and superbly creased slacks, he had the air of someone who has seen his share of the active side of security work.

When I reached the table, he did not get up. Instead, he nodded and placed his hand palm upwards on the table cloth. As I sat down, I placed mine on his in a half handshake. We exchanged greetings and Alvarez said: 'The lamb is excellent.' It was obviously my cue that preparations had been made and no time was to be wasted on restaurant routines. Within a minute, a whole lamb, delicately roasted and spiced, was brought; within five minutes, our table looked as though we had been in the restaurant for an hour.

For such a momentous occasion, the conversation was remarkably low key. My Spanish was good enough to understand most of what was said, but the interpreter put it into English anyway, using rather flamboyant and formal phrases, as though we were discussing a contract to organize an opera tour instead of one to go outside the legal process and attack the Basque terrorists on their own ground.

The phrases all referred to 'confirmation of agreements' and 'implementing earlier understandings'. The sole purpose of the meeting was for 'Richard', to make a personal assessment of me and decide whether I could be trusted with a mission which could – if it went wrong – bring down the government or cause a break in relations with France, or possibly both.

My views on dealing with terrorists had become known to the Interior Ministry through what is known in Spain as 'the channel of the colonels'. In the Spanish military, colonel is the level at which things really get done and there is a lot of mobility between the services. The Guardia Civil, for example – the paramilitary force which does rural policing, border control and is responsible for institutions in urban areas which are of national concern, such as banks, post offices and embassies – recruits its men direct, but members of its officer corps are all transferred from the army. So a retired colonel who works as my commercial agent in Madrid negotiates an equipment deal with an engineering colonel who used to command a battalion in the

Spanish Sahara where he fought alongside a parachute commander who is now with the Guardia Civil, attached to military intelligence. In the process, I am introduced along this line of contacts and we discuss military matters of current concern.

At that period, nothing was of greater concern than E.T.A. terrorism. E.T.A., which stands for Euzkadi Ta Askatasuna, meaning Basque Homeland and Liberty, is fighting for the creation of an independent Basque Marxist state. It is a sophisticated and skilled terrorist organization which had already successfully carried out hundreds of murders, bombings, kidnappings and bank raids. Apart from its international connections, especially with the I.R.A. and the P.L.O., E.T.A.'s biggest asset was the mountainous Pyrenean border between Spain and France which divides the area the Basques consider to be their homeland. Just as the United States failed to seal the border with Cambodia during the Vietnam war, and the British face the continuing nightmare of trying to close off Northern Ireland from the Republic, the Spanish have never managed to block the hundreds of paths through the valleys, pastures and high passes of the Pyrenees.

E.T.A. operates with a cell structure; E.T.A. members captured in Spain know little or nothing about the activities and identities of other cells. Only the leaders know the overall picture and they control their operations from the safety of the French Basque region, around the resort city of Biarritz.

Spain had never managed to persuade France to take decisive action against E.T.A. Successive French governments had promised increased co-operation in rounding up and extraditing known terrorists, but effective action was never taken. The Basques had repeatedly threatened that they would begin terrorist operations in France itself – including Paris – if the French moved against them. Faced with this threat, the French attitude was to tolerate the Spanish Basques as long as they made no trouble on French soil.

The Spanish security authorities also faced serious problems internally in dealing with the Basques. With the general loosening up of political life which followed the death of General Franco in 1975, the increasingly liberal attitude towards the Basques and the policy of encouraging them to participate in national life had allowed E.T.A. sympathizers to infiltrate every area of government and all the security services and police forces. Conversely, it was virtually impossible for a non-Basque to penetrate the Basque milieu, making counter-intelligence a nightmare. As liberalization continued, the left-wing press, released from the constraints of censorship in the post-Franco area, were constantly praising Basque 'freedom fighters', and the student community was, as always, quick to grant the terrorists heroic status.

But men like 'Richard' and Juan Alvarez had had enough – and their voices in favour of direct, extra-legal action were beginning to be heard more sympathetically as the Basques themselves grew more and more ruthless.

The trigger which made the secret war possible was probably the attempt on the life of the Prime Minister, Adolfo Suarez, a few months earlier, using an RPG-7 rocket. Publicity about the attack had been suppressed but only a failed firing mechanism saved Suarez's life. The RPG-7 is a shoulder-held, man-portable anti-tank weapon which fires a high-explosive round. It is a bit like a miniature bazooka, extremely effective and, as it is cheap to buy and easy to use, it is favoured by terrorists over much more sophisticated American and British hardware. It is a Soviet design, copied by the Chinese and manufactured in five or six different countries under licence.

An E.T.A. unit, helped by an I.R.A. instructor, brought one into Spain, mounted it on the back seat of a private car and aimed it at Suarez's bedroom window at the Prime Minister's residence in Madrid, set to be triggered by a timing device, powered by a 24-volt battery. Luckily, there are two safety devices on the RPG-7 and only one of them had been switched to the armed position. The rocket was fired and struck just below the bedroom window, but it failed to explode and clattered down harmlessly into the garden below! A good joke for the Guardia Civil mess hall, but one told through clenched teeth, because the security experts knew how close it had come.

There had also been, in the same period, some dramatic ambushes of Guardia Civil personnel in the Basque country, and an attack on the Guardia Civil barracks in San Sebastian which had shaken the security community badly. An E.T.A. squad had simply pulled up in cars on an elevated stretch of motorway which ran above the barracks and had opened fire over the parapet onto units on the parade ground below.

Police counter-measures were also becoming more and more tough. At that time, it was not uncommon to drive through the Basque country and suddenly have a police helicopter swoop down onto the road in front of your car; you would be ordered through a loud-hailer to get out of your vehicle and spread yourself on the bonnet, and in seconds you would find yourself surrounded by three policemen with submachine guns.

But the Basques were winning, mainly because of their ability to use France as a safe haven, and my attitude to adversaries like that hasn't changed since I had my first real experience of guerrilla warfare in Indonesia and in Vietnam. I take the view that there is no point in needlessly complicating the problem, you take them on their own ground.

The Basques were operating completely outside the framework of the law. Because of French obstructionism, the legal processes of extradition and trial were completely impotent – but that does not mean that those responsible for national security have to simply sit there and wring their hands!

Up to that point, Spanish military and police intelligence had limited their activities in France to gathering information about the Basque exiles. The only attempt at direct action had been by a loosely-knit group of right-wing fanatics, former Franco activists whose style was to get drunk, then charge across the border in a fit of alcohol-induced patriotism and shoot up some bar or other where E.T.A. supporters were know to congregate. Some of them were former Guardia Civil troopers and the Guardia had given its unofficial blessing to some of their raids, occasionally helping them back across the border. But their efforts were disorganized and clumsy. There was no advance intelligence-gathering; innocent people got hurt and the raids placed a severe strain on Franco-Spanish relations without achieving any real success.

Alvarez and others who had supported the plan to hire me knew they were buying a totally different level of professionalism. I already had a good track record with the Spanish. I had established myself over several years as a reliable supplier of military equipment and as a tactical adviser to the Spanish security forces, the G.E.O.S. I had also supplied them with good intelligence on the movements of E.T.A. people in the Middle East and they were aware of the Marbella assassinations and the operation against Gavrades.

These last two operations had particularly impressed Alvarez and, I had been told, 'Richard' also; but because they had been carried out for British Intelligence, they had also raised doubts about whether I could give my primary loyalty to Spain.

I could understand their concern, but I had no personal doubts at all. I am not really a 'pure' mercenary. I choose my causes carefully and have refused many paymasters over the years, but once I make a decision to accept an assignment, I make a full commitment. I consider the Queen to be my Queen, and in time of war that is where my priorities would lie, but I hold no overriding accountability to Britain. As far as the British were concerned, this was an offshore problem which I was dealing with, in commercial terms, for a Spanish client. In fact, successful operations against E.T.A. could only benefit Britain, given the tight liaison between E.T.A. and the I.R.A., but that was a secondary point, and did not influence my decision to accept the Spanish contract.

'Richard' was bothered because of the widespread disillusionment in Spanish intelligence circles about liaison with British Intelligence. Two recent events had soured them in particular. Several weeks before the Madrid dinner, I had visited the police morgue in Madrid to be shown the body of an Irish-American who had been killed in a shoot-out between the Spanish police and an E.T.A. terrorist group. The Spanish had established that he was an I.R.A. instructor who had trained E.T.A. cadres in Libya and had been brought in to Spain to advise on a particular terrorist operation. Presumably because of the political sensitivity of having an American citizen working for the I.R.A. and active in Spain, the British had clammed up and virtually refused to co-operate in further investigations, which had infuriated the Spanish.

During the same period there had also been yet another foul-up which had allowed an arms shipment to slip through. Madrid had warned London that some weapons destined for the I.R.A. were on board a cargo ship which had recently docked in Bilbao. The ship had sailed on, with the weapons still on board, and the Spanish had warned Britain that they were going to be offloaded in France, put into container lorries and shipped by road to Rotterdam, then on to Holyhead in Wales. The British had checked with French Intelligence who reported having no knowledge of any such movement. The British had trusted the French over the Spanish and, as a result, the arms shipment had gone through.

I had been briefed on the background to all of these problems by Alvarez and his associates and when they were raised, in veiled terms, at the dinner, I was able to give 'Richard' reassurances – but not too many. One of my principles in these kinds of negotiation is not to come on too strong: I am not in the business of hard-selling my services. Many people in the mercenary world can talk a good game, but in the end only performance counts.

I stood out especially firmly when 'Richard' himself attempted to come on strong at one point. Essentially, he was hoping for some kind of 'proving operation' – a demonstration run almost, which he could point to and say to his Minister and the Prime Minister, 'This is what Rivers can do. This is what you're paying for.' In the stilted commercial language we were using in the restaurant, it was described as 'confirmation of value'; but I knew what he wanted and I made it clear in no uncertain terms that the covert warfare game is not played like that. The difference between my kind of operation and the right-wing hooligans who shoot up E.T.A. bars shouting 'Viva Franco!' is that I lay the groundwork carefully, check and double-check my intelligence data, and recruit exactly the right personnel for the individual missions. I do not dash off quick 'demonstration projects', any more than I talk tough or make macho noises during pre-contract negotiations.

I did give 'Richard' certain undertakings which I could see pleased him: I gave him, above all, the absolute assurance that I would seek no Spanish help for the operations in France. I would use my own people, my own weapons and equipment, and my own transport, and I would launch no operations from the Spanish side of the border. Madrid would be completely divorced from the missions once they had assigned them. In return, it was understood that my liaison with the government would be only through Alvarez.

'Richard' understood the importance of this. 'You will report to Colonel Alvarez,' he said. 'Colonel Alvarez will report to me. I will report to the Minister. There will be no other links in the chain.'

It was agreed also that no attempt would be made to stop the activities of the fascist crazies. It was felt they might become useful as possible scapegoats for my activities. In fact, the Francoists caused me several headaches once our operations got underway, but there was not really any option; if we had asked the Guardia Civil to shut down their activities, it would have tipped them off that alternative operations were underway and the Guardia, like the Policia Naçional, was too heavily penetrated by the Basques to risk that. I was also to have very serious problems with the British during the secret war against E.T.A., but not through anything that was predictable at the restaurant meeting in Madrid.

Overall, despite my refusal to provide evidence of my skills for his superiors, I could see that 'Richard's' reactions to me were positive. After less than half an hour he said simply: 'I am satisfied. Thank you, Mr Rivers. Now, if you will excuse me, I have to leave.'

When he had gone, there was a feeling of elation at the table among Alvarez and his colleagues. I deliberately did not share in it. They had just won backing for their faith in me; I had never doubted my ability to carry out the operations, so there was no cause for elation.

It might seem odd to an outsider, but the rest of the meal was taken up with what can best be described as my educating the Spanish in how to pay me! One of the refreshing things about dealing with Spanish security is that they are not pretentious. If they don't know something, they admit their ignorance and try to remedy it. Alvarez was concerned at how to disguise the payments to me. I had told them that, for my part, an absolute, inviolable requirement was that I should receive regular monthly transfers to my bank account in Geneva; the operations in France were going to be expensive, with several people on my payroll, and I had to make it clear that the minute the payments stopped, the operations stopped also.

Alvarez now had his authority for obtaining the funds, but he did not see how he was going to get the money to me through the Spanish civil service bureaucracy, especially the Finance Ministry, while preserving total secrecy.

I explained to them how other countries handled the problem: using dummy companies and phoney contracts. Alvarez listened carefully and, in the event, the Spanish proved extremely imaginative at the covert payments game. I was paid over the coming months for such varied activities as consulting on the marine architecture of a new dock at Bilbao and advising a fabric company in Madrid.

But the real work which remained could not be carried out in a restaurant. We ended the meal with a formal toast and adjourned until the next night when I met Alvarez and his deputy in a police safe house in Madrid.

I have used the house often since. It is in the Madrid student quarter and the police have the top floor of a building which houses prostitutes and assorted lodgers – a generally transient population which is, unknown to them, controlled by a seedy-looking, elderly woman concierge who is a fully trained and armed policewoman attached to police intelligence.

At this meeting, Alvarez revealed for the first time the full extent of Spanish Intelligence's penetration of the Basques in France. Though they had never carried out any direct operations, they had been extremely active in intelligence-gathering, with no co-operation from the French.

I was shown about thirty *pro formas*, with photographs, of the people who were to be on my 'short-list'. Written in Spanish, each had an English translation appended, in language that sounded much more formal than the original.

One in particular caught my eye: 'Rodrigo Ibarguren also known as "Zarra". Born 6.11.42 in Zarauz/Spain, son of Geralde and Pilar. Terrorist. Unmarried. His address in Biarritz is unknown. Nevertheless he can spend the night in some of the following addresses: Biarritz: 11 Rue de la Mer and 342 Boulevard de Paris. He can drive any of the following cars: Renault-4, blue colour; registration number 26023-YT-91, registered to his name. Renault-5, white colour, registration number 65732-YT-91, owned by a girlfriend, the militant Teresa Maria Ansola (27 years old, short, plump, with a pretty face).

'He is the highest responsible of E.T.A.-Militar at all the levels. He is a very difficult and dangerous target, of big mobility. He is always escorted by the militant Marcos Olazaguirre, born 3.7.51 in Bilbao/Spain, reputed to be the best shooter in the organization. Zarra is a regular visitor to the apartment of Ansola, a building of two floors, on Pannecau Street. He is accustomed to visit on Monday evenings, about 22 hours, at the Bar Restaurant des Sports.'

I did not know how soon, or in what circumstances, but as I read the *pro forma* I had no doubt that at some time, not too far away, 'Zarra' would be one of my targets.

TWELVE

TARGET: THE PROPAGANDA CHIEF OF E.T.A.-MILITAR

Immediately after the restaurant meeting, the Spanish government paid more than £60,000 into my account in Switzerland as advance expenses, and I began my recruitment.

The first stage of my mission – which I did not confide even to Colonel Alvarez – was to verify through my own resources the intelligence data that the Spanish security forces had provided. I had no intention of carrying out a series of assassinations and abductions on the strength of the *pro formas* handed over in the safe house in Madrid, as I had no way of knowing how accurate and current they were. The mission was dangerous and sensitive enough without risking innocent deaths. With careful planning, we had a reasonable chance of getting away with the kind of killings which could be blamed on inter-Basque rivalries or put at the door of the Francoist crazies; but if innocent bystanders started getting killed, nothing would stem the uproar.

My own intelligence-gathering had to be done by Frenchmen – or at least by fluent French-speakers – and I put together the nucleus of a team, which could be expanded later when I was satisfied that the Spanish funds would continue to flow. One of my favourite partners, Yves Kergal, was not available. He prefers the quick 'in-and-out' jobs and the secret war was clearly going to stretch on over many months. Instead, I chose another stalwart of the Marseilles mercenary world, a Corsican called Jacques Cesari. Surprisingly, Kergal and Cesari have never worked together. They know and like each other and I have often drunk with them, together, in one of the little bars off the Vieux Port in Marseilles where the mercenary fraternity likes to hang out. Professionally, though, their worlds do not overlap. Cesari is a member of a prosperous Corsican business family. He runs a successful auto spares firm in Marseilles but ever since his early service in North Africa, as an officer seconded to one of the French Foreign Legion parachute regiments, he has been bored by day-to-day business dealings and has worked as a mercenary in the Congo, Nigeria and in the Middle East. He was delighted to come in on the Basque assignment as it gave him an excuse to leave the car spares firm to his brothers and take what he likes to call an extended 'action holiday'. But the flippant language is misleading. Once Cesari walks out of his auto dealership in Marseilles, he becomes a soldier. My own reputation is based on using only real professionals; there is no room on missions as delicate as this one for adventure-loving thrill junkies.

The other advantage of hiring a man like Cesari is that I can safely delegate recruitment to him. In many ways, mercenaries are like the terrorists they are fighting: they work well in cells. For bigger operations, where large numbers are involved, I will recruit a sergeant-major figure who will be responsible for putting together a unit under his discipline and answerable to me. On the missions requiring smaller numbers of personnel, I usually recruit everyone personally, but for the intelligence-gathering in Biarritz, the main requirement was for people who could liaise smoothly with Jacques. He would be based in the city resort more or less permanently, while I flew in and out and carried on with my many other activities.

Cesari rented a house in Biarritz, a pleasant old-fashioned two-storey structure, with a courtyard whose walls were covered in climbing plants and a trailing ornamental vine. Access from the street was through heavy iron gates, and a vehicle could be taken straight into a fully enclosed garage which formed part of the ground floor of the house. During his first three weeks there, Cesari spent a lot of time preparing hiding-places for weapons and explosives. He fancies himself as an amateur carpenter and was very proud of the various false ceiling sections and movable floorboards he managed to construct. For the kind of work we were to do, the remotely-detonated car bomb is one of the most effective and anonymous weapons, and we ferried to the Biarritz house a good stock of materials. I brought the detonators and remote-control gear in myself from England as I strongly favour certain equipment which I have designed to my own specifications, but to save unnecessary Customs problems, the explosives were purchased in Marseilles. In order not to draw too much attention to Jacques' activities in his home ground, however, I arranged for a Belgian contact to bring in pistols and submachines from a stock he was holding on my behalf. He was paid for carrying them over the frontier and they were collected from him in Nantes. I drove them down myself to hand them over to Jacques.

Meanwhile, Jacques was organizing his intelligence-gathering. I took very little part in it – except when, once every three weeks or so, I visited Biarritz and was taken on a 'tour' of Basque terrorist hang-outs with Jacques as my guide. He had found the Spanish data both sound and up-to-date but he had expanded the dossiers considerably.

I estimated that we would be ready for our first hits between five and six months after the initial briefing in Madrid. I wanted that length of preparation because I felt we should go after several targets simultaneously. Once we made our first move, the E.T.A. organization in Biarritz would be alerted that there was an operation underway and they would quickly change all their patterns.

In the event, we were forced to move earlier. Three months after Jacques installed himself in Biarritz, I received a phone call at my office in London. Would I please come to Madrid urgently? Mr Richard wanted urgent discussions about a contractual difficulty.

On the flight to Madrid, I had no trouble anticipating what it would be: the Interior Ministry wanted action. They had paid over large sums of money and they wanted to see something for them.

I went preparing to resist the pressure. Professionally, it made sense to prepare the ground thoroughly, then hit a big section of the E.T.A. leadership at one time, but after a tense meeting with 'Richard', this time in the Madrid police safe house, I allowed myself to be overruled. When you understand, as I have learned to do, how intelligence and security bureaucracies work, you know there are times where there is no alternative but to give in to their internal procedural imperatives.

'Richard' was under unbearable pressure from the Interior Ministry. During the winter of 1979 and the early spring of 1980, the Basque terrorists seemed to be developing a status almost above the law. There had been two recent killings in San Sebastian which had shocked even a hardened public. In one, a police inspector had been drinking with his fiancée in a café when two young men – kids virtually – had drawn up in a car and almost casually gunned him down. The kids had been so confident, they had not even bothered to mask their faces and had stood, watching the man die on the café floor, for a good minute before making their escape. In another, an off-duty policeman had had the tyres of his car shot out; the car had swerved and the policeman had been thrown against the windshield. As he lay, bleeding across the steering wheel, a gunman on a motorcycle had drawn up beside the wrecked car and finished him off with a bullet in the head, laughing as he fired. While all this was going on, the Spanish government was not unaware that large sums of money were being laundered through the Finance Ministry to pay for 'special operations' against E.T.A., but nothing was happening. All Alvarez could report was that I was establishing 'an infrastructure' on the ground and was making good progress.

I could feel at the meeting that 'Richard' had no leeway for manoeuvre. He had a name for me. He wanted an assassination. I could see that it was no longer a question – as it had been at the restaurant meeting – of 'confirmation of value'; this was an absolute imperative, or funds were going to dry up. I took the name, flew back to London and passed it that night by telephone to Jacques.

Two days later, I was sitting beside Jacques in his rented Peugeot, watching a bathing party; or, to be more precise, watching our target, José Arizguren, aged twenty-eight, watching his girlfriend take a swim. It was, according to Jacques, a regular morning ritual. They came always to this remote little cove, about six kilometres out of Biarritz, and stayed for between half an hour and an hour. It was the first week in May and not yet swimming weather by the standards of the southern European races. There was the usual blustery prevailing wind from the west which created white-tops far out to sea and blew sand around on the low dunes surrounding the little cove. The girlfriend, Suzanne Caccia, was a heavily built girl who swam daily, thrashing about in the surf, making a show of taking vigorous exercise. Arizguren did not even undress. He sat, Jacques said, as he was sitting that morning, at the foot of the dunes on a boulder, watching the girl. He was dressed in a dark grey sports coat, with the collar turned up, and a grey scarf trailing around his shoulders. He obviously cultivated the intellectual look, with heavy-rimmed glasses and a curved pipe which he often held, unlit, in his mouth.

Jacques had spent two days and two nights watching him and was not impressed with him either as a human being or as a target. In the original *pro formas* I had brought from Madrid, he was listed as propaganda chief of E.T.A.-Militar; Jacques had run across him several times during the first months of surveillance but had not paid him particular attention until my phone call.

I would have preferred to begin our operation with a target like Zarra but 'Richard' had given me a specific, direct instruction, and afterwards, Alvarez, who was aware of my annoyance at being rushed, had emphasized that Arizguren was a very important target to the Ministry of the Interior. 'Don't pay any attention to the intellectual appearance,' Alvarez had said. 'He's a deadly bastard. He's killed twice personally and had a hand in others.'

I was prepared to accept Alvarez' word; it was beginning to look as though any wet-nosed kid could become a gunman or bomber in E.T.A. Anyway, 'Richard' had been determined, despite my warning that we might blow months of work by hitting one target, sending everyone else to ground.

As we followed Arizguren's car to the beach, Jacques had given me what he had been able to glean about the man from his brief period of round-the-clock surveillance and from discreet but intense questioning in the areas the Basque frequented. According to Jacques, Arizguren seemed to spend most of his time screwing. He had two girlfriends – the French girl who was now in the water, and a young Spanish girl, another Basque militant, Dorotea Corta. The Basque seemed to devote a lot of energy to keeping Suzanne and Dorotea from finding out about each other, and whatever his activities were on behalf of E.T.A., they could not have occupied more than a few hours a day – the hours he was not in one bed or the other. 'Ça baise beaucoup chez les militants,' Jacques said with a grin.

On the floor of the Peugeot, beneath my feet, covered in a heavy cloth, I had laid out enough explosive to blow Arizguren's Renault right out to sea if necessary, together with an effective little remote-control system that I had used successfully on several occasions. In Jacques' opinion, now was a good time to place the charge under the car – the girl was still in the water and showed no sign of coming out; when she did, if Arizguren repeated his usual pattern, there would be some fooling around while she dressed, then a little walk, then they would come back to the Renault and drive back to Biarritz.

I had already asked Jacques if he thought we should hit the girl too if necessary and he had answered with a shrug. 'Why not? She's no innocent. She knows who Arizguren is. According to the people I talked to, she's a terrorist groupie. She gets turned on by the excitement.' He grinned. 'It's only fair she should share the risks too. No?'

On that assessment, I agreed. I have no time for women who find terrorists exciting. Many of the terrorists themselves only get into it because of the macho image they think they project to the women. I've known more than one bombing done specifically as grandstand play to impress some female hanger-on.

If the other girl, Dorotea, got in the way of our plastic, she was fair game too. As far as I was concerned, once a female joins a terrorist organization, in whatever role, she loses all consideration for her sex.

As we were to use my own special remote device, I told Jacques that I would fix it in position. The Peugeot was parked about twenty yards from Arizguren's Renault and Jacques could watch the Basque and the girl almost all the way back from the beach. Once they started back, he had only to signal me just before they went out of his line of vision and I would have plenty of time to get clear of the Renault. In any case, the fixing would not take long. I had plenty of cover; there were no other cars parked close by and the handful of other people around were all on the beach, so the dunes provided total cover.

I ran between the cars at a low crouch, holding the equipment into the hollow of my stomach like a rugby ball. When I got to the Renault, I lay down flat, with the equipment pushed well under the vehicle so that if another car did happen to come anywhere near, I would look simply like someone with a mechanical problem.

In all, the job took not much more than five minutes. I put one plastic charge at the front, right under the driver's position, and a second one at the back, under the petrol tank. With each charge I put an electrically-fired detonator, both of which were connected to a single, magnetized receiving unit placed under the main frame of the car, to receive the radio signal for detonation. No mess, no fuss, no wires, and nothing to see from the sides of the vehicle. According to Jacques, Arizguren was not in the habit of making safety checks on his vehicles and there was no way he would spot this layout accidentally.

I went quickly back to the Peugeot and did my final checks. I verified the strength of the battery and did a receiver module check – a refinement I always like to incorporate in my equipment, which allows me to use the transmitter to check that the receiver is ready to pick up the signal.

We were all set, but there was a major snag at the last moment. The girl came out of the water and towelled herself dry, but as she started to pull on her jeans and blouse, another car, a battered white Citroen, arrived and drew up right beside the Renault. Jacques grinned at me. 'Good job you're a fast worker,' he said in his heavily accented Corsican French.

The driver parked the Citroen almost bumper to bumper with the Renault and four young people got out – two men and two women.

'Do you know them?' I asked Jacques.

'I've seen one of the men before with the crowd at the Bar des Sports. He's E.T.A. for sure and the car is on the Spanish list.'

'What about the others?'

'No idea,' Jacques said. 'Probably, but I can't be sure.'

'We'll have to get Arizguren later,' I said. 'They may just be innocents.'

Jacques grinned. 'Pity, *mon cher*, six at one go would have made a nice opening gambit.'

I nodded. If the four people in the other car had been on the E.T.A. list in any capacity, I would have gone ahead with the detonation. The charge under the Renault would have easily destroyed both cars and I would have considered it six justifiable deaths, but there was no question of doing so with doubts against three of the group.

We watched as they went down to join Arizguren, played around for a while, laughing and joking, then came back up to the cars, as a group, separating only at the last moment as they climbed into the vehicles and drove away.

We let both cars get a good start, then Jacques backed the Peugeot onto the narrow sandy coast road and we set off to follow Arizguren's Renault.

'I know where they'll be going,' Jacques said. 'Her apartment – 48 Rue de l'Atlantique. Second floor. You could set your watch by this guy's screwing habits.'

Any chance we could detonate at the flat?' I said.

'Not likely. They'll park at the back of the apartment building. There's a square. It'll be packed with cars; everyone parks all over the place. Too many people around.'

We followed the Renault without any difficulty and Jacques was right: they did go to the French girl's apartment. They pulled into the square and Arizguren parked in the true French tradition, slotting the Renault into the last space on the block by getting his front wheels onto the kerb and dropping into a gap that was not more than a couple of inches longer than the car was.

'Lucky bastard,' Jacques said. 'He'll be in there for hours and we've nowhere even to put the goddamn car. No one ever leaves a parking space around here. At least not till after lunch.'

I looked around and saw that every inch of the three sides of the square was taken up with vehicles that were virtually touching front and back.

We double-parked for a while, but I wasn't happy and neither was Jacques. The Peugeot was too conspicuous out in the middle of the roadway. On this kind of mission, it's the really basic things, like an argument with a traffic policeman, that can cause you problems. Apart from the risk of being remembered by the policeman, Jacques had rented the Peugeot on a phoney licence and I.D. and there were weapons in the trunk.

'You'd better drop me and find somewhere to park,' I said. 'I'll wait at that café on the corner. Get back as quick as you can.'

By now it was almost eleven o'clock. Despite the cool breeze, the café terrace was crowded. I managed to get a table right on the road edge of the terrace, with a view of the entrance to the girl's apartment. I ordered a glass of white wine and settled back casually, making sure that the transmitter was well-concealed in the pocket of my lined jacket.

The unit I was using is a very handy little device. It measures only six inches by three and is barely an inch or so thick. The antenna is about eight inches long and I had detached this and put it in my sock, inside my trouser leg.

We could make the hit any time, it was merely a matter of waiting until Arizguren was in the Renault and the vehicle was positioned where no bystanders were at risk.

I was on my second glass of wine before Jacques got back, complaining irritably that he had had to park several streets away.

'He's been in there more than an hour already,' I said. 'He might not be too much longer.'

'Maybe,' Jacques said. He gave me a dry little smile. 'Let's hope it's a good fuck. It may well be his last.'

It was a little over two hours later that Arizguren reappeared. He was alone and looked cheerful, and made his way quickly to the parked Renault.

'Any chance you can get the Peugeot?' I said.

'No. Not a hope,' Jacques said.

'O.K. I'll follow him in a taxi,' I said. 'Go back to the house. I'll call you when I need the car.'

There was a small taxi rank on the near side of the square and I found a driver before Arizguren had manoeuvred himself out of the tight parking space.

I knew I would have no trouble with the pursuit. French cab drivers love to follow people. I gave him the usual line about the guy in the Renault having it off with my wife, and the taxi slid into the lane behind Arizguren.

The drive took about ten minutes and Arizguren pulled up outside another apartment building right in the heart of the student quarter of Biarritz. I had been there once on one of Jacques' 'guided E.T.A. tours' and I knew that there were several suspects living in the apartment blocks along the street. Really, it is misleading to call this part of town a student quarter; most of the lodgings are by no means shoddy and the building which Arizguren had entered consisted of fairly high-rent accommodation. But the students who lived around there had set their style on the area. Many of the flats were occupied communally and there was constant movement between one apartment and another, instead of the usual box-like isolation that goes with apartment living.

The street was a broad boulevard, lined with plane trees, planted right into the flagstones of the pavement. It looked as though no road maintenance had been done for years and the pavement was broken and bumpy, with the kerb almost merging with the roadway at several points. I had reason to notice this aspect of the local architecture because of Arizguren's incredible parking technique. The area outside this apartment block was not as crowded as the last one had been, but parking was still fairly tight and again, Arizguren had put his wheels onto the kerb to manoeuvre into a slot. Because of the uneven flags and his careless handling of the car, he managed, while reversing, to get his left rear wheel into one of the small beds of earth round the base of a plane tree. The earth had hardened and shrunk in the heat and the wheel went right down and I could hear the underside of the car scrape against the flagstone. I was paying off my cab only a few yards up the boulevard and I heard Arizguren curse as he got out of the car to look. I was so close that it would have seemed unnatural if I had ignored the incident, so I walked down too to see what had happened. The first thing I noticed was that the petrol tank of the Renault, and therefore one of the explosive charges, was almost touching the kerb. There was no danger of the plastic going off, but it could easily be discovered if Arizguren started getting down under the vehicle to see how badly he was stuck.

As I approached, Arizguren started talking to me in French, which he spoke with a heavy Spanish accent. Though I knew he wanted me to help push the Renault out, I made out that I couldn't understand.

I said, in English, 'That looks a bit of a mess.' Arizguren didn't understand. He spoke again in French, then lapsed into Spanish. At that point, I said in deliberately poor Spanish, '*Oh. Habla Espanol?*' We exchanged a couple of phrases about the car in Spanish, which made Arizguren more comfortable, but he was still agitated about the situation and he said finally, 'I have a friend in the building there. I'm going to get him.'

Immediately cautious, I said, 'The car is very heavy. How many friends do you have?'

'Just one,' Arizguren said. 'Will you help too?'

There was a phone booth just up the street beyond where I had paid off the taxi, and I said, 'I'll try, but I've got to make a phone call first.'

Arizguren walked off into the apartment building and I strolled up the street to the phone box. At that point, I hadn't decided whether to risk making the hit. There was clearly a chance the taxi driver would remember me, and he could well have made a note of the number of the car I had asked him to follow. On the other hand, that was a risk that might apply equally if I followed Arizguren on to somewhere else and did the hit later in the day. If I left it too long, there was always the chance that the Basque might find the charges – or, given the way he drove, knock the damned things off the vehicle altogether!

I had even fewer doubts when I saw the face of the man who was with Arizguren when he came back out of the apartment building. He was a short, plump man of about thirty with a heavy black beard that I remembered clearly from Alvarez' *pro formas*. His name was Martin Garmendia and he was listed by the Spanish as being concerned with E.T.A. intelligence activities.

As I looked down the slightly sloping boulevard from the phone box at the two figures approaching the car, I thought to myself: 'Why not?' My only concern was whether I was too close. The transmitter I was using can send a signal over a distance of two kilometres. At very close range, in an enclosed urban environment, there is always a slight chance of attenuation in the antenna which makes it difficult for the receiving module to decode the incoming signal.

As they approached the car, Arizguren looked up the boulevard and spotted me in the phone box. He waved and I pushed the heavy door of the kiosk open and waved back, pointing at the same time to the receiver to indicate that I was still making my call. I made a further sign to indicate that I was coming, then went back into the kiosk. With my back to Arizguren and the receiver crooked in my shoulder, I crossed my legs, slipped the aerial out of my sock, and fitted it quickly to the transmitter. Before leaving the box, I dialled the channel I had set the receiver to, then palmed the unit in my hand, shielding the antenna behind my back as I stepped out of the booth.

The two men were already working at freeing the car. Garmendia was in the driving seat and had already started it up. Presumably he had decided that since Arizguren had got the car into the hole, he should be the one to do the heavy work of pushing it out. Arizguren was standing at the front of the vehicle, his arms under the front bumper, preparing for an attempt to rock the car and allow the rear wheel to get some purchase on the pavement.

As I came out of the phone box, Arizguren saw me. He straightened up and waved. I waved back with my left hand, then brought up my right hand, which was holding the transmitter, and pressed the button.

The explosion was spectacular. The rear charge under the petrol tank sent up a spiral of flames and sparks like an enormous Roman candle, the front charge scattered pieces of metal right across the boulevard, and the noise was as great as though a whole building had gone up. Through the smoke and flames, I could not verify the kill, but I had no doubts that I got both targets. In seconds, the Renault was a fiery ruin and the two vehicles next to it at the front and the back were also burning.

Immediately, heads began appearing at apartment windows, then the first figures started coming out into the street and running towards the scene. I walked away from the wreck, up the slope of the boulevard and turned into the first side street.

As soon as I was out of sight of the gathering crowd, I broke into a spring, then went up a gear and ran like hell.

As I ran, I disconnected the antenna from the transmitter and stuck it up the sleeve of my jacket. The transmitter unit went into an inside pocket and I buttoned the coat up to stop it flapping about.

The side street sloped slightly downwards, and at the bottom an elderly man came out of a small house. He stared upwards and pointed at the column of black smoke that was visible now right above the level of the buildings.

He shouted at me, 'What is it?'

Using bad French, I said. 'Fire. Fire. Gas.'

'*Ah, oui. Propane. Propane*,' he then said.

As I couldn't see a phone box anywhere, I thought I might as well make use of the old fellow and I asked, by sign and with a broken phrase or two, whether I could use his phone.

But the old man didn't want to get involved, except strictly as a spectator. He made a show of barring the gate to me. '*Je regrette. Pas possible*,' he said.

By now there were plenty of people out in the street, so instead of rushing away, I simply joined them. You could hear sirens from practically every direction and the police had already set up a roadblock to seal off the end of the street and prevent access to the boulevard.

I watched the scene for a while, like any other normal curious citizen, then, after a decent interval, when anyone might have got bored with the spectacle, I turned away and strolled down the hill to look for a phone box to call Jacques.

THIRTEEN

MIXED SUCCESS IN BIARRITZ

I observed the aftermath of the first Spanish assassinations from my home base in Switzerland. Two hours after the hit, I took a train from Biarritz to Bordeaux, then an internal Air France flight to Paris, and Jacques drove in his back-up vehicle to Marseilles. I had arrived for the mission in a Range-Rover, but I decided that it was too conspicuous a vehicle for the departure, especially as it had non-French plates, so it was left locked in the garage of the rented house, which was also closed up. Jacques wanted to stay away from Biarritz for a while, but he was not happy at leaving the house empty so he sent back a man who is known in Marseilles underworld language as a 'runner' – a trusted but minor associate who re-opened the house and made a show of carrying out some maintenance work.

From Paris, I called Alvarez who was jubilant and four days later I flew to Madrid for a de-briefing. I learned that Arizguren had died instantly but Garmendia had survived, despite being in the driving seat of the Renault; the point was academic, however, as he had lost both legs and an arm, and was permanently out of action. The Spanish government was delighted with the outcome, despite general condemnation in the press and a strong protest from Paris.

Alvarez' people were watching the situation on the ground in Biarritz and they reported that the French police investigation had not come close to either Jacques or myself. Some of the pressure had been taken off us by the arrest by the French – apparently on a tip-off – of two of the Francoists who had been involved in one of the earlier incidents. The French police had no evidence against them, but they had been found to be armed and they were being held for questioning for the illegal possession of weapons. I knew very well that the tip-off had come from Alvarez himself, though it was never said directly. Like many of the senior Spanish policemen I had dealings with during the 'secret war', Alvarez was to reveal a very subtle touch in covert operations – the kind of finesse, in fact, not often credited to the Spanish.

But, as I had predicted, the murder of Arizguren did throw the E.T.A. network in Biarritz into a panic and they tightened security and went collectively to ground. This was accepted by 'Richard' as the necessary price for an operation he had needed to justify his personal decision to authorize the use of foreign mercenaries; more funds were released, Jacques returned to Biarritz with authorization to hire more people to develop his intelligence-gathering network and I turned my attention to other activities and contracts for the next six or seven weeks.

One of the features of my life is that I am always busy. When I do slow down, it is usually in the company of a woman, but I rarely take holidays in the conventional sense. For most people, time off is measured in long weekends and weeks; I usually take time off on the move. If I am not involved in a serious relationship with a woman, I will go off alone and do something active – a day's hunting if I am in Kenya or a couple of days' riding the trails in the Superstition Mountains when I am in the United States. I like doing different things in different places and I've never been able to collect them altogether in one place. Some sociologist once coined the word 'transilient' to describe someone who has experienced the high points and best features of so many different places and cultures that he can never be satisfied settling in one place. That certainly describes me and I find myself constantly moving on, creating my own environment as I go.

At the period of the Spanish contract, I used to use my business activities as recreation from my covert operations and the mercenary side of my life as a break from business. I find that less easy to do now as I get much less enjoyment out of business – except for the aviation side – but in the late 1970s, much of my recreation consisted in switching back and forth between being soldier and covert operations specialist on the one hand and president of my various companies on the other.

Switzerland, though, always makes up one part of my lifestyle. The Swiss environment is totally functional; everything works and nothing changes radically. You go back to it and it is as you left it, except that everything has been slightly updated. I also, of course, like the Swiss tax system. When you do what I do to make money, you believe in keeping what you make and the Swiss place few restrictions on the kind of complex financial arrangements that are necessary for my activities. Also, Switzerland is convenient. It is a perfect jumping-off ground for the rest of Europe, and it provides me with easy access to my absolute favourite sport, skiing, and allows me to indulge my love of the mountains.

Fortunately, though, I can enjoy all of my sports for the pleasure of the sport – I don't have to do anything special to keep fit. I need to be permanently fit and I am always fit, but that is much more a matter of mental attitude than physical conditioning.

When you are really fit, to begin with you subconsciously keep certain muscles in your body toned up without thinking about it. I never climb stairs one at a time, for example; I'm much too impatient, and always going up two at a time does contribute to muscle toning. My weight has not altered since

I was eighteen years old, give or take a couple of pounds, because I never abuse my diet. I'm not a health fanatic; I eat normally but I don't overindulge in heavy foods. Years of training and active operations with the S.A.S. provided the basis for my fitness – maintaining it is really a matter of mental habit.

If there is time before a big operation, I will spend three or four days in the gym in Geneva, but by that I don't mean indulging in frantic sessions of pumping weights and running round exercise tracks. You have got to relax to be fit; tension destroys muscle toning, and bulging muscles have nothing at all to do with fitness.

I might spend half an hour in the sauna, then take an ice-cold bath, then relax for ten minutes to get my heart rate down, then go into the eucalyptus room and just breathe in the eucalyptus air which puts your respiratory system into an open and receptive state. Then it's time for some work with weights and the exercise bicycle, but the object really is not to strain myself but to get myself into a physical frame of mind.

After that kind of routine, you find that your body objects to poisons in foods and you just want to eat such things as muesli, yoghurt and fruits – things that sit lightly in the gut.

But there are no eucalyptus rooms in Vietnam or my other theatres of activity, and that kind of conditioning session is an extra refinement. On operations, endurance is what counts, and that is, more than anything else, a question of mental approach. Fitness is essential but fitness alone does not create endurance. In warfare there are so many tests of endurance that fitness simply will not carry you through; in the end, you either have the mental capacity or you don't.

In Switzerland, when I am not skiing, I am more likely to be found enjoying music than in the gymnasium. I love all kinds of music. Few of my military friends know that I studied classical piano for a period as well as racing motorbikes and flying crop-dusting aircraft! I have also been a session drummer with a number of rock groups and even made an album with a well-known rock group. Nowadays, I play very little but I collect all kinds of music and I edit tapes for my own listening. In my apartment in Geneva I have the very best sound equipment available. I never talk about it or show it to anyone – a casual visitor will simply notice that there is a good stereo – but every item from pick-up to pre-amp is the best, and often I will sit up all night using records to create tapes of perfect quality. Creating the tapes is not a mechanical exercise. Music, for me, provides an emotional escape. It is a vehicle through which I can recall the turbulent events of my life. Sometimes it helps me to get them in perspective. At others it drives me deep into introspection and soul-searching isolation.

All of these activities have to be fitted into a life of constant movement. If I undertake a contract like the one with the Spanish government, I supervise the overall operation but I do not spend months on end in Madrid or Biarritz looking after every detail. Because I fly myself, I always have mobility, and I use private aircraft and helicopters to fill in the gaps that the scheduled airlines leave. During the Spanish operations, I was also developing my activities in Iraq and elsewhere in the Middle East; Madrid was only one point on a non-stop circuit which included London, New York, Baghdad and a dozen other cities.

I would have preferred to leave more of the groundwork to Jacques than I was actually able to, but in the early months of 1980, the level of E.T.A. terrorism reached one of its periodic highs. In the first half of the year E.T.A. terrorists killed fifty-two people, by the official count, and there were numerous other woundings during a spate of ambushes, random shootings and bank robberies.

There was also one incident which was kept very quiet at the time but which badly shook the security forces. In Barcelona, a group of E.T.A. terrorists hired a room on the ground floor of a building opposite a residential block for Guardia Civil families. They tunnelled under the road and put nearly two thousand pounds of explosives under the Guardia Civil residences. If the charges had gone off, it would have demolished the building, which housed about six hundred people, most of them women and children. By pure chance, the janitor of the building that the E.T.A. people had rented found the tunnel and gave the alarm. Two of the E.T.A. team were caught but it was an appalling security lapse which could have led to the worst outrage of the whole Basque separatist campaign.

There was also in this period an attempt on the life of Colonel Alvarez which by pure chance I became personally involved with. I had flown into Madrid for a meeting to discuss progress in Biarritz and I had spent the evening talking to Alvarez and the chief interpreter José-Martin Bolivar at a safe house in the centre of the city. We finished just after one o'clock in the morning and the three of us strolled down the street together, chatting before looking for taxis. A couple of blocks ahead of us, on the other side of the street, there was a big newspaper kiosk and, though it was closed, a youngish man was standing beside it, apparently looking at some of the magazines which were hung in rows behind the glass panels. When Alvarez spotted him, I heard him draw breath sharply and very quietly he told me to look at the man's coat. The man was tall and thin and wearing a fairly fashionable raincoat with a belt that was tied at the front instead of being buckled. I saw immediately what Alvarez had spotted: in the light from the window of a nearby shoe shop, you could see, reflected in the glass of the kiosk, that the man had a light submachine gun under his raincoat.

Alvarez' first reaction was that he did not want to get me involved. He said loudly, in Spanish, 'O.K. I'll see you at the car. I just want a word with

Bolivar.' I appreciated the courtesy, but I had no intention of leaving Alvarez to handle things alone.

I took the cue and walked on a little way, and I could sense that it was definitely not me that the waiting man was interested in. There were cars parked on both sides of the street and I carried on, using them as partial cover, watching closely for any signs of movement. Alvarez and Bolivar had stopped to talk, then Alvarez moved on slightly ahead, following me down the street. Though he was armed, the interpreter had very little experience of firearms and certainly none of street gunfighting, but Alvarez, as a member of General Franco's personal bodyguard, was one of the fastest and most accurate shots in Spain and he had not lost his eye.

As Alvarez drew level with the kiosk, the man turned and started to bring up his submachine gun, but Alvarez downed him with a single shot to the chest before he had the weapon fully raised. But it was not that simple. As soon as the man fell, a second man appeared in a doorway further up the street and opened fire in the general direction of Alvarez. It was pretty wild shooting, but bullets ricocheted off cars and it was a good job that that part of the street was deserted or passers-by would certainly have been hit. The interpreter and Alvarez both fired back and I ducked down between two cars to watch the other direction. My instincts told me that the attempt was not as ill-conceived as it appeared to be and I found out very quickly that I was right.

While shots were bring traded between Alvarez and the second attacker, a third man appeared from behind a tree and started to sprint towards the scene, and I could tell from the way he was moving that this was a serious and experienced professional.

He was young and sinewy and wearing a loose raincoat and tennis shoes. He ran with a loping stride and made scarcely any noise. He didn't show any sign of excitement at the noise of the gunfire. He was concentrating on approaching quietly, and if I hadn't been there, there is a good chance he would have got off a burst at Alvarez from close range before being spotted.

I came up from between the parked cars and fired a 9mm round into his shoulder. It spun him backwards; as he fell, I fired a second round straight into his head. After that, I checked that there were no further surprises coming to Alvarez, then I slipped quietly into a side street and put a lot of distance between myself and the shooting.

The incident did me a great deal of good with the Spanish because it was the first time they had seen me in action personally, and I had handled myself with just the style Alvarez appreciated. I had got off the shots that counted, but I had not been around to cause embarrassment when police reinforcements arrived to help finish off the second attacker.

Three more E.T.A. terrorists had been added to the security forces' tally but the direct attack on Alvarez and E.T.A.'s apparent knowledge of the safe house added to the urgency of the need for more results in Biarritz.

In a second meeting with Alvarez the following day, I promised to speed up my own operations again, but our fortunes in Biarritz in the coming weeks were to be mixed.

We began with an easy success. I had allocated more funds to intelligence-gathering in Biarritz and Jacques developed a very sophisticated little network. He had called in another Corsican from Marseilles, a really amusing character called Paolo Carlotti. He was a small wiry ex para who was dark-skinned enough to pass as a member of almost any of the Mediterranean races and he had established himself as a street gipsy – the kind of Romany who wanders around southern resort towns in the holiday period doing a bit of stealing, pimping, and general mischief. He had brought two young Corsican girls with him – at Spanish government expense – and they had become flower-sellers working the streets and cafés in the area that the Spanish Basques frequented.

Paolo had picked out an easy target from my E.T.A. list, a man called Luis Michelena who had become really careless about security – as usual because of a woman. Michelena was an important figure in E.T.A. According to his Spanish intelligence *pro forma*, he was responsible for distributing E.T.A. funds among the exiles in Biarritz; he looked after apartment rents, arranged transport for operations and generally acted as paymaster to the terrorist cells. He spent most of his time with the other Basques, living an almost communal life in their various apartments and bars and cafés, but Paolo quickly discovered that he had acquired a French girlfriend whom he apparently wanted to keep to himself. To achieve this, Michelena had developed a very elementary, almost childish security routine.

He lived in an apartment on the Boulevard des Explorateurs which ran down from the student district towards the sea. One of the E.T.A. hang-outs was almost directly opposite – a little seafood bar called the Café de la Coquille, and Michelena, like many of the E.T.A. activists, used to spend some part of several evenings a week drinking and occasionally eating there. Since beginning his affair with the French girl, Michelena had taken to going to the Café de la Coquille until about 9.30 in the evening, when he would leave and, apparently, go back to his apartment in the building opposite. In reality, Michelena never actually went up to his own place. Instead, he would come out of the café, cross the street, enter his apartment building, walk down a long corridor which went right through to the far side, emerge in the Boulevard Gambetta which ran parallel to the Boulevard des Explorateurs, then take a taxi to his girlfriend's house.

Jacques and Paolo decided that it was too good a routine to waste and, with my permission, they organized a trap. There was a taxi rank on the

Boulevard Gambetta, but in the evening many of the drivers used to hang out in a little bar, playing dice and cards. Co-ordinating by radio, Paolo waited until Michelena came out of the Café de la Coquille then followed him at a discreet distance. On receiving Paolo's signal, Jacques hot-wired and stole a taxi from the rank, choosing one belonging to a driver who was having a meal.

When Michelena walked along the corridor through the apartment building, Paolo followed, letting the Basque become aware that he was closing in on him. Michelena hurried on nervously and as he emerged into the Boulevard Gambetta, Paolo started shouting after him: 'Hey. Do you want a woman?'

Michelena was nervous and irritated by the intrusion and, as Paolo had intended, he started to cross the street to get away from him, instead of pausing to look for a cab.

When he saw the stolen taxi, he tried to hail it and Paolo kept up his harassment, shouting obscenities to keep Michelena distracted. Jacques put his foot down and the taxi struck Michelena at almost sixty miles an hour, killing him instantly. Before anyone had seen anything, Jacques had roared off into a side street and Paolo had simply melted into the alley at the side of the apartment building.

That same night, Jacques fixed an explosive charge to one of the cars that the E.T.A. people used regularly, and he deliberately did it really clumsily, leaving a wire trailing which no one could fail to spot. The aim was to lay the blame on the Guardia Civil Francoists and, though simple, the ruse worked very well. Since we couldn't stop the fascists blundering around, I decided we might as well make use of them and try to accustom the Basques to expecting unsophisticated attacks, like hit-and-run killings and badly-laid booby traps. It worked for a time, but though the Francoists made excellent scapegoats, they also caused us very serious problems on our next big operation: an attempt to get the E.T.A. leader in Biarritz, the man known as Zarra, with a car bomb.

There had never been any doubt that Zarra – as Rodrigo Ibarguren was always referred to – was a prime target.

He was responsible for co-ordinating the activities of all the cells in France and many across the border in Spain. He was in Biarritz less frequently than the others and it was presumed that he often went into Spain, but he always eluded the Spanish police. Unlike many of the Basques in Biarritz, Zarra was no café terrorist. He could not be cut out from the herd while womanizing like Michelena; his girlfriend Teresa Maria Ansola was a dedicated and experienced E.T.A. terrorist, and Zarra himself was rarely seen in the street without his bodyguard-cum-driver, Marcos Olazaguirre, who was rated by the Spanish as an outstanding marksman.

Also, Zarra rarely went to the addresses given to us by the Spanish: 11 Rue de la Mer and 342 Boulevard de Paris. Both were still used by E.T.A. people but Zarra seemed to have moved on to new haunts.

I told Jacques and Paolo to concentrate on Zarra and went on a business trip to the Middle East. When I came back to Biarritz, three weeks later, I was astonished at the progress they had made. By a combination of up-front street work done by Paolo and his two 'gipsy' girls and painstaking covert observation by Jacques, they had discovered what was currently Zarra's permanent residence: a third-floor apartment in a stylish building several blocks away from the student area. That night, Jacques took me to his observation post. He had found a garage with a flat roof almost opposite the building, and each night, when the garage closed, he had taken to shinning up a rear drainpipe and settling there, concealed under a layer of dark sacking, with a light-intensifying night-vision device trained on the apartment building and the surrounding street.

Both he and Paolo were keen to try for a quick hit. Zarra's habits were much more professional than many of the people he commanded. It was quite likely he would soon move on, perhaps vanishing over the border into Spain. I agreed and authorized an immediate attempt.

Zarra was very conscious of safety routines and the loyalty of the bodyguard Olazaguirre was such that after checking the car each morning for wires and devices, he would turn on the ignition and warm up the engine before his boss came anywhere near the vehicle. But Jacques has a refined touch with a car bomb. We decided on remote detonation rather than a timing device and Jacques said he would like to plant the charge personally. He had had enough of lying under dirty sacking and he reckoned that as I had been enjoying myself around Europe and the Middle East I should take a turn on the garage roof.

We did the job the next night, at about 1 a.m. Paolo watched from the road, I took the garage roof, and Jacques placed the charge, detonator and receiving device. He approached by crawling under a long line of cars to where Zarra's Peugeot was parked and came out the same way. It was a very neat job and Jacques came back convinced that the bodyguard would not spot anything when he did his morning check.

Usually, Zarra left the apartment about 7.30 when the street was fairly quiet but we could not risk him being called out in the middle of the night, so we settled in for a long night of observation.

The trouble came about ninety minutes later. I was getting a bit stiff from lying under the sacking. Jacques relieved me and I took a turn round the block to stretch my legs. We kept in touch by pocket radios and I had only been gone about fifteen minutes when Jacques came in on my receiver. 'You'd better get back here,' he said urgently. 'Someone's coming to the car.'

When I got back to the garage roof, I found Jacques staring intently down into the street. I looked down too and the scene was totally incredible. Right there in the middle of the street, making no effort at all at concealment, two men were busy packing what were obviously explosives into Zarra's car. One had forced the door on the driver's side and had opened the bonnet and the other was busy stuffing charges under the rear axle!

'Jesus Christ!' I said. 'What a fucking circus.' The sight was so incredible I almost burst out laughing.

'Francoist cunts,' Jacques said furiously. 'They might as well sell tickets.'

Amazingly, no one saw them, but when they had finished there was not the remotest possibility that their handiwork would not be spotted. It would not take a sharp-eyed bodyguard either – one of the men had actually bent back the rear number plate to stuff plastic under it and he had left it twisted and hanging off at a forty-five degree angle!

'We get the hell out of here,' I said. 'We get right away. We can't touch the car. They'll find the charge – and ours too. We'll just have to hope they think it's all the same attempt.'

As it turned out, they didn't find our equipment, only the remains of it. After calling Paolo on the radio and telling him to get out of the area, we removed all traces of our vigil at the garage and set off too. We had barely gone four or five blocks when there was a mighty explosion which shook the whole neighbourhood. The Francoist bomb had self-detonated without anyone coming near the vehicle.

By the time we had got back to the rented apartment, my sense of humour had surfaced. We listened to an all-night radio station which reported the confusion and the panic. No one had been injured but several vehicles had been totalled, trees damaged, flowerbeds and roadside gardens ripped up, and the archway entrances to two buildings cracked by the blast.

It was chaos, total bloody chaos, and Zarra had not come near to having a hair singed.

'We'll get the bastard,' Jacques said.

'Yes,' I said with a wry grin, 'if those Francoist assholes don't level Biarritz first.'

A month passed before the second attempt. Once again, I spent most of the time travelling, and while I was in Baghdad I received a phone call to say that two E.T.A. Basques had been shot in a street fight – apparently by right-wing extremists. In fact, the killings were the work of Jacques and Paolo. Both the targets were middle-ranking members of E.T.A.'s intelligence unit and both deaths were blamed on the Francoists.

By this time, though, the press was beginning to hint that there were people at work in Biarritz other than the right-wing Spanish fanatics. Stories began to circulate that anti-Basque right-wingers were using former mem-

bers of the French O.A.S. – the secret army organization – to carry out assassinations. They were getting closer to the truth but our cover was still holding well enough.

At a meeting in Madrid, there was some tough talking over the Francoists.
Had it not been for the depth of our cover inside Spain, the obvious move
would have been for 'Richard' to exert pressure on the Guardia Civil to withdraw their support for them, but I accepted finally that we had to live with
the problem on the ground. Alvarez convinced me that, for the first time
ever, they had managed to maintain absolute security within Spanish intelligence circles about our operations and the Guardia could not be pressurized without compromising that.

My response was to go back to my original proposal for a major operation
to try to take out as much of the command structure as possible at one time.
Alvarez was in favour but 'Richard' urged us to have one more quick try for
Zarra on his own. Eventually, I allowed myself to be talked into it. Partly, it
was a question of morale; getting Zarra had become a point of pride with my
team in Biarritz. Also, I was receiving reports that Zarra had become quite
cocky since the explosion. He was apparently cool-nerved enough to use his
survival to boost his own macho image within the E.T.A. community – especially as he felt he was up against incompetents.

I alerted Jacques that we were going to try again, and made another trip to
London and Geneva, then returned to Biarritz about ten days later. Jacques
had done the groundwork thoroughly, as always. Zarra had switched apartments, moving about a quarter of a mile from the scene of the previous
attack to a small three-storey building where he lived on the middle floor.
The bodyguard, Olazaguirre, had the bottom apartment.

Reconnaissance had shown that their most vulnerable point was still the
car. It is one of the facts of terrorist life that however much pressure you are
under, you constantly have to use transport. Zarra spent a good half of the
day driving round the city and already his initially thorough security checks
were becoming careless. Now, though, there was an added complication:
since the explosion, Zarra had been under surveillance by the French police.

Still, Jacques did not regard them as a major threat. His own observations
had shown that the French plain-clothes people obviously regarded their
detail as a bore and cut corners whenever they could. Instead of carrying out
the kind of discreet observation that Jacques himself was doing, the French
would simply park outside the apartment in an unmarked car. When Zarra
returned they would wait for a while, then check inside the building to
satisfy themselves that he was home for the night, stay another half hour for
good measure, and then drive off – probably to a bar or café – returning in
the morning.

The main problem was the morning check on the vehicle by Olazaguirre.
Zarra had acquired a newish Renault-12; before driving off, the bodyguard

checked under the bonnet and in the boot and got right down onto the pavement to look beneath the vehicle.

I decided that the answer was to make a shaped charge using a combination of plastic and semi-liquid explosive, which can be moulded almost like cake mixture. I checked on the configuration of that particular model of Renault and designed a charge that could be slipped round the rear section of the engine and the petrol tank without being visible either from underneath or from the top when the bonnet was open. The explosive was put into a clear plastic bag, packed like a long, thin sausage which could be tucked away out of sight, with a detonation cord and detonation device inside the bag itself.

This time, I opted for a booby-trap detonation rather than remote control and went with Jacques to rig the device. Paolo had been watching Zarra for most of the evening. The Basque had made two calls at different apartments in the city, then gone to meet his girlfriend at the Café de la Coquille. After supper, he had stayed, drinking, until after eleven o'clock, then gone back with her to his own apartment.

We watched as they went inside, leaving Olazaguirre to park the little blue Renault about fifty yards from the main entrance. The cars along the kerb were not quite bumper to bumper but they were close enough to make a fairly easy approach, and we decided to go in under the vehicle; but we settled down first for a long night's wait.

We did the observation partly from our own two vehicles, with occasional strolls into side streets to stretch our legs and compare notes with Paolo. The French police came and went, carrying out their cursory routine exactly as Jacques had described it. Half a dozen people entered the apartment building between midnight and 3 a.m. but no one came out and the street itself was virtually deserted after two o'clock.

Just before five o'clock, we decided the time was right. I took the explosive charge and approached the Renault from the front. Jacques slipped under a car parked several vehicles down behind the Renault and we gradually worked our way towards each other. Manoeuvring under cars is never very easy. With some you can slide straight under; others have bulky differentials or awkward track rods and you have to try to squeeze between the wheels and the kerb. You end up covered in road dirt and oil but if you take your time it is much safer than approaching the target vehicle from above, especially when there is an outside chance that it might be under unexpected observation.

When we both reached the Renault, I set about placing the charge, wedging it round the gearbox and the drive unit, then passing the rear end of the sausage to Jacques to press up by the petrol tank.

The system I had designed involved a combination switch attached to the detonation device inside the plastic bag. On the tightening of a nylon wire the switch-activated firing cap ignites the safety fuse. On the end of the nylon wire was a small fishhook which I inserted into the rubber of the offside front wheel. With this kind of booby trap, you have to make very fine calculations. The theory is that the driver checks for wires or other devices linked to the ignition, starts the engine, then, when satisfied, drives off, and as the wheel turns, the nylon wire tightens and the explosive is detonated. But you can allow only an inch or so of slack if the wire is not to be seen by anyone looking under the vehicle, and if the angle is wrong the hook can be knocked off the wheel during the initial start-up.

Olazaguirre had parked facing the wrong way and I had to work out exactly what his manoeuvre would be to get out of the row of parked vehicles and into the flow of traffic. As a further complication, the wire was made slippery by blood from a bad gash on my hand caused by an inconveniently-placed heat plate round the car's silencer.

When the job was done, we both crawled back the way we had come and rendezvoused later in Jacques' car to try and clean ourselves up.

It was already almost light and if Zarra stuck to his routine, we would not have long to wait. At 6.30, the French police car returned and parked up the street. They made no special checks and the two men in the car just sat, watching the entrance, looking bored and waiting for Zarra to come out.

At 7.15 exactly, Olazaguirre emerged and looked up and down the street.

'He's a cocky swine,' Jacques said quietly. 'He likes to put on a show for the French cops.'

The bodyguard walked nonchalantly up to the Renault and, sure enough, he began his safety routine, using exaggerated gestures that were obviously for the benefit of the policemen in the car. But there was more show than substance in the safety checks themselves. Olazaguirre had been doing this every morning for a month and had found nothing. It had become almost a game to him.

He began by checking under the car, but he looked only briefly and, finding nothing suspicious hanging down, he opened the driver's door and released the catch for the bonnet. Again with a grand gesture, he opened the bonnet, looked inside, then slammed it down again with a triumphant smile.

'Bloody hell,' I said, 'he's going to knock the fishhook off.'

We couldn't tell whether he had or not and we could only watch as the bodyguard continued his routine. He opened the driver's door fully, wound down the window, and got inside. Then, glancing down towards the police car, he put in the ignition key and – with the bravado of a matador – turned it once and started the engine. When nothing happened, he let it run for a few moments, then, when he was satisfied that all was well, he sat back to wait for Zarra.

The Basque leader came out of the building a couple of minutes later. He too glanced up and down the street, noted the presence of the police car, then looked across at the Renault. The engine was ticking over nicely, Olazaguirre looked relaxed and Zarra started to walk towards his own vehicle.

'We've got him,' I said to Jacques. 'We've finally bloody got him.'

But I had spoken just a second too soon. Zarra had taken only a couple of steps when another man came out of the entrance and walked up to say hello. They shook hands and stood chatting on the small driveway in front of the building.

I could see Olazaguirre's impatience, and Zarra's, and when the conversation continued and showed signs of becoming animated, the bodyguard leaned out of the car window and shouted to him that they were late.

Zarra waved, indicating that he was coming, and in the same moment, Olazaguirre started to pull out of the parking space. He obviously intended to reverse and manoeuvre into the line of traffic to try to hurry Zarra along but he got only as far as drawing level with the car in front.

The explosion split the Renault in two, sending fragments of metal right across the street, staving in the other vehicles and shattering some windows in the nearest apartment building. Through the smoke, I could just make out Zarra. He paused for only a second – not even long enough to make sure that his bodyguard was dead – then sprinted back into the apartment building to make his second escape.

FOURTEEN

PREPARING FOR THE CLIMAX

It was several months before we went after Zarra again and then it was part of the kind of operation I had wanted from the beginning: a concerted attack to damage the whole E.T.A. infrastructure in France – one which became the climax of the secret war against Basque terrorism.

For such an operation to become possible, several factors had to come together. The most important of them, to put it callously, was that the security situation had to deteriorate enough for the government to agree to release the kind of funds necessary – over £160,000.

The Spanish government faced a continuing dilemma in dealing with E.T.A. On the one hand it was committed to encouraging gradual progress towards Basque autonomy in the more liberal context of post-Franco policies. On the other, the government was in constant fear of military disaffection if it was seen to be too soft on E.T.A. violence.

The signs in the early part of 1980 were promising. Apart from our own successes in Biarritz, the intelligence division of the Policia Naçional uncovered an E.T.A. plot to renew its summer campaign of violence at Spanish holiday resorts in order to damage the tourist industry. There was a plan to place bombs at Malaga airport, in several well-known discotheques along the southern coast, and in two yachting marinas. The official line put out by the police was that the plot had been foiled with the arrest of five E.T.A. militants and the discovery of three E.T.A. safe houses, one of them, in Madrid, packed with weapons and explosives.

Alvarez and others knew, however, that finding documents does not necessarily mean the end of a conspiracy and, sure enough, by June the bombing had begun. Four bombs went off in the resorts of Alicante and Javea, and though there were no injuries, the explosions caused extensive damage and sent shock waves through the tourist industry. One depressing aspect of this particular campaign was that it was not the work of the hardliners within E.T.A., the E.T.A.-Militar people who we were going after, but of the so-called moderates, the politico-military faction.

In the same month, E.T.A.-Militar assassinated the chief technical officer of the Michelin tyre plant at Vitoria and the company was forced to close the whole plant for a time because it could not guarantee the safety of the 4,000-strong workforce. E.T.A. had also stepped up its fund-raising through blackmail, forcing Basque businessmen to pay its so-called 'revolutionary tax'. Faced with the apparent inability of the security forces to contain the terrorists, most businessmen and companies paid up.

The overall intelligence picture which Alvarez confided to me looked bleak. There were now about 200 E.T.A. terrorists living in France; seven countries – Ireland, Czechoslovakia, Cuba, Algeria, Lebanon, Uruguay and South Yemen – were known to be training E.T.A. personnel, and funds were being received by them from the Soviet Union, China and Libya.

By this time, the refusal of the French government to offer any real help in dealing with the sanctuary problem had brought about a serious deterioration in relations between Madrid and Paris.

In June, Spain decided to try to exert some pressure by making its grievances public. The Interior Minister, Juan José Roson, arranged a special briefing for foreign correspondents based in Madrid at which he directly accused France of harbouring terrorists, including those responsible for the holiday resort bombings. He also said Spain had evidence that French non-Basques as well as French Basques were helping E.T.A.

The police then picked up the cue from their boss. In July, *Tribuna Policial*, the official publication of the Spanish police union, carried an unsigned article which stated firmly that the general staff and the executive committee of E.T.A. were based in Biarritz. It also described how young Basques were being put through a training programme in France, beginning with a course of Marxist-Leninist political indoctrination and going on to training in shooting, weapons handling and the use of explosives.

The publicity did very little good. France made noises promising increased co-operation but nothing effective was done, and by the middle of the year E.T.A. had killed more than fifty people and injured many others.

All of these developments were providing increasing weight to my proposal for a major operation against the Basque leadership in France but there was one other development which finally clinched the Spanish approval for the funds, and ironically it was one which also soured my relations with British Intelligence for some time afterwards and was to cause me very serious difficulties with them later on.

Early in the year, the Basque regional administration had received grudging authority from the Ministry of the Interior to set up a local Basque police force. It was intended that they should be strictly regular policemen, with no paramilitary functions, but the Conservative leader of the Basque administration, Carlos Garaikoetxea, quietly set about creating the nucleus of a force capable of combating E.T.A. terrorism. A training camp was set up at Berroci, in Alava province, and a German security company was hired to provide instructors. The company recruited five specialists in small arms and special warfare tactics – all of them British. When the story was leaked to the press in July, it was reported that the five were ex-S.A.S. In fact, they were former members of the Royal Marine Commandos.

The leak caused an uproar and Britain denied any official connection with the camp. But by this time Spanish police intelligence were even more worried about the situation. They had managed to infiltrate the camp itself and had discovered that known E.T.A. sympathizers were actually being trained there!

The effrontery of E.T.A. stunned even Alvarez. He decided to enlist my help but he was uncertain how I would react to moving against British nationals. To test me, he arranged a meeting to review the overall security situation and, as was his custom, he handed me an updated set of security *pro formas*, listing details of the latest movements and activities of people who were on his E.T.A. target list. Among them, he included two Britons at the Berroci camp.

I could feel myself being watched as I examined the *pro formas*. Alvarez was making a personal assessment of whether I would be prepared to kill British citizens. I had always maintained my objectivity but it had never been tested quite so brutally before. I looked at Alvarez and made my own assessment of the position. Alvarez is a subtle man, not a brutish killer, and I knew that while he was testing my loyalty, he would not assume that it could be proved only by making the Marine instructors automatic targets.

'You want me to deal with this situation?' I asked, indicating the two British *pro formas*.

'Yes. It has become very urgent. The army is furious that the government has let itself be manoeuvred into allowing the E.T.A. people to mock us in this way.'

'All right,' I said, 'I'll deal with it.'

The same night I flew to London and arranged an urgent meeting with Sandy Haldane, my liaison man with MI6. We met in an office belonging to his defence company in Threadneedle Street. After the pleasantries, I simply put the two British *pro formas* on the table in front of him and said, 'What do you make of that, Sandy?'

Sandy looked at the photographs and the passport details and the record of entries and exits on Spanish soil.

'Yes,' he said, 'I know them both.'

'I thought you might,' I said. 'Trouble is, do you know what it is you're looking at?'

'Well, someone's done their research.'

'But do you know why people have done that research?'

Sandy thought for a minute. 'I've got a pretty good idea,' he said finally, then he added, looking straight at me, 'Are you going to do this?'

'I gather from that that you know what we're talking about?'

'Of course I do,' Sandy said. 'Are you going to do it?'

'Well, I'm showing them to you, aren't I?' I said. 'You have a choice. Either you do something about them, or I have to. All I'm giving you is forty-eight hours because that's all I have.'

Sandy nodded. 'Leave it to me.'

In less than forty-eight hours the British instructors were out of Spain and my short-term problem was solved, but in the intelligence world, nothing is ever that simple. The ripple effect of my meeting with Sandy went on for months and contributed to a later situation which nearly ended my effective career as a mercenary. The British did not like being forced to pull the instructors out. It was said they were being used partly as a cover for intelligence-gathering on I.R.A. activities in Spain and, in addition, getting them out that quickly had meant blowing the cover of the resident MI6 man in San Sebastian. The resentment of my loyalty to my Spanish clients resurfaced and it had taken Sandy considerable effort, I learned later, to convince his people that I meant business. The instructors also bore me a personal grudge because they naively believed I had acted to protect my own commercial position in Spain in relation to the German firm that had hired them, and had got them thrown out of very lucrative jobs, with top-rate allowances, for selfish reasons.

On the face of it, I had achieved very efficiently exactly what Alvarez wanted and my handling of the instructor situation took me one step nearer to gaining approval from the Spanish for the large-scale anti-E.T.A. operation I was recommending in France. But when that approval finally came, in August 1980, and I was faced with one of the most interesting logistical and planning problems I have had to deal with on a mercenary operation, I discovered that the whole project now had an extra dimension of complexity because of some British concern at my position in Spanish employ.

The final element needed to persuade the Spanish to give the green light to the operation was supplied when Spanish Intelligence discovered that the E.T.A. group had rented a farmhouse outside Biarritz which they intended to use for their high-level planning sessions. The farmhouse provided the focus for a major attack which would be outside the city and therefore less likely to bring about a total breakdown in relations between France and Spain. Alvarez and 'Richard' quickly came round to my belief that a concerted attack was now possible – but they also refined the mission in a way that presented a real challenge to my organizing skills. Very rapidly, it all came together: Alvarez wanted an attack on the farmhouse and I was given the mandate to eliminate as many E.T.A. terrorists as possible, but I was to capture two men – Zarra, and his deputy Julio Larranaga, who was known by the nickname 'Chempe' – and bring them back to Spain for interrogation.

The deadline set was less than a month away. Spanish Intelligence had established that the E.T.A. leadership was holding a series of meetings, leading up to a full-scale planning meeting in early September. Funds were released and I was given a free hand – though, in fact, I took an even freer one than 'Richard' had intended.

Two things were clear immediately. First. I would have to operate entirely outside the Spanish orbit; secrecy had been maintained reasonably well so far, but if I started looking for logistical support from the Spanish side, leaks to other arms of service were inevitable. Secondly, it would have to be a tactical mission; in other words, it was not going to be possible to infiltrate people into France disguised as civilians and have them in place and waiting. Instead, it would have to be a military raid, with personnel who were smuggled in immediately before the mission and extracted straightaway afterwards.

My first move was to get hold of my best logistical expert, a Belgian arms dealer and general fixer, Paul Reynaud, who was based in Antwerp. From the moment I put him 'on hold', Reynaud came onto the payroll; it was essential to have someone standing by, ready and available to help me bring the various components of the mission together.

My first plan was to use a fixed-wing aircraft to carry an assault team in and fly them out, over the Pyrenees, with the two Spanish prisoners on board, but the minute I started to take soundings on the practicalities, I realized that I was going to run up against major difficulties.

One was that the internal security situation in the Basque country had been thrown into turmoil by the capture by E.T.A. of two Spanish undercover operatives who were tortured, then killed and left by a roadside near the border. The Guardia Civil reacted with sweep and search patrols all over the area, and security at border posts and airstrips – which was already tight because of the cross-border raids carried out by the Francoist extremists as well as by E.T.A. – was screwed up yet another notch.

Also, I was beginning to discover the extent of British displeasure over the affair of the Royal Marine instructors. It is very easy to tell, in my profession, when you are out of favour. Nothing specific is said but the signs are as easy to read as tracks in the jungle. I began to have trouble getting licences and permits for some of my cargo flights; as my movements around Europe speeded up, I began to notice some harassment by Customs and Immigration at Heathrow airport. Next, I found myself under surveillance in London, to the point where my shadows were even deliberately letting me know – by bumping into me in pubs where I was not supposed to be known – that I was being closed in on.

At the same time, I began to pick up comments through my network of social contacts – including one or two 'gipsy warnings' during casual encounters in the S.A.S. mess at the Duke of York's barracks – that it was a pity I had sold out to 'foreigners' like the Spanish. Didn't I know where my real interests lay? Finally, on one trip to Spain, I had some trouble in Paris and I knew that I was going to have to take extreme measures to preserve the integrity of the mission.

At that point I resolved that I would do the mission my own way, with minimum consultation, and simply deliver the goods to the Spanish. I divided the planning into separate compartments. I put Jacques in charge of the surveillance of the farmhouse and of the movements of Zarra and his immediate circle. I also delegated to Jacques the recruitment of a back-up team. I had decided to lead the attack with a five-man assault team consisting of Jacques, myself, and three other men chosen personally by me. As the farmhouse was in a remote stretch of country south of Biarritz, on a track between the coast road and the sea, I knew I would also need extra personnel to cover the approach and retreat, and I charged Jacques with finding nine men through his Marseilles contacts. That is the normal recruiting procedure for this kind of mercenary operation. The back-up team would be selected by Jacques, paid by him and disciplined by him. They would not know me or the exact nature of the mission; their task would be to cover an assault team carrying out an unspecified mission. They would provide their own weapons, rendezvous with Jacques at an agreed point and disperse afterwards without ever being told the full extent of the operation.

For the main assault team, I recruited three men I knew well and trusted to have at my side at the sharp end. I selected two Britons, Bill Dillon and Ray Kenna, both ex-S.A.S. troopers, and a Rhodesian-born Briton, Mark Austin, who had served in the Rhodesian Special Forces and who now lived in the south of France on a French passport.

In the meantime, I gave very careful thought to the infiltration and extraction of the team, and, abandoning the idea of a fixed-wing aircraft, I decided to use a helicopter. The machine I wanted was a Gazelle which had all the right tactical characteristics for this kind of operation – including a convenient noise signature which means that it is possible to fly in swiftly without advance warning.

The main problem, though, was still where to fly out to. A Gazelle would give greatly increased mobility over a fixed-wing plane but there was still the problem of security on exfiltration. Because of the intensive police operations going on over the border, the Spanish Basque country had become virtually a no-go area. It was not going to be possible to land a helicopter anywhere in the area with a group of armed foreigners on board and remain undercover long enough to complete the interrogation of the two captives – which Alvarez wanted done away from any of the main police installations in Madrid or San Sebastian.

Very soon I was working on an ambitious alternative plan: to fly the team and the captives straight out by helicopter and land on a cargo ship off the Spanish coast. That would provide a secure landing point after the operation, as well as enabling the interrogation to be carried out on board the vessel. After that, Zarra and Chempe could be dumped on Spanish soil for disposal by Alvarez in whatever way he chose.

I knew already that Reynaud, my Belgian contact, had access to a suitable ship which made regular runs out of Antwerp with a crew that was used to this kind of illegal operation. The difficulty was to bring all the pieces into place inside three weeks – a task which involved my practically living on aeroplanes in a whirlwind shuttle around England, Belgium, France and Spain.

I had my first breakthrough when one of my oldest friends in the mercenary world, Martin Rostand, managed to get hold of a Gazelle for me. It was a civilian helicopter – and there are not many civilian Gazelles around – but it had all the performance of the military version and, if stripped down, could carry the loads I wanted at the right speed.

Rostand is someone you would never normally spot as a mercenary. He comes from an aristocratic Parisian family and he has a large private income, as well as a share in widespread family business interests. But he served with the French forces in Indo-China and developed a taste for the excitement of military life. I didn't use him directly in the attack, but he organized the French end of the logistics with a flair that was peculiarly his own.

In Antwerp, Reynaud managed to organize the cargo vessel – a 3,500-ton coaster called the *Sainte Marie*, with an aft deck hold-cover suitable for use as a helicopter landing pad. It was a slow vessel, needing several days to get down off the Basque coast, but Reynaud was prepared to answer for the Master and crew and it was available for a charter fee of £33,000.

Officially, I had told the Spanish that I was planning to exfiltrate from France by road after the mission, but I also had a very private conversation with Alvarez whom I had grown to trust personally during the earlier Biarritz operations.

'Juan, you realize we won't be coming out by road, don't you?' I said.

Alvarez grinned. 'I had gathered that,' he said.

'Tell me a beach where you'd like to collect the merchandise.' I said, 'and I'll give you a delivery time.'

After consideration, Alvarez chose a tiny beach about fifty miles inside the Spanish border. It hadn't even got a name of its own. It was just a patch of sand with a track leading to a village consisting of half a dozen houses.

At the same time, we established an emergency communications centre in Bilbao. If anything went wrong, each member of the assault team was to try to reach Bilbao by whatever means he could. Anywhere else, he was likely to be arrested by the Spanish authorities; no one in the Guardia or the mainstream Policia Naçional had been briefed on the mission.

By this stage, my own movements were being watched by far too many people for comfort. I took to meeting Alvarez in Bilbao instead of Madrid and we agreed a code to protect me on arrival. We arranged that if I arrived wearing my watch on my right wrist instead of my left, Alvarez' men were to move immediately on the man behind me. Similar signals were fixed to cover other emergencies.

British Intelligence was making life thoroughly uncomfortable for me in England and I did most of the final planning from either Belgium or France. Spanish Intelligence finally confirmed the date of the E.T.A. meeting at the farmhouse with only six days' advance warning, and it took all of my energies, as well as Martin's and Reynaud's, to bring all the pieces into place in time.

When the *Sainte Marie* sailed from Antwerp, Reynaud put a complete set of weapons on board, duplicating those we had already stockpiled in Biarritz, in case the situation became too tense to risk going back to our rented house right on the eve of the mission. The ship sailed for Brest where four of Jacques' Marseilles back-up team – who were all Corsicans – went on board to reinforce the crew. Our weapons and ammunition were unloaded and taken south to Biarritz by road, together with some stun grenades which I had got hold of from contacts in England.

Martin arranged for me to pick up the Gazelle at a small airfield south of Paris and came with me for a test flight. It had been a very long time since I had flown a Gazelle; I was determined not to make any mistakes through unfamiliarity and for a couple of hours I flew it through various tactical manoeuvres until I was completely at ease at the controls and was reminded of my delight in this beautiful, fast machine. During the flight, we touched down at a farmhouse owned by a friend of Martin's and stripped out the seats. Then we flew back to Paris for the final briefing.

Reynaud's last job was to organize the illegal entry into France of Bill Dillon and Ray Kenna. I had done the hiring in Belgium and they had stayed there, waiting for the signal to move.

Reynaud brought them in by road and Mark Austin flew up from Nice for the final briefing which took place in Martin's flat in Paris.

The four members of the assault team were being paid £25,000 for the mission, and I was satisfied that each of them would be worth it. They were very different in background and temperament: Bill Dillon was a rough-mannered countryman from the north of England; Ray Kenna was an Irish-born Cockney who had been used by the S.A.S. under cover in Northern Ireland and had been at a loose end since his discharge; and Mark Austin was a film director's idea of a great white hunter, blond and fit-looking and as bronzed by his life on the southern French beaches as he had once been by the Rhodesian sun. But their Special Forces training and experience gave them their most important common feature: they were all capable of thinking fast and improvising during an operation.

After introductions to Jacques and Martin, I laid out the details of the mission and, finally, I handed each man a set of intelligence *pro formas* – the very latest provided by Alvarez and annotated by Jacques with his own comments and Paolo's.

'We're going there to take only two prisoners,' I said, pointing out the profiles of Zarra and Chempe. 'The rest are to be dealt with in any way you can.'

FIFTEEN

CONCLUSION OF THE SECRET WAR

Three nights later, I was sitting at the controls of the helicopter on the ground, in a clearing in a pine forest ten kilometres from the farmhouse, waiting to give the signal for the assault.

For me, it was the tensest moment of the whole operation. I was alone; in the stillness of the night I felt as though the scream of the Gazelle's turbine could be heard all the way to Spain – and we had lost contact with our principal targets Zarra and Chempe.

Everyone was in position for the attack. Jacques, Dillon and Kenna and three of the Marseilles Coriscan back-up men were at the farmhouse, ready to go in on my command; the Rhodesian, Mark Austin, and two more Corsicans were lying in wait for Zarra's car, ready to lay flares on the road to guide me in so I could set the helicopter down on the road and seal the ambush of the E.T.A. leader. But Zarra and Chempe – as far as we knew – had not left Biarritz and we had lost radio contact with Paolo who had been tailing them all day. They were due at the farmhouse shortly – that much had been firmly established through surveillance – but without confirmation from Paolo that they were on their way, I dared not give the signal for the attack on the meeting and, meanwhile, the noise of the helicopter seemed to be filling the entire landscape.

I did not want to shut down the Gazelle's turbine. If I did, and the noises had already attracted the attention of the police patrol or some passing local, I would not be able to lift off fast enough to get out of trouble. The risk was not too great. The Gazelle had remained hidden in another wood not far away for two days without being spotted, but then it had been silent and camouflaged skilfully and guarded by the two Corsicans who were now with Mark Austin. The Corsicans, tough, disillusioned veterans of France's Algerian war, had guarded many a drugs cache and were skilled in the art of concealment. They had reported the whole area virtually deserted apart from a few passers-by who never strayed from the two minor roads which were some distance away. But small or not, the risk still seemed unacceptable as I sat scanning the trees which were illuminated only by a faint gleam of moonlight and the glow of the lights of Biarritz over the horizon.

As I reviewed the situation, I could picture every detail of the preparations. Since flying down from Paris and concealing the helicopter, I had spent much of my time undertaking personal surveillance – lying in the pine trees beside the friend of Paolo's who had been watching the E.T.A. people assemble at the farmhouse, and sitting in cars and rented rooms in Biarritz with Paolo himself, listening to audio surveillance of Zarra and his aides.

The farmhouse would already be full. Though it still had the layout of a typical farm of the region, with a steeply sloping tiled roof and a walled courtyard with a small pond, it had long since been converted into a comfortable country residence with many of the stables and outbuildings refurbished as guest bedrooms. In the past three days, seven people from our *pro forma* target list had been arriving, and at the last count there were eleven people there altogether, including four women.

Two men at the farmhouse were French but were clearly members of E.T.A. The four women were all Spanish and two of them were listed as active militants, but it was obvious from our audio surveillance of the preparations that the weekend was to be a party as well as a planning meeting.

Quantities of food and good wine had been brought in from Biarritz and a celebration meal was being planned for that night before the working sessions got under way.

Our biggest break thus far was the discovery that Zarra's status within E.T.A. required a late entrance and he would arrived with Chempe only when all the preparations at the farmhouse had been made. The meal was set for ten o'clock, which meant that they should have been en route, but Zarra was a hard man to judge.

At one level, he seemed careless for a terrorist leader. After a second attempt on his life, he had, for a while, taken scrupulous care with his security arrangements and Paolo had been forced to keep his distance. At that point, Paolo had brought in yet another Marseilles Corsican, a really seedy character called Ricco who was one of the most anonymous-looking people I have ever met, the kind of guy who can sit at the same café terrace as you for three days in a row without you noticing him. Gradually, they had closed in on Zarra again and watched him growing more and more casual.

The Basque had acquired a newer and bigger car – a white Peugeot-504 which was much easier to tail than the nondescript Renaults that most of the E.T.A. people used, and he travelled regularly in the company of Teresa his girlfriend, Chempe, and another Spanish girl who lived in the same flat as the deputy. That kind of observable pattern was very unprofessional – as was his apparent willingness to let a major meeting of his command structure turn into a weekend social occasion.

Yet his record as a terrorist was undeniable. Alvarez reckoned that Zarra had personally taken part in at least eight assassinations – including a bomb attack in which the baby daughter of a Guardia Civil officer had been crippled. Chempe, too – belying his nondescript 'intellectual' appearance – had, like Zarra, managed to make numerous operational trips across the Pyrenees into Spain without being detected. Such men could not be underestimated and I knew that even a minor departure from the plans E.T.A. had made for the weekend could seriously disrupt our operation.

My immediate concern, though, was the noise of the Gazelle. I cannot remember when I have felt as conspicuous. It seemed as though I was sending a siren message over the whole countryside to come and inspect my hiding-place. The sound was just too distinctive; there was no way it could be taken for a car, or even a heavier road vehicle. I checked by radio with Mark Austin who was the one, theoretically, in radio range of Paolo, but there was still no word and I decided that I had better lift off.

I reasoned that I might be less conspicuous in flight, and for a while I circled over the eastern edge of the forest on low power, setting up a loiter pattern within my map grid, using natural cover to watch for signs of movement in the trees below. But I soon set down again. I could see no one in the immediate vicinity of my clearing and, anyway, I simply could not spare the fuel. This time, I switched off the engine on landing and the silence was truly deafening. With the mission already under way and my adrenaline running strongly, I felt as though every policeman and E.T.A. terrorist for fifty miles around knew exactly where I was, and I sat, poised for emergency lift-off, willing Paolo to confirm that Zarra and Chempe were on their way.

It was as well I did set down because the signal did not come for fifteen long fuel-expensive minutes. I learned later that when Zarra had set out for the farm, the Peugeot had made several detours, criss-crossing through the outer suburbs of Biarritz, apparently as a routine precaution against being followed by the French police. Paolo and Ricco, tailing in two separate cars, had managed to stay with them, but Paolo, who had the radio, had not been able to call Mark Austin because of the high buildings and the contours of the outskirts of the city.

Once they were out of Biarritz, Paolo sent the message, in the form of an excited yelp. Mark relayed it to me in a clipped, more military tone, but I could still hear the note of relief and anticipation now that we were finally 'off and rolling'.

When the signal came, I knew I had about fifteen minutes to reach the rendezvous with Mark and spring the ambush. For the first time, I opened the general radio channel, and told everyone that I was lifting off and the assault would begin, on my command, in approximately ten minutes. I flew the Gazelle slowly without lights, using nap-of-the-earth technique, hugging the contours of the terrain, staying close to and below the tops of the trees in a dog's-leg path to the rendezvous, which would keep me out of sight of the road until the last moment. This was not the time for kick and rush tactics; I had planned it so that the sudden appearance of the helicopter in the path of the Peugeot would be one of the great shocks of Mr Zarra's life – and probably the last.

Now that Paolo was back in radio contact I was receiving progress reports every three or four minutes. Zarra was apparently satisfied that he was not being followed and the Peugeot was making steady progress along the lonely minor road, with Zarra at the wheel, Chempe beside him and the two girls in the back seat.

During the journey, there was only one moment of tension. I received a message via Mark that one of our surveillance cars had broken down and had had to be abandoned. I discovered only later that it had not in fact broken down at all – it was simply that Ricco's nerve had cracked. He had no radio and he felt isolated and lonely and wanted to join up with Paolo! Ricco was at that point closest to feigning a breakdown, forcing Paolo to pick him up. It was the kind of moment of weakness that could have jeopardized the mission, but you have to make allowances for such normal, human reactions when you are forced to use people whose military skills are not tuned up to the pitch needed for this kind of mission. Paolo, though a former para, was not really current either, but they were both there for their surveillance ability not their combat skills and no one could have handled that side of things better.

As it turned out, the manoeuvre delayed them by a couple of minutes; Zarra noticed nothing amiss and continued his steady progress towards the farmhouse.

From the air, I spotted the Peugeot when they were about two kilometres away. Paolo's car was hanging well back and the E.T.A. vehicle was the only other one visible in any direction. I tracked it by its headlights as it moved in and out of the wooded slopes. Then I opened the radio and gave the signal for the attack on the farmhouse.

From my position close to the ambush point, I could now just see the farm. It was practically the only lit building in that part of the landscape but I saw it only as a smudge of light, off to my right, as I prepared for my descent on Zarra. But Bill Dillon described the scene to me graphically later in his rough northern England dialect and I gathered that though the whole assault was over in less than ten minutes, the firefight was tense and bloody.

When I had given them the 'ten to run' signal on lift-off, they had moved from their positions in the pine trees and infiltrated in ones and twos into the inner courtyard. There were two guards in the grounds of the building but there had been no need to deal with them in advance of the final assault. Inside, there was virtually a party going on, with several people, carelessly silhouetted against brightly lit windows, sitting round the massive farmhouse table in the main ground-floor lounge, drinking wine and laughing and joking as they waited for the arrival of their leader. The outside guards made periodic circuits of the wall but, in Bill's phrase, they were 'too bothered at missing out on the booze' to take their task seriously and kept going back to join the revelry.

By the time I gave the final signal for the attack, Jacques and the two British ex-S.A.S. men were lying under parked cars almost under the window of the lounge and the three Corsicans were beneath other vehicles, spaced out along the length of the farm.

There were several machine-guns and pistols lying around the room, against the wall and chairs and on the table – clearly visible from outside – but no one had a weapon in their hand when Jacques threw the first stun grenade. 'They were damned sloppy, thank God,' Bill said, and he mentioned that they had even heard the noise of the Gazelle in the distance just before the attack but had not bothered to check it out.

In all, three stun grenades were thrown. One bounced off the wall, but two got through the partially open windows and that was enough to give the assault team time to smash their way through the huge French doors at the end of the house. This particular type of stun grenade gives off eight reports and eight flashes in lightning sequence and totally disorientates everyone within range by creating temporary deafness and breathlessness and an inability to move.

With no one to isolate and keep alive, they were able to open the attack by raking the room with automatic fire and four people died in the very first burst.

The resistance came from the bar end of the room. At the end of the lounge, there was a large bedroom, which was being used as an annexe to the main room and was stocked with food and drink. The intervening wall shielded some of the Spaniards from the effect of the stun grenades and three managed to reach their weapons and return fire into the lounge.

According to Bill, the firefight lasted about three minutes. At the end of it, nine E.T.A. terrorists, including two women, were dead, and two other women were seriously wounded. But we had also taken two casualties. Ray Kenna had been hit in the chest and one of the Corsicans had taken a burst in the stomach.

The wounded women were left alive. Bill reported quite dispassionately that there had been a brief discussion about whether to finish them off, but as they were not on the Spanish target list and as all the assault team were masked by balaclavas, it was agreed they could be left. They were dragged into a side room, then Bill organized a search of the house while Ray and the Corsican dealt with their wounds as best they could. Finally, when Jacques and Bill were satisfied that the situation was secure, the team withdrew into the woods to prepare to move out.

Long before that stage was reached, of course, we had got involved in our own action on the road four kilometres away.

The spot we had chosen for the ambush did not make for easy flying. It was a sudden bend in the road after a low ridge when approaching from Biarritz. On one side, the ground sloped away to where rolling fields began about twenty feet below. On the other, it rose more sharply so that, from the air, the ambush area formed a shallow hollow, set against a dark hillside.

Five pinlights had been arranged in the road to mark out the landing zone for the helicopter. These lights are set in little cups so that they are invisible from ground level. From the air, they can be seen only from directly above or from an acute angle at certain low altitudes. I was to be guided to the pinlights by two brighter flares, one at the back, marking the end of the curve in the road, and one at the front, which was to be lit only at the very last moment.

Mark did not like this part of the plan; he was the front man and it meant that right at the moment when Zarra's car was approaching he would be exposed in the middle of the road. To avoid this, the Rhodesian had anchored the front flare to a stake and had run a lanyard from it, across the road, so that he could activate it from his ambush position.

When he had confirmation from Paolo that the Peugeot was coming into range, Mark radioed to me to hold myself ready for the ambush and signalled to one of the Corsicans to light the back flare.

The flare lit first time, but it fell on its side and lay burning with reduced intensity. I could still see it, though, and I radioed for the front flare. Mark pulled the lanyard out but that flare failed to ignite.

I was left with a very tight flying situation. The car was approaching the last hilltop and would soon be coming into view – there was no time for Mark to run to the flare and try again to light it; I was going to have to come in by one flare and the pinlights alone.

The single flare did not really help. It gave me no clue to the direction of the pinlights and I dared not use its light, as staring at it would ruin my night vision. There was no question of using my landing light and I ended up jinking up and down above the road, trying by trial and error to find the height at which the pinlights would become visible. The pinlights were set in a tee formation – three down the centre of the road and two at either side.

Eventually, I spotted the middle three and though I never did find the outer two, I swung the tail of the Gazelle in the general direction of the brighter flare. By this time the machine was swaying and I was beginning to flare out. I put the nose of the machine up and went into hover effect, the final stage before landing, and, using the contour of the ground to help me situate the roadway, I eventually managed to bring the Gazelle down safely, with barely a minute to spare.

Instead of shutting the machine down, I locked the controls to keep it on the ground, and left the turbine running, throttled back to flight idle. I jumped out and stood beside the cockpit, with one arm reaching in to the control panel and the other gripping my MP-5 submachine gun; then, at the second that Zarra's Peugeot came over the low hilltop, I hit the landing light, bathing the whole hollow in a spectacular dazzling glare.

I saw Mark right next to the car. He raised his submachine gun and raked the car, firing low to knock out the vehicle without killing the passengers.

Zarra had no chance to grasp what was happening to him. One second, he was driving along chatting to Chempe and the girls; the next, he had come upon a helicopter in the middle of the road, then he was blinded by the light and immediately under fire.

The Peugeot swerved to the right and started to veer up the slope. Zarra wrenched the wheel and the car careered back down onto the road and kept on coming.

I thought, 'Oh Christ, he's going to hit the chopper,' but another burst of fire from Mark forced the Basque to spin the wheel again.

This time, the car stalled and skidded to a halt on the verge of the road. I could hear the women screaming and I raised my own weapon and opened fire. Then Mark shouted: 'Hold it. We're going in.'

I stopped firing, and as I did so I heard the first return shots. I could see Chempe firing his pistol blindly in the direction of the light and one of the women also had a weapon and was trying to aim through one of the side windows.

I switched off the helicopter light so as not to blind Mark, and in the last seconds of illumination I saw Zarra in silhouette struggling to get a submachine gun from under the dashboard.

Then Mark opened fire and with the first burst killed both of the women. I could not see at first why he had fired at them and not at Chempe, then I realized that the deputy was now half slumped in the passenger seat – I had hit him with my original burst.

Zarra threw open the driver's door and rolled out but he was too late to have even the beginnings of a chance. Both I and the Corsican on his side were on top of him before he could raise his weapon, and through the noise of the helicopter turbine I made signs to him to leave it on the ground.

At that moment, Paolo and Ricco came roaring over the hilltop in the Renault. They both jumped out, weapons trained, but there was nothing left to do. Chempe was badly hurt and no longer a threat, and Zarra was so overcome with terror that every thrust from the muzzle of our weapons produced an instant, grovelling response.

Mark and one of the Corsicans lifted them both up against the side of the car, frisked them, then forced them to drop their trousers which were tied round their ankles to complete the immobilization. Finally, they were hauled acros the road and thrown onto the floor of the helicopter, Chempe whining with pain and Zarra effectively paralysed with fear and shock at the speed of what had overtaken them.

The next step was to link up with the assault team but we got no response to a radio call. We could not tell whether they were too preoccupied to answer or whether reception was being interfered with by the configuration of the landscape and I sent Paolo and Ricco down to the farmhouse to investigate. The Corsicans were organizing their own exfiltration but the plan was for me to lift Mark and the two Britons out with me to the ship.

I estimated that it would take Paolo at least twenty minutes to get to the farm and back and I could not leave the Gazelle on the road for that long. We had intended to roll the Peugeot down the slope but I decided there was no need, and we left it, as a wreck by the roadside, with the two women concealed in the back seat.

After that, we were free to lift off. The two Corsicans set off across the country to find their own vehicle and I took off, with Mark squatting in the stripped-out rear cabin to watch over Zarra and Chempe, and cruised back down the road, with the landing light on, hoping to meet the team from the farmhouse.

After just over two kilometres, we found them; I put down again beside Paolo's Renault, and we took the two Britons on board, with Bill half carrying the wounded Ray Kenna.

It was the first indication I had had that we had taken casualties and, once I was airborne and the bearing set for the flight out to the *Sainte Marie*, I ordered Bill to give me a detailed briefing. Talking through the headset from the Gazelle's co-pilot seat, Bill gave me his account of the attack. Our final tally was nine dead terrorists. One of the things that sticks in my mind from the debriefing was Bill's description of moving carefully from body to body checking the identity of each of the victims against the target *pro formas* provided by Alvarez.

He was convinced that Ray Kenna would pull through but he was sure also that the Corsican who had been hit in the stomach would not last more than a few hours. His death, if it happened, would, I knew, be reported to me later only if the Corsicans chose to do so. They were a self-contained unit and they had already left the farmhouse, their part in the mission over, bearing away their own wounded.

The flight to the ship took a little over an hour and by the time we reached her, just after midnight, Ray Kenna was already much more comfortable. He had taken a bullet in the upper chest but it had exited cleanly beside the collar bone and he had cleaned it and bound it and was sitting quietly, conserving energy for the final stage of the mission.

Chempe was in much worse condition. Mark Austin had staunched the bleeding, but though we had painkillers with us, he was not given any. His interrogation was about to begin and the kind of pain he was in would make him all the more ready to talk without resistance.

My biggest remaining problem was to put the Gazelle down on the deck of the *Sainte Marie*. I found the vessel exactly at the rendezvous position but she had cut her engines and was drifting in a moderate sea. The landing would have been much easier if she had been under way and a landing on a rolling deck was anyway a manoeuvre I had never had to try before.

My team did not help. Their adrenaline was running and they were high with the success of the mission. They didn't give a damn about the danger and had no patience with my efforts to line up the helicopter safely with the pitching and rolling of the makeshift helipad on the stern of the vessel. Each time I made a pass over the deck there were shouts of 'Go on. Put the fucking thing down,' but I just grinned and ignored them, until I had got the angle exactly as I wanted it.

Three of the crew threw sandbags over the helicopter's runners the moment I touched down, two others concentrated on refuelling the machine, and the four Corsicans who had boarded at Brest to guard the ship stood by the rails, waving and cheering.

For the rest of the night, the main task passed to the Spanish interrogators and I won't pretend it was a pleasant business. The Spanish treat terrorists with the same brutality that the Basques mete out to their own captives and Alvarez had sent two experts who knew they had only a few hours to try for the biggest haul of intelligence data since the start of the struggle against E.T.A.

They worked in the galley, with tape-recorders turning, while we rested and cleaned ourselves up and prepared for the return to France. They did not report to me afterwards and it was only later, from Alvarez himself, that I learned just how much they had found out. Chempe, who was already dying of his wounds, offered no resistance, and Zarra did not hold out for long. They revealed for the first time the details of the cell structure within E.T.A. and the names of key individuals in half a dozen cities. They also gave information on arms shipments and the links between E.T.A. and the I.R.A. and the ways in which the terrorist operations were funded on both sides of the border.

Shortly before dawn, the chief Spanish interrogator came to find me in the Master's cabin and announced that he was almost ready to take the two terrorists ashore. 'We have one more tactic,' he said. 'I would like you to come on deck, please.'

I went up with Mark Austin and found Zarra and Chempe, their hands bound behind them, slumped against the rail of the ship.

Without saying a word, the Spaniard raised his pistol and shot Chempe through the head. There was no doubt Chempe was already close to death; his wounds and his interrogation had left him barely enough strength to support himself against the rail and the shot in the head was almost an act of mercy rather than an execution.

Without showing any emotion, the Spaniard turned to Zarra and said in Spanish, 'Do you want to join your friend, or shall we continue our talk?'

Zarra, his face bruised and bleeding, managed the strength to grunt and nod his head, and the Spaniard led him below.

The tape-recorders turned for another twenty minutes, then the Spaniard came on deck and announced that he was ready to go ashore.

I had left to Alvarez the details of the final scenario and it was obvious that the two Spanish interrogators were working to detailed instructions.

Chempe's body was wrapped in an uninflated rubber dinghy and stowed in the back of the Gazelle, then Zarra was brought, half carried and half dragged by the second Spaniard, and made to lie face down beside him. Two canvas bags containing weapons were brought and put in, then the two Spaniards climbed in beside them. I said brief goodbyes to Bill Dillon and Ray Kenna who, like the Corsicans, were going with the ship, first to Bilbao and then back to Brest and Antwerp. Mark Austin was flying back to France with me and he took his place in the passenger seat.

But first there was the final flight for Zarra. I took off just after five o'clock and headed straight for the beach which had been designated by Alvarez. I landed right on the water's edge, on a narrow strip of grey, dirty sand, and remained at the controls, as the Spaniards, helped by Mark, unloaded Chempe's body and laid it on the beach, still wrapped in the dinghy.

Finally, Zarra was pulled out onto the beach, almost fainting with fear, and as Mark climbed back into the cockpit and we lifted off, I watched the Spaniards carefully untying his hands.

At the debriefing in Madrid, I was never told the exact details of Zarra's execution. I do not know who fired the final bullet or when, and the police record makes no mention, either, of the time of Chempe's death.

The official record shows that a Guardia Civil uniformed patrol – which just happened to be at this godforsaken, un-named beach at five o'clock in the morning – came upon two Basque terrorists who were trying to enter Spain illegally in a rubber dinghy for the purposes of committing a terrorist act. Both were killed in the subsequent gunfight and weapons and ammunition were found.

For us, it was the end of the secret war against E.T.A. The Spaniards were so satisfied with the outcome that I have maintained a close commercial relationship with all arms of the Spanish security services ever since. The ripple effect of the Biarritz raid went on for months, though, long after our team had dispersed to their home stations – Kenna to recover completely – and all of them to wait for further mercenary assignments.

Alvarez estimated later that over 150 arrests resulted, either directly or indirectly, from the data gathered during the interrogations on the ship. The Spaniards also learned a number of lessons from our techniques which they later began to put into practice for themselves.

Nearly four years later, in March 1984, I happened to be listening, during one of my trips to the Middle East, to a broadcast on the B.B.C. World Service which contained more than a few echoes of the style we had taught our Spanish clients.

The radio said that four alleged members of E.T.A. had been shot dead by police as they entered the port of Pasajes, near the French border, by boat, shortly before midnight. 'The police operation was clearly well planned,' the B.B.C. correspondent in Madrid reported, 'and had resulted from a tip-off. Shortly before midnight, a fisherman's motor launch, which was coming from France, according to the police, entered the port. Police say the boat was challenged and ordered to freeze. A gun battle ensued, spotlights were switched on and the bodies of four occupants of the vessel were recovered from the harbour by police using rubber dinghies. The operation was carried out by members of the crack Spanish anti-terrorist unit, known as G.E.O.S., modelled on Britain's S.A.S.'

Well, maybe there was a tip-off and maybe there was even a raid. Still, I could not help smiling and wondering just which of our lessons the G.E.O.S. had been putting into effect.

SIXTEEN

REMANDED IN CUSTODY

British Intelligence took its revenge for my Spanish involvement in, of all unlikely places, the Channel Islands.

It was through a series of coincidences that they happened to choose that particular location but there was no doubt that they had been looking for an opportunity to teach me a lesson since the affair of the personnel who had had to be pulled out of the Basque police training camp.

Objectively, I understand their resentment. It was not just the professional embarrassment. Because they had only forty-eight hours to get the instructors out, they had to blow the cover of their resident man in San Sebastian to do it. With Spanish Intelligence watching the situation so closely, once he had surfaced his usefulness was at an end and he was to all intents and purposes exposed. But I gathered through Sandy Haldane that what had really irked MI6 was the firmness with which I had put my ultimatum. They had understood – as I intended – that I *would* have moved against the Britons if they were not extracted, and that jolted quite a few people who were not used to receiving ultimatums.

Their resentment increased yet further a few months after the Biarritz helicopter raid when I started working for the Spanish inside Britain. It was not a major assignment – in fact, it amounted to a few weeks of very routine undercover enquiries – but the authorities abviously decided that I had yet again overstepped what they considered to be 'the mark'.

The assignment grew out of the interrogation of an E.T.A. suspect in Madrid. He was engaged in gun-running for E.T.A. and for the I.R.A. and he disclosed that one link in the European network involved moving both weapons and people through the container port at Southampton on the south coast of England. Irish dockers with I.R.A. sympathies were handling the British end and linking up with Spaniards working in Spanish and French ports. Alvarez asked me if I would take a look at the Southampton end and I agreed, partly to keep my association with him warm and partly because it's part of the world I enjoy being in anyway.

In my 'transilient' movement around the world in search of the ideal lifestyle, there always have to be plenty of spells in England and I am particularly fond of the rural life in the stretch of countryside behind that southern coastal area. I have a lot of friends there, including one who runs a flying school, and I can take a very full part in the local life – flying, sailing, riding and enjoying the countryside – without laying down formal roots in Britain which I would not want to do.

There is a certain sanity about English country life which has always appealed to me. There is a kind of gentleness and charm about the way people deal with each other. Not everyone, of course. As in all countries, there are plenty of people who live boring, limited and superficial lives, but there are also a great many who make the most of their cultural background and create an environment that is very easy to feel comfortable in. For one thing, the art of discussion hasn't been lost. There are plenty of people who really know how to talk, not just educated people but farmers and coun-tryfolk generally. For me, naturally, the language is a huge bonus. In most of the countries I live and work in, language makes me a foreigner. In England, at least I have a common tongue, something I find very restful.

If I did not live the violent life I do, and need, I am sure I would want to set-tle in a harsher land than Britain – somewhere like Kenya, for example, or South Africa. As it is, Britain provides the perfect gentle contrast to the rough side of my life and as long as I have other places to shake me out of my 'gentility', I'm always happy around southern Britain.

Yet I do not want to integrate completely into the British way of life. I do not really want to have to worry about its politics and its strikes and its other economic problems. Over the years, I have developed an almost cynical detachment from day-to-day problems, which has been reinforced by exten-sive reading of history. I believe there are certain powerful currents in human development which create turning points and changes of direction over the centuries. Most of the issues that obsess the media and ordinary citi-zens seem to me to be merely transitory.

That does not mean that I don't follow current events. In my business you have to be informed. I detest ignorance in others and will not tolerate it in myself. I am probably better informed than most Britons about their prob-lems, just as I have to be able to debate Zionism or Arab nationalism in the Middle East with people who are almost obsessively well versed in every aspect of them. But I try not to lose my detachment.

Anyway, in the spring and summer of 1981, I was very happy to spend quite a lot of time in the Southampton area, fitting in some investigations for the Spanish, while making trips to the United States and the Middle East, and flying myself around Europe, as well as doing some flight instruction at my friend's flying school to help repay his hospitality.

It was through a combination of these activities that I finally came up against British Intelligence and, as is common enough in my profession, the circumstances were complex and full of intrigue.

It began pleasantly enough with a chance meeting with a young woman – at least, it appeared to be a chance meeting; I found out only months later that it had been planned. At the time, I simply walked into a country pub in the New Forest with a flying friend and we struck up an acquaintance with two girls at the bar.

The woman I was attracted to introduced herself as Jenny and she told me, over a couple of drinks, that she was a physical training teacher in a school not far away. The evening ended with my driving her back to her home and arranging to see her again.

So far, it was a very pleasant and very conventional encounter; she was in her twenties, attractive and intelligent, and I enjoyed her company from the outset. Then the meeting developed into an affair which continued over several weeks and I began to be aware that there were certain aspects of the situation which might have some bearing on my professional life.

With hindsight, I now know for certain that Jenny became more emotionally involved with me than she had ever intended and I was very quickly drawn to her in a way that went beyond picking up a pretty girl in a pub.

One of the myths that has developed around people who do the kind of work I do – fostered by the glamorized 'agents' and mercenaries and S.A.S.-types in cinema films and on T.V. – is that we like glamorous, empty-headed women whom we can use for sex and recreation.

In my case, the reality is very different. There is nothing I like better than becoming involved with a woman – but involved emotionally as well as sexually. Jenny had the kind of sensitivity that I find particularly attractive and she was able to respond to my need to relax and free myself of the tensions of my work, without being able to talk specifically about what I do.

One of the biggest problems with my work is that you have too many secrets. I force myself to forget more than most people remember, and when a mission is over I cannot unburden to friends or women companions. But there are some women who are able to perceive that inner dimension to your life without having to know what you have been doing to make you like that.

I really enjoy counter-balancing the pushing, driving, violent side of my life by seeing a good lover. There has to be a soft side to existence and I find that the kind of perceptiveness that helps keep me alive in the middle of intrigue and undercover action also makes me able to read a woman quite well too. If there is no one on the right wavelength to allow me emotional release, then I keep everything tight inside me. Subconsciously, I never waste anything. I just keep on rolling and, of course, the pressure builds up.

Jenny was on the right wavelength. I am not saying that she was one of the great loves of my life, but our affair was a great deal more than skin sex, and it was only after a few weeks that the disturbing incidents began.

The first happened at two o'clock one morning while I was in bed with

Jenny at her flat. She lived over an agricultural implement showroom in a very original little studio flat which she had decorated with great flair. Its main feature – apart from the bed – was a huge clothes rack of the kind used to display garments in department stores. Instead of being in wardrobes, all her clothes were hung on this rack and she had made it a decorative feature of the bedroom. Because of the open-plan layout of the flat, it was very hard for anything to happen without being aware of it, and that night I had a pretty good view of the man who knocked at the door of the flat in the early hours of the morning.

He was a tall, very fit-looking man in his thirties, with sleeked down black hair and a little Mexican bandit moustache. When Jenny opened the door, he was surprised to find that she was not alone; he seemed quite accustomed to being there at unusual hours. Jenny got rid of him quickly, but I was curious and a bit irritated. I assumed it was another lover Jenny had not told me about and I made it pretty clear to her that I was not interested in playing those kind of games.

Jenny apologized and sounded sincere. She said the man was called Alan Vass and he had never been a lover.

'Then what the hell is he doing wandering in as though he owns the place at two o'clock in the morning?' I said.

Jenny fudged her answer. She said they were engaged in a project together and it was strictly business and they met at odd hours because he travelled about a lot and often got back late in the evening. I asked what he did and she said he had been at the same college of physical training as she had; he had begun, like her, as a P.T. teacher but now worked for a sporting goods firm as a salesman.

I had a definite feeling that that was either not the truth or only part of the truth but I didn't press the issue then.

A couple of weeks later, she introduced me to Vass, who had wandered into a pub we were drinking at in Southampton. I was sure it was not a chance meeting, especially as Vass showed a lot of interest in my work. I told him that I had quite a lot of different business activities but at the moment I was doing casual flight instruction at a flying school nearby.

Immediately, Vass started talking about taking flying lessons. He said he had always wanted to and asked what it would cost and so on. I gave him some details and suggested that he come over to the flying school to talk to the principal.

He did make some enquiries at the flying school, at a time when I wasn't there, then at our next meeting – he invited Jenny and me over to his flat for drinks – out of the blue he offered me some cannabis.

I said I didn't smoke grass and I was surprised he did if he was thinking of taking up flying, but he made a big thing about how harmless he thought it was and did I really think it would affect my judgment as a pilot.

I did not let him pursue the subject and I sensed that Jenny was very uneasy, as though she had known it was going to come up.

In the week after the conversation, she behaved even more oddly. Instead of preserving her usual discretion about what I really did – apart from teaching people to fly – she started making remarks like: 'You know, people are really bothered by you. You're so much of a mystery man. You ought to talk a bit more about yourself, then people wouldn't be so suspicious.'

She made the remarks in a tone that suggested she was trying to warn me and I know now – after the event – that she was trying to do exactly that.

What I did not know then was that I was becoming involved, as a suspect, in a major drugs investigation by the narcotics division of Scotland Yard. Jenny herself was working under cover for the police, and was one of a number of people who had been recruited to help investigate drug trafficking in schools. She was not a policewoman, only a long-term informer who had been contacted during her training college days and who did the work because she believed very strongly in the need to protect children from drugs.

Vass, however, was a policeman – a drugs squad detective – and he had me marked down as a prime suspect. What was happening, I found out later, was that my enquiries for the Spanish were getting mixed up with the drugs squad enquiries into narcotics shipments through the port of Southampton. More particularly, the point of contact between the two investigations was a man called Paul Amesbury.

Amesbury was a wealthy businessman, with a bit of a reputation as a fast operator, who was not too fussy about how regularly he paid his taxes. My interest in him was that he employed a number of Irish labourers who drank regularly with the Irish dockers who were suspected of handling the container racket in Southampton docks. I thought the Irish were moving arms and terrorists in the containers; Vass and his associates believed they were moving drugs. My problem – though I didn't know it at the time – was that Vass didn't know I was investigating Amesbury; he thought I was working with him.

When I had started to suspect Amesbury I had made an effort to get close to him which had proved very easy because he was a keen amateur pilot who used my friend's flying school for advanced flight and navigation lessons. The drugs squad was very bothered by Amesbury's rapidly advancing flying skills, believing he would make use of them for drug trafficking. Since I was making it my business to do more and more of the instructing, I was putting myself right 'in the frame', as the British police say, as a suspect by association.

The situation came to a head over a flight Amesbury wanted to make for a long navigation exercise. I had some business in Bordeaux and I said I would fly him there as his instructor. We flew to Bordeaux, I completed my business and we stayed the night, and the next morning Amesbury asked if I would be willing to go on to Tangiers for the weekend instead of flying back.

I had nothing special on for the weekend and I didn't mind being paid to holiday in Tangiers for a couple of days so I agreed. We flew direct from Bordeaux and checked in at the Holiday Inn. In Tangiers, we virtually went our separate ways, meeting only for a drink at intervals when we happened both to be in the hotel. On the first night, he came back to my room for a nightcap and to my astonishment he produced a packet of 'hash cookies' which he had bought in Tangiers during the day. A few hash cookies are no big deal in a place like Tangiers – the kids practically stuff them in your pockets at every street corner – but I was still surprised and I said to Amesbury: 'What the hell do you want that stuff for?'

'Oh, it's just for fun,' he replied. 'I'm just trying out a bit of local colour.'

The next day we flew back to Bordeaux, with the intention of refuelling and flying directly on to Southampton, but during the second leg, the weather closed in over the south coast of England and after the usual air traffic communications I diverted to Jersey.

I didn't know it at the time, but I really set the police chasing their tails. They had intended to arrest Amesbury on his return to Southampton, and the weather and my flight diversion had set them a considerable problem.

In Jersey we took a taxi from the airport and agreed to meet for a drink after we had checked into a hotel.

We met an hour later and Amesbury was looking white and shaky. I asked him what was the matter and he said: 'Look. I've got a problem, can we go for a walk and talk about it?'

And he did indeed have a problem. After checking in at the hotel, he had called his wife in Southampton and learned that the police had been to the house. They had asked a lot of questions about his movements and activities, and had generally thrown his wife into a state of panic.

'Look, Gayle,' Amesbury said, 'I've been a bit silly. I've got involved with some people who use drugs. Nothing big, just hash and grass for parties, and I've been buying stuff for them because I travel about so much. I've got a couple of tins of hash in my luggage.'

'What kind of tins?' I asked.

'Just small tobacco tins. Enough for me and a friend.'

'They're not likely to do you for a tiny bit of hash,' I said.

'They're after me,' he said. 'They're convinced I'm a big trafficker.'

'Well, that's your problem,' I said firmly. 'I don't want anything to do with the situation. I'll fly back by commercial airline tomorrow. You're quite capable of flying the plane on your own. And if I were you, I'd just dump the tins in the sea on the way across and forget about the whole damn business.'

We walked along the seafront for a while and Amesbury begged me not to leave him on his own.

'You won't be involved,' he said. 'You fly the plane back. I'll dump the hash in the sea. They'll be waiting in Southampton. We can file a new flight plan and land somewhere else.'

Eventually, I agreed. I had several reasons. I felt a bit sorry for the guy. The amount in his possession seemed very insignificant. His panic was obviously genuine and whatever he was into, he had obviously got in much deeper than he originally intended. I was already fairly sure that he wasn't involved in the I.R.A. arms shipments or the illegal entry of terrorists, and there was, too, the practical consideration that I was responsible for the aircraft – we were supposedly on an instruction flight – and anyway, I didn't really want the trouble of returning to England on a commercial plane.

Ah, well. We all make mistakes!

The next morning, we went to Jersey airport and I filed a new flight plan to Gatwick airport. I had barely handed the document over when I was called into the office of the head of Customs, a big burly Scot.

'Are you the Captain of this aircraft?' he asked.

Yes.'

'Have you anything to declare?'

'No,' I said. 'There is nothing in the aircraft outside private ownership that I have any knowledge of to declare.'

'Would you sign this form please?'

I looked at it and pushed it back to the Customs officer.

'This form is for freight,' I said. 'This is a private flight, I am not carrying freight and I personally have nothing to declare.'

'But you are the Captain of the aircraft?'

'Yes.'

'Then I must ask you to sign this form,' the Customs chief said.

'No,' I said. 'That form is for freight-carrying aircraft and I have no manifest.'

'This is the form we use here,' the man insisted. 'It's standard Customs procedure in Jersey.'

Finally, I agreed to sign it and beside my signature there was a space for flight destination, so I wrote 'LGW' for Gatwick airport, London.

The Customs officer took it back and I was immediately approached by two men who had been standing to one side at the end of the office.

'Are you Mr Rivers?'

'Yes.'

'And you are the Captain of this aircraft?'

'Yes.'

'You are going to Gatwick?'

'Yes.'

'And your passenger is Mr Amesbury?'

'Yes.'

'Weren't you originally going to Southampton?'

'Yes,' I said.

'Why did you change your mind?' one of them asked sharply.

I didn't like his tone so I said equally sharply, 'That's my business.'

They they impounded the aeroplane, and arrested me and Amesbury.

I was taken to the local police station near the airport and the questioning began. I said over and over again that it was a private flight and that although I was Captain of the aircraft, I had no responsibility for the contents of the private belongings of my passenger Mr Amesbury – any more than the Captain of a commercial airliner is responsible for what is in the luggage of his passengers.

I met a complete stone wall. I was taken back to the airport and marched out to the plane. Amesbury was already there, but we weren't allowed to speak to each other – only to watch as they searched the aircraft.

By now all my professional instincts were coming into play and I could see all the signs of a carefully pre-arranged set-up. The whole process went along like a well-rehearsed play – except that there were far too many characters, including a couple of plain-clothes policemen, obviously special branch and strangers to Jersey who did not know any of the local layout or procedures.

In the search, they found two flat blue tobacco tins Sellotaped together. That afternoon we appeared before a magistrate and on the evidence table there was a plastic bag full of cannabis that would barely have fitted into the bloody aircraft!

Amesbury was charged with conspiracy to import drugs and I was charged with making a false Customs declaration.

Amesbury, to his credit, made no attempt to involve me. He denied possession of the huge quantity of dope on the table, but he also stressed that I had nothing to do with the situation whatever.

Ironically, when I started to maintain that I was innocent, I found my flying skills were one item which counted strongly against me.

I was questioned about the movements of the aircraft and I said we had flown from Southampton to Bordeaux, then Bordeaux to Tangiers in two hops. The magistrate turned out to be a retired R.A.F.-type who probably hadn't been at the controls of a plane for years but he insisted that, given the specification of the plane, such long flights were not possible. I explained patiently that by skilful use of fuel-saving techniques and convenient winds, I had managed to extend the range of the aircraft, but he wasn't having that. From his knowledge of twenty-odd years previously, he knew better and decided that I was lying about the whole venture.

I was remanded to Jersey prison and it was there that my troubles really began. For three weeks, I was questioned incessantly – and, I soon discovered, not just by the drugs squad or the Jersey police.

I realized very quickly that they had been watching Amesbury from the beginning of the flight, but I also discovered that I had been watched as well – thanks to the efforts of Mr Vass – and special branch, acting as leg men for London showing great interest in matters other than drugs, had also become involved. During those three weeks, they exerted every bit of leverage on me they could muster. They threatened me with transfer to Winchester prison on charges of conspiracy to import drugs; they brought up the conversation I had had with Vass when he had offered cannabis and they tried to make out that although I didn't use it I was seen as a type who was certainly willing to transport it. I was told that word would be passed to the S.A.S. that I was going down on drugs charges if I didn't show a more helpful attitude, and step by step they got around to questioning me about what I was doing for the Spanish. They threw everything at me – honour of the regiment, loyalty to my country, and the risk of losing my pilot's licence which would effectively wipe me out commercially.

I got a lawyer and he told me that they were planning to try to get me three months. The lawyer said I would certainly win an appeal as the document they had insisted I sign at the airport was not the correct one, but the courts were going into recess and I would have to stay on Jersey for another three or four months to wait for an appeal hearing.

Then the special branch man came back. He said that if I were charged with a drugs offence, my belongings could be impounded. My office in Britain could be searched and cleaned out. Did I want the police and the security service taking that close a look at my affairs? Wouldn't it be better to tell them all about my activities for foreign powers?

Meanwhile, I learned later, the drugs squad was actively rounding up people who were involved in drugs trafficking in the Southampton and London areas – a gang which Amesbury had accidentally found himself on the fringe of.

At the end of three weeks, I was told that the charge would be dropped, provided I left the island immediately, and I was put on a ferry to France. I had £15 in my pocket. I hitchhiked to Paris, organized some money from friends, and flew back to London.

The same day, I went to see Sandy Haldane. He was embarrassed and awkward, but I wasn't having any hedging. MI6 had had their fun, but I wasn't going to lie down for it.

During the three weeks, I had told no one what I was actually doing for the Spanish. Now, I told Sandy most of it and suggested strongly that he pass on the information about the I.R.A. connections. I could have made it easier for myself in Jersey by letting special branch have the satisfaction of winning their little game. The Spanish would not have minded – and in fact Alvarez authorized the passing on of the information without any hesitation. But I cannot afford to be seen to be giving in to that kind of pressure.

Personal reputation counts for too much in the circles where I have to do business.

In exchange, I made sure that Sandy worked personally to clear my name in regimental circles of any association with drugs. But I still had one more important hurdle to cross – an interview with the Civil Aviation Authority at which I had to show cause why my pilot's licence should be reinstated, after its automatic suspension on arrest.

The interview took place at the C.A.A. office on Kingsway in London. I took along a lawyer and the proceedings passed off quite straightforwardly. I had been convicted of no offence in the end and the reinstatement was automatic. But after the interview, I was called into an adjacent office for a second interview, this time with an elegantly suited silver-haired man from MI6 who started yet again to question me about my 'real connection' with Mr Amesbury.

He reeled off a whole series of pieces of so-called evidence that had been collected in Southampton linking me to drug activities. By this time, I had figured out that Mr Vass was the man who had been at work on me, and I realized now that he had really gone out of his way to incriminate me – no doubt as a favour to my 'friends' in MI6 and certainly for his own promotional self-interest.

I let the interviewer finish, then I said very quietly and coldly: 'You have known all along that I have nothing to do with drugs. There is no need for me to answer any more of this nonsense. You'll be receiving a report in due course from Major Haldane. That will answer all of your questions. Just tell your masters that it's been an interesting three weeks – and I won't forget it.'

After that, I still had one score to settle. In my profession, you cannot allow people to set you up and get away with it. It isn't just a matter of pride. It is a matter of survival. If people think they can do it to you, they will try. It is much safer to be known as someone who cannot be messed about with impunity.

I went back to Jenny, took her to bed, then asked her, gently, where I could find Mr Vass. 'I don't know,' Jenny said, sounding nervous.

I just smiled at her. 'Look,' I said, 'I don't bear you any grudge. You tried to warn me and I know you believe in what you're doing. But Mr Vass is a different matter. People who go too far must take the consequences.'

She still would not tell me where I could find him. He had apparently been moved out of the area and all Jenny would say was, 'I think it's somewhere near London. Richmond, Kingston, Putney, somewhere like that.'

The tip was close enough. With the help of a couple of police friends, I learned Mr Vass had a new assignment, working out of a West London police station.

Apparently he was a man who did make enemies. I subsequently learned that he suffered an accident and that he was crossing the road near one end of Kingston Bridge when he was knocked down by a blue saloon car – a rather anonymous vehicle, the kind that rental companies hire out by the hundred. A leg and an arm were broken in the accident, but the driver did not stop.

SEVENTEEN

MOSSAD MAKES A MOVE

It is not often that two attempts are made to kill me in the course of one assignment. I get into firefights and other combat situations often enough but that is not the same as having someone come specifically after you personally. Those kinds of attempt on my life are much more rare but there were two within a few weeks in 1975 while I was involved in a deal to sell Mirage aircraft to the Egyptian government.

The background to the story is best explained by this article which appeared in the *Washington Post* on 30 January 1975, under the headline SADAT REPORTS GOALS ACHIEVED IN FRANCE:

Paris, Jan 29 (UP) by Jonathan C Randal

Egyptian President Anwar Sadat left for Cairo today, declaring that he had achieved all his objectives during his three-day official visit to France. The French agreed to sell Egypt Mirage jets and other sophisticated war material.

Discussing the first major Egyptian arms purchase in the West since 1955, Mr. Sadat said at a news conference that the details were a 'military secret'. But Egypt was reported to have bought $2.32 billion worth of arms for which Saudi Arabia and other Persian Gulf oil producers will provide cash payments.

Mr. Sadat and French President Valéry Giscard d'Estaing avoided trumpeting the arms agreement, which is designed to make up for the Soviet refusal to replace Egyptian losses in the 1973 Mideast war and to stake out French claims for a role in the Middle East . . .

Both countries want to avoid Israeli intransigence and provoking the wrath of the United States and the Soviet Union in advance of the Mideast visits of Secretary of State Henry Kissinger and Foreign Minister Andrei Gromyko early next month.

French officials and Mr. Sadat sought to play down the immediate effect of Egyptian purchases of French planes – said to number about 50 – by suggesting that a Middle East settlement could well be achieved before all the planes were delivered.

The article is balanced, accurate and well written, but, as is so often the case with sensitive politico-military stories of this kind, it leaves out all the important bits.

If what the *Washington Post* printed had been the whole story, I would not have been invited to a meeting at the London Hilton, Park Lane, in the suite of Sheikh Abdullah Ousmani bin Ousmani, a wealthy businessman and member of Saudi Arabia's ruling establishment and frequent emissary for the Saudi royal family.

The invitation to the meeting came through an old commercial friend of mine, Robert Hemsworth, a tough, hard-driving Yorkshire engineer with a thriving business in aircraft components, who had extensive interests in Saudi Arabia and was well known to Sheikh Ousmani.

Ousmani was a gaunt, dignified individual who looked as though he would be more at home in a tent in the desert flying his hawks than exchanging endless Arab pleasantries with me over tea and titbits in the Hilton. He played out the whole sequence of courtesies appropriate to the occasion of a first meeting, then – in more Western style – he came straight to the point: would I be interested in arranging the transfer from France to Cairo of the flight and technical manuals for the Mirage aircraft which were to be purchased?

The request did not surprise me even though it may seem odd, to someone not familiar with the military aircraft world, that clandestine negotiations with a civilian third party should be necessary to arrange the hand-over of technical manuals.

Military flight manuals are very different from car manuals. When you buy a car, the dealer takes you for a demonstration spin and hands you a booklet which tells you how all the gadgets on the vehicle work. With a military aircraft it is a very different story.

To say you have bought a Mirage jet fighter-bomber doesn't actually mean very much. The Mirage is a basic type of aircraft which at that time was already in service with a number of air forces, but there is an almost bewildering range of what – to borrow a term from the auto industry – might loosely be called options. In fact, it is the 'options' that really count. When you fly your Mirage into battle, the electronics and the weapons system on board are far more important than the basic plane itself. President Sadat may have revealed to journalists that Egypt was buying Mirages from France, but one of the best kept secrets in the defence establishments of both countries would be what the 'performance graphs' were.

When you sell an aircraft to another country, you don't necessarily equip it for maximum performance. Countries get what they can afford, within their specific combat needs, and I gathered early on in my conversation with Sheikh Ousmani that France was preparing to sell a much more sophisticated weapons and delivery package than had been made available to the Middle East previously.

The Israelis – who would be the target if the Mirages ever saw combat service with the Egyptian Air Force – would be desperate to know what France was supplying their enemy. And I was aware also that the Israelis would not only be trying to gather intelligence on the deal; they would be doing every-thing possible, both politically and clandestinely, to stop it going through.

I was not at all surprised that Sheikh Ousmani had chosen to ask Robert Hemsworth to find a reliable outsider to deal with such a sensitive question as the aircraft manuals. I could imagine only too well the intrigue and savage infighting that the Franco-Egyptian deal would have sparked off within the French defence and intelligence communities.

Every country has its defence interest groups and intelligence factions but in France the divisions are exceptionally bitter. The Mirage is manufactured by Dassault Industries which is, in itself, an extremely powerful force within the defence community. Generally speaking, it is right wing and Gaullist in sympathy, with strong links to the French aristocracy and the elite of the Grandes Écoles-Polytechniques and the École Normale Supérieure which vir-tually run the French government and civil service. But that does not mean that it always shares the views of the government in power – even when it is headed by Giscard d'Estaing. Dassault tends to be a law unto itself. It believes that whatever sales it makes are its own business – and business done by Dassault is good for the French economy and therefore for France.

There are, too, the lobbies of the various armed services which have vary-ing perceptions of what should be the country's defence priorities and where it should place its overseas, and especially Middle East, allegiances. But the single most powerful sub-faction in the armed services and the milit-ary-industrial complex, as the Americans call it, is undoubtedly the pro-Israeli lobby. The Israeli intelligence service, Mossad, has always had strong ties with the various arms of the French intelligence services, the D.S.T. and S.D.E.C., as well as the Sûreté, the domestic criminal investigation depart-ment. Yet there are also powerful Arabist interests, individuals and groups who have served in North Africa and the Middle East who have developed pro-Arab, rather than pro-Israeli, sympathies. They are not as powerful, but they are a force.

Finally, in relation to this particular deal, there are the pro- and anti-American factions in government and the administration. Normally, one thinks of the French as being anti-American – and certainly the faction which urges France not to follow American attitudes slavishly is by far the stronger. But the United States does have extensive commercial influence in France and the American-Jewish business community has ties with the French Zionist groups.

When I finally agreed to accept Sheikh Ousmani's proposition, I was aware that I was entering a fraught and tense situation in which I would need eyes pointing in all four compass directions. As always, I made my acceptance in stages, feeling my way by professional instinct as I went.

At the initial meeting, we talked directly only about transporting the manuals to Egypt, but it was obvious from his line of questioning that Sheikh Ousmani had a much bigger role in mind for me. He was clearly looking for someone with the capability to instruct the Egyptian Air Force on the weapons and electronics profiles in the manuals – a task which would involve flying the Mirage at Dassault's testing grounds at Istres in the south of France under the supervision of the company's test pilots, then going to Egypt and organizing conversion courses for the pilots chosen by the Egyptian Air Force.

I did not commit myself initially to this wider role, but I did agree to fly to Cairo to explore ways of shipping the manuals.

My first Cairo visit was brief and highly secret. I had several hours of talks about shipping manuals and my main contact there was a man who would play an important part in my later troubles. His name was Colonel Khaled; he was close to President Sadat, and although technically retired, was obviously still very much current.

I ran my own check on Khaled and discovered that he was a very tough and sinister figure. He had been a colonel in military intelligence and had served with the President in the army, when Sadat had also been an army colonel. Khaled was a crude animal of a man, of peasant stock, who had a reputation as a ruthless interrogator – which is to say torturer – and as a master of intrigue, and he had acted as Colonel Sadat's chief henchman within the army.

When Sadat became President, he had rewarded Khaled with a foreign car dealership for Egypt – an enormously lucrative position which had made him a millionaire. The result was that, even more than before, Khaled was Sadat's man, totally committed to the service of the President and as active in intelligence matters as he had been during his military service.

Colonel Khaled's main showroom overlooked Soliman Bacha Square (now known as Talat Harbe), the bustling, deafening noisy heart of downtown Cairo, an area which seems to be eternally packed with decrepit Leyland buses and two-thirds of the population of Egypt!

The showroom was a place where I was to live some tense moments in the weeks to come, but the initial visit passed off smoothly and it was agreed that I would arrange to transport the manuals from Paris to London in transit, then ship them by airfreight to Cairo as office equipment for the dealership.

I flew back to London and immediately further talks began with Sheikh Ousmani which ended with my agreeing to take on the wider role of carrying out the flying coversion programme.

The assignment had many attractions. It was lucrative – worth £75,000 plus expenses, a very good fee in the currency of 1975. It was also a genuinely interesting assignment in my favourite field – aviation. The Mirage is a beautiful aircraft. It is bigger and faster than anything I had ever flown before but I felt well up to the challenge, especially as Egypt was buying it for use in a ground-attack role. During a long spell as a reserve captain in the South African Air Force I had flown several types of plane for ground attack as well as doing conversions to that role on aircraft which I had bought abroad and ferried back for them.

I was aware, though, that it was an assignment during which I would have to watch my back – especially as I was picking up more and more indications that there were even deeper ramifications to the deal than I had already reckoned with.

Two weeks later I flew out to Istres to begin my training on the Mirage. Istres is a very lonely but beautiful spot, situated on the Estang de Berre, the vast inland lake which lies parallel to the Mediterranean, westwards along the French coast from Marseilles.

I was given a warm welcome by the test pilot fraternity, allotted a villa for my accommodation, and assigned a senior pilot who would be responsible for my instruction. He was a very likeable, devil-may-care fellow called Alain Deissart, who had obviously been a bit of a hell-raiser as a young officer but who had sobered up – at least a little – with the responsibility of testing aircraft like the Mirage in extreme flight conditions.

On the aviation side, the whole programme progressed smoothly and quickly, from classroom instruction on the weapons system to the early familiarization flights. But at the same time I began to pick up indications of trouble that the other pilots – who did not have my special warfare instincts – were not really aware of. They were concerned solely with flying. I was concerned also with reading the atmosphere of the situation and there were some very tricky cross-currents.

To begin with, there were obviously some people in the flight programme itself who did not like the idea of the Mirage being sold to a foreign air force with the advance weapons system that I was being trained on. Though they tried to shield me from it, I also picked up hints that union trouble might be impending at one of the manufacturer's facilities over the Egyptian deal.

I got the first hint of real trouble, though, away from the Istres base. During a weekend break in the flight programme, I went to Marseilles to see some mercenary friends and straightaway I started getting warnings about my involvement.

Most of the Marseilles mercenary crowd are tough veterans of Indo-China and North Africa who will go anywhere for a good fight. Many of them are Corsican and have links with the underworld, but only a few have any real sense of the politics behind their missions.

I was astonished that everyone in Marseilles had any idea what I was up to. I had told no one what I was doing at Istres. Officially, I was down there for a few days to talk about a business deal of my own, but I had barely downed the first few Pastis in one of the bars near the Vieux Port that the mercenaries like to use, when one of them – Robert Buisson, an old friend from the Middle East – said casually, 'I hear you've been in Cairo lately. Seems a few people didn't like that.'

He was too close a buddy for me to let him get away with that, so I took him aside later – as he knew I would – and insisted that he spell out what he meant.

'I don't know what you're doing down at Istres, my friend,' Buisson said, 'but whatever it is, our Israeli friends don't like it. They're watching you. They knew you were coming here.'

He didn't say any more but he didn't need to, and as soon as I got back to Istres, I had a further sign that Mossad was taking a close interest in me.

One of my business associates in Geneva called me to confirm that the instalment of money due from Sheikh Ousmani had been paid into my account. At the same time he managed to convey in roundabout terms that a certain influential Swiss Jew who was known to have Mossad connections had been trying to find out about the new inflow of funds.

He had got nowhere. Swiss banking secrecy can defeat even Mossad, but his enquiries told me a great deal. Mossad is a very efficient intelligence service. If it was moving in such a way that its traces could be picked up so easily in Marseilles and Geneva, that meant it was pushing very hard.

From the information I had, there was time for the Israelis to move more subtly – it was likely to be months before the Egyptians actually got any aircraft. I decided then and there that there was something about the deal that I did not know and I also decided that I would proceed no further until I found out what it was.

The same day I called Robert Hemsworth in London and told him I wanted an immediate meeting with Sheikh Ousmani. I arranged with Alain Deissart to take a day off from the flight programme, flew to London and – after the usual round of formal courtesies – I told Ousmani coldly that I was pulling out unless he gave me a full and proper briefing on the situation to enable me to assess correctly the risks I was running.

Ousmani did not come clean immediately, but over three meetings with him, spaced out throughout the day, and two 'heart to hearts' with Robert Hemsworth, I finally managed to piece together the full picture.

By the end of the day, I knew very well why the Israelis were panicking. It was not going to be months before the Egyptians started receiving their aircraft.

The essence of Sheikh Ousmani's deal was this. The French government had agreed in principle to the sale but there were no Mirages available for immediate delivery. President Sadat was not interested in waiting until the Middle East peace negotiations progressed. He wanted insurance against the failure of the Kissinger mission – in other words the capability to attack Israel on realistic terms immediately, if the situation deteriorated.

The solution that had been devised was to persuade Libya to transfer to Cairo some Mirages which had already been delivered to Tripoli. Anyone who followed Middle Eastern politics only from the newspapers would find such a suggestion unbelievable. Only the previous year there had been – at least officially – a blazing row between Libya and Egypt over some Mirages which had been loaned during the 1973 Middle East war. But that was only the public posturing. Money speaks with a powerful tongue.

The Saudis, who wanted Egyptian capability built up rapidly, had agreed to pay Libya greatly inflated prices for the Mirages and the deal involved huge commissions for the Sadat family interests as well as for Libyan interests. The French had sweetened the pot by offering the Libyans another advantage. In the original sale, the French had delivered the Mirages to Tripoli with a relatively unsophisticated weapons system; now, part of the covert deal was that Libya would be offered the same high specifications on its replacement delivery as the Egyptians were getting now.

But the resistance against the sale of Mirages to Egypt by any means was becoming extreme. Washington was exerting fierce pressure on Paris to delay the delivery of any Mirages – preferably indefinitely – to give the Kissinger peace shuttle a better chance. The U.S. Administration itself was under relentless political pressure from the American-Jewish community to stop Egypt from being able to threaten Israel. The result was a diplomatic effort which was making even the normally independent Giscard d'Estaing government waver.

Dassault wanted the Egyptian sale to go ahead but were obliged to respect official dictates. The Saudis also wanted the sale to go through, but according to Robert Hemsworth the royal family was getting panicky at going so blatantly against America's wishes. Their solution was a typically Saudi one: they were pushing the responsibility out onto Sheikh Ousmani, who could be disowned if the situation got too hot to handle. Mossad, meanwhile, was using every trick it could muster to try to block the delivery of the Mirages – including taking steps to expose the enormous personal financial gain that was likely to accrue to certain members of the Sadat family from the deal.

The upshot of all this was that I agreed to go back to Istres – but with a new financial deal from Ousmani which took into account the obviously escalating risk factor.

I now knew how touchy the situation was, and it was less than a week before I discovered just how real the threat from Mossad was.

I found out as I was flying as co-pilot over the N.A.T.O. missile range off Sardinia with Alain Deissart at the controls of a Mirage. We had had a fine session on the range, testing the MATRA 520 missile system which discharges anti-tank rockets from underwing attachments. We had successfully completed two runs over the targets floating on the range below but as we pulled away from the target on our third run, terminating our running dialogue with range control, we realized that we had not completed the rocket rail discharge. Range control were immediately advised of our problem.

The instrument panel indicated that firing had been completed, but we knew we had a live rocket still in the rail under the port wing, and there was a further malfunction in the system preventing us from disarming and dumping it.

Deissart radioed to ground control that we were leaving the range with an armed munition on board. Ground control responded with a recommendation for us to continue our climb out and eject.

After a brief discussion, we decided not to eject immediately. We had no idea whether the rocket was in a condition that was dangerous in flight or only with the impact of landing; it could go off at any moment. But we wanted to stay in the cockpit as long as we could. We knew we would probably have to eject – landing at Istres with a live missile on board would put too many lives, apart from our own, in jeopardy – but we wanted to eject nearer the coast to give ourselves time to collect as much data as possible on the malfunction before the aircraft was lost.

In any event, we did not have much time. We had limited fuel for manoeuvring, as we had used a great deal during the attack runs over the range and, anyway, the distance between Sardinia and Istres is not very great in a Mirage!

We had left the range in a climb, which meant that we could eject during a descent to bring us nearer to the coast. Deissart began with a high-speed run at altitude but immediately found that serious vibration was set up in the aircraft, so he switched to a powered descent so that we could carry out our ejection at a lower altitude.

A powered descent is not a dive. A Mirage-3 does not glide, you really have to fly it, but we found that the whole aircraft was becoming increasingly unstable.

The instability could not have been caused just by the presence of the rocket in the pod. The most likely explanation was that the launcher itself had become unaerodynamic. We could not actually see the pod under the wing but it seemed likely that something was hanging off the launcher – possibly the rocket itself in a semi-discharged condition. There is a function on the MATRA to dump the missile and we tried that several times, but with no result. The instruments in the cabin were showing everything on the missile system functioning properly and it was becoming obvious they had been tampered with. Events were happening very quickly and were being handled systematically and calmly.

While Deissart was flying the aircraft at various speeds to try to stabilize it, I worked at updating the navigation system and trying to make radio contact with Istres. Then Deissart passed the controls to me to enable him to make a final check on all the possible solutions within the system. I discovered by experimenting that a speed of 600 m.p.h. gave us the least vibration and I decided to try to hold out at that speed for as long as possible. Meanwhile, Deissart had contacted Istres and was feeding data to them to analyse to see if they had any suggestions.

Then came the explosion in the port wing. It obviously came from the missile pod, but we never did find out whether the rocket had exploded spontaneously or whether, as we later suspected, there was a pre-timed explosive charge to help it along. Either way, the explosion took a fair hunk off the end of the wing and we went immediately into a flat spiral rather like a fast roll.

For an experienced jet pilot, that is not as disconcerting as it sounds. Going inverted is a fairly familiar sensation, and it is quite common to do weapons release practice from an inverted position. But within seconds, it was obvious that we were out of control. We were gyrating longitudinally now and I couldn't correct it even using full opposite aileron. As you spin over and the nose rises in the inverted position, you can suffer an instant inverted stall; the only option now was to eject.

I had never ejected from an aircraft before – and luckily have never had to since – but like all pilots I had trained for it often enough. The first lesson is to eject immediately. Once the decision is taken, there is nothing to be gained from even a brief delay. As I was at the controls, Deissart hit the button first, leaving me to follow immediately.

But I have to admit that I did not follow the drill and go after him instantly. For a few moments I had the wonderful sensation of enjoying being alone in this rather fast, brutal aircraft. It was spinning and gyrating in a horizontal plane at an alarming rate and my head was being banged solidly against the canopy frame but I had the illusion – and it was only an illusion – that I was still flying the aircraft. The nose began its descent below the horizon.

I felt no fear at all. Many times in my life when I have faced a dangerous situation for the first time, I have had the strange feeling that I have done it all before. I had that feeling now; I knew exactly how to eject and there was no need to worry about it.

In reality, only about twenty seconds elapsed between Deissart's ejection and mine. Following procedure, I pulled my feet away from the controls and held them hard against the seat, then pulled hard on the lever.

Explosive bolts hurled away the canopy. The seat moved slightly in a preliminary adjustment of the angle, then it punched out of the aircraft and I was in the open sky. I actually ejected downwards, which is not a very comfortable sensation because you are upside down when you hit the slip stream. In theory it doesn't make all that much difference, but in fact you experience a quite unnatural whiplash – a feeling of disorientation.

After that, the seat fell away and the chute opened and I was free to watch the Mirage hurtling seawards.

I deviated from the ejection procedure only at the last moment. Pilots are taught to hit the water before they disengage the chute but I've done too many combat jumps to go along with that. I prefer to release before entry to avoid any risk of being caught under the canopy.

I hit the water smoothly, inflated my life jacket, and floated off to begin what was to be two long hours in the Mediterranean – plenty of time to reflect on how it felt to be the target of Mossad sabotage.

EIGHTEEN

DOUBLE-DEALING IN CAIRO

I was already in Cairo by the time investigations concluded that the Mirage had been downed by Israeli sabotage. In any event, I had not needed to wait for their verdict. I knew already that it was the work of Mossad. It was not simply instinct; that would be understating it. In my profession, you just *know* that certain things are done in certain ways; there is a definite logic to certain patterns of events. I did not need proof, I was quite sure Mossad was responsible.

This visit to Cairo was intended to be much longer than the previous one. I was now there in my role as technical adviser to the Egyptian Air Force. The manuals were due to arrive almost immediately and I was supposed to start ground instruction with selected Mirage pilots and engineers but, as usually happens in the Arab world, the trip got off to a slow start.

I was booked into Shepheard's Hotel and as soon as I checked in I decided that I would agitate to be moved. Shepheard's is a nice enough hotel; it is not as well equipped as the more modern Hilton or the Sheraton, but it has a pleasantly romantic atmosphere and a delightful setting on the Nile, with its own landing stage for the dhows to draw up at, and views across the water to the luxurious white barge which is the Egyptian officers' club. The problem is that being an old hotel it does not have lots of little bars and coffee shops in which you can hide away discreetly; outside of the bedrooms, the population of Shepheard's is centralized in one huge lobby. Everything happens there. People gather and watch each other and meet – including several international journalists who come to pick up gossip and see which dignitaries and businessmen are in town.

It was hardly suitable for my kind of mission so I sent a message to Colonel Khaled that I would like to be moved; he agreed straightaway but no action was taken for two days.

I visited the car showroom for a preliminary meeting but we just sat around drinking mint tea and talking about hunting, and Arab courtesy rituals stretched the visit out to over two hours. I was treated as the honoured guest, but that had no real substance to it; you go through the motions knowing that you are no more honoured than the camel in the back yard.

I was given a sleek blue Chevrolet and a driver and invited for drinks here and there, but I am not very fond of that kind of time-wasting and I was also very keen to get out of Shepheard's where I felt exposed and vulnerable.

On the second evening, I was promised firmly that arrangements would be made the next morning to move me. Unfortunately, the people who were given the job of organizing it arrived at my room at 6.30 a.m. – and set me my first security problem.

I answered the knock, thinking it was a maid who could be sent away. Instead, three members of Khaled's staff walked in and announced that they had come to move me. My problem was that I had a weapon lying in the bed, which I did not want to be seen.

I had brought only a small weapon – a Beretta.25 pistol – but I did not want to disclose to Khaled that I was armed at all. I was playing the role of visiting technician and, as such, had no reason to have a weapon. The three men pushed their way into the room and settled themselves down, waiting for me to complete my toilet and organize my luggage. I had slept that night with the Beretta beside me and now it was lying under the bedcovers, together with a small leather ankle holster and a spare clip of ammunition.

One of the men sat down on the end of the bed; if he had moved his backside another few inches he would have sat on the Beretta.

I went into the bathroom, showered and shaved, and instead of packing my toilet bag afterwards, as I normally would, I brought all the bits and pieces back into the bedroom and threw them on the bed. On the pretext of packing my toilet bag, I managed to slip the holster and the spare ammunition clip inside it, along with my razor and shaving kit. That still left the gun itelf, which would not fit in. Fortunately, one of my habits is always to lay out my clothes for the next day – I suppose it comes from wanting to be ready to jump out of bedroom windows in my youth – and I had a suit and shirt and other articles on a chair close to the bed. I managed to pick up my suit jacket and lay it out on the bed without attracting attention. The last manoeuvre was to fold the jacket quickly and slip the Beretta into the outside pocket. I managed to carry it off only inches from the man sitting on the bed, who had remained where he was throughout the proceedings, but it was an unpleasantly close moment.

After that, I was taken yet again to the car showroom. I discovered later that my early call had not been accidental. That morning, President Sadat had flown to Aswan with Henry Kissinger to begin the shuttle and it had been decided that I should be kept under wraps.

I was given a sort of breakfast at the showroom, then Khaled arrived. After the usual pleasantries, he suddenly produced a .357 Magnum revolver with a pearl handle and offered it to me to admire. The purpose was soon clear. Khaled wanted to raise the subject of guns and to ask me if I liked weapons and whether I usually carried one. I said that I did not need to be armed, but later that morning I found out the real purpose of the questioning: my luggage, which had already been taken from Shepheard's Hotel to the flat I was to occupy, had been searched and the holster and ammunition clip taken from the toilet bag.

Khaled knew I had a weapon somewhere but he could not insult me by insisting on searching me.

It was the first of several signs that the various protagonists in the deal were very keen to know the full extent of my involvement, but Khaled was always the man to watch. He was a skilled interrogator who was experienced in the techniques of oblique questioning.

The flat, at least, was much more to my taste. It was in the old quarter of Cairo, near the Nile, and it had a terrace with views right across the city with, as the centrepiece, the American building which is festooned with aerials and is known to everyone as the 'C.I.A. tower'. The entrances and exits to the flat were unobtrusive and it was altogether a safer place to wait around in than the lobby of Shepheard's.

During the next three days, it became obvious that everyone wanted to make me keen to stay in Cairo. There was clearly some delay – even though the flight manuals themselves had arrived safely on the second day – and no one wanted me to get bored and take off for Geneva or London.

The flat was run by a woman called Nadia, a plump Egyptian lady who never removed her headscarf, and apart from cooking and cleaning, she obviously had instructions from Khaled to keep me supplied with women. Her source was the nearby university and she brought to the flat a succession of pretty – and not so pretty – students who offered themselves for my entertainment. One of them took my refusal as a personal affront and began to act out in dumb show all the sexual delights I was turning down. I told Nadia as best I could that this was not what I liked with my breakfast eggs, and the girls started to get more beautiful. But fortunately, as it turned out, I had found my own companion.

With so much time to kill, I paid several visits to the prestigious Gizira Club on the island of Zamalek on the Nile, and I met a young woman called Anna who had lived for a time in London while her father had been military attaché at the Egyptian embassy there. I had spoken to her once in London, at an embassy reception, but now I got to know her, during two very pleasant evenings of dining and dancing at the Gizira Club.

Anna was tall and lean, with Gulfari eyes, and a classic Egyptian profile – a world away from the student-hookers Nadia was offering me; but more importantly for my survival, she was employed during the day at the British Airways office in Salambashi Square, very close to the dealership showroom. Her job was a stroke of luck for me of the kind everyone is entitled to occasionally during this type of operation, and I certainly had reason later to be more than grateful for it.

In the meantime, however, Sheikh Ousmani, who was pulling strings from London and Saudi Arabia, arranged for me to have another companion of a very different type.

The day after my first meeting with Anna, an old American friend, Dale Brinton, flew into Cairo. Dale is in his forties, an international salesman for the McDonnell Douglas Aircraft Corporation which at the time was engaged in negotiations to supply DC10 aircraft to the national carrier, Egypt Air. McDonnell Douglas was not making much progress with its bid and Dale had been surprised to get a summons to come to Egypt for urgent consultations.

In fact, neither Dale nor his company were aware of it, but he had been summoned to act as cover for me. It was a very smart move by Sheikh Ousmani; I am quite well known on the commercial side of the defence and aviation industries and the longer I stayed in Cairo, the more questions were likely to be asked about what I was doing there. Ousmani was aware that, being old acquaintances, Dale and I would be quite happy to go about together for part of the time, and it would seem quite plausible to any observers that I was also in some way involved in the Egypt Air negotiations.

I approved of the cover and I liked Dale's company well enough but I was already becoming concerned about the tensions that were showing around the Mirage deal. Something was going wrong. I did not know what yet, but Khaled was getting very edgy, in addition to which I had also noticed that I was being followed.

I had assumed, naturally, that Khaled's people were watching me throughout my stay, and without a doubt Nadia was reporting on every detail of what she observed at the apartment. But I had noticed another man – a European, not an Arab – who had been keeping an eye on me for three consecutive days. He was a hard-looking character in his thirties, wirily built with tightly curled black hair, who wore grey and tan tropical suits on alternate days. I had noticed him especially around Soliman Bacha Square; whenever I was with Khaled, he waited for me, hanging about outside a backgammon parlour across from the showroom.

I decided to take a closer look. As I came out of the showroom after one of my visits to Khaled, I told my driver to wait and I walked across to the backgammon parlour and went inside. In the parlour there were rows of cement tables with the backgammon boards painted on their surface, and deep indentations where the shuffling of the counters had worn them down over the years. The constant hum and excited chatter of competition filled the room. The Arabs were playing so intently that they barely looked up as I walked through to the back to look for a toilet, aware that the European 'shadow' was following me.

The toilet was absolutely filthy. There was crap everywhere and the stench of urine was overpowering. I stood at the stall, holding my breath to stop the smell from filling my nostrils and watched as the shadow came in and stood beside me. We eyed each other from a few yards apart, then I zipped up my fly and started to move towards the exit. The door was a heavy wooden slatted structure, which was hanging freely on metal hinges. I hesitated so that the shadow would come up close, then I swung the door back with all my strength. It caught him full in the face, gashing his forehead and sending him stunned to the floor of the washroom.

For a minute or two he did not know where he was, which gave me time to do a lightning frisk and discover that he had a French passport and was carrying a gun. I didn't touch either of them because he started to come round very quickly. I pretended it had been an accident and apologized profusely, helped him up and made a big show of trying to make amends as he walked through the backgammon parlour.

He knew what I had done. He wasn't fooled for a minute, and I had his measure too. He was definitely a professional; the coolness of his reaction gave him away. He wasn't hurting enough and he wasn't angry enough. If an ordinary passer-by had been knocked down like that and left with a huge gash between his eyes, he would have behaved quite differently.

This man just stayed silent and concentrated on collecting himself as we walked between the lines of impassive Arab backgammon players. Outside in the street, I kept on apologizing and even invited him to meet me at the Hilton for a drink! He did not respond but simply left sullenly and walked off across the square.

I did not know yet who he was, but I was sure that he was an agent of some kind and almost certainly did not work for Khaled.

Though there did not seem to be any connection with the incident in the backgammon parlour, that same afternoon I was summoned to the long-awaited first meeting with Aswan Sadat, the President's brother who, I discovered, was maintaining a particular interest in the negotiations.

I was taken to his apartment in the new suburb of Heliopolis and, I must say, I took a pretty strong dislike to him. He struck me as being a peasant in king's clothing; a crude, overfed, uncultured man whose principal obsession was money.

The apartment was modern and luxurious but it was an absolute mess. Despite the comfortable furnishings, we ate dinner Arab-style off the floor, then talked, with the men all sitting in a circle fingering their worry beads.

Khaled was there, together with his brother, a mountainously flabby man, dressed in voluminous robes, who seemed to spend a lot of time with his finger up his nose.

One thing above everything else was evident from the discussion: this was a very worried group of men. The main theme of the talks was how to organize the official acceptance of the Mirages by the Egyptian Air Force. The acceptance procedure would involve a long series of detailed briefings

by me, followed by simulated flight instruction, followed eventually by proving flights in the Mirages themselves. If the aircraft were not delivered
direct from France with the usual product support, the Egyptians would be
forced to convert to the systems using detailed ground instructions from the
technical manuals. But by the end of the discussions I had got a very clear
picture that the real problem was how to get the Air Force to co-operate discreetly without exposing the deal.

The Air Force, which was headed at that time by Hosni Mubarak who succeeded Sadat as President, was not an accomplice in the corrupt profit-tak-
ing which was appearing as a crucial part of the deal. Aswan Sadat's concern
was, without a doubt, the huge commissions that would be earned by
interested members of the Sadat family; national security was a secondary
issue.

As the Air Force was not involved in the corruption, Aswan Sadat and
Khaled could not ask the officers outright to hush up the acceptance procedures, yet if news of the deal did get out, it would certainly sabotage the Kissinger peace shuttle. The news that Sadat was secretly negotiating a huge
escalation of his Air Force's striking capability would make nonsense of Kissinger's efforts to obtain from the Israelis guarantees of withdrawal behind a
buffer zone. I sensed, too, that all was not well on the Libyan side of the
negotiations and I was beginning to feel distinctly like the pig in the middle
in a deal that was going sadly wrong.

Nevertheless, two days later I did begin my briefings with the Egyptian
Air Force, though 'briefings' really is too mild a word for what took place. It
was more like an interrogation under pressure; I have rarely been grilled so
intensely on a technical project.

The meeting took place in a classroom-like hut in a Military of Defence
complex on the outskirts of Cairo. At one end of the long room, the Mirage
flight manuals sat in large boxes behind the rows of officers ranged at
wooden desks to listen to my introductory briefing. There was a tremendous
sense of urgency about the meeting. Khaled had clearly managed to convey
to everyone present that formal acceptance had to be made quickly and the
officers gave me the impression that they were expecting the Mirages to
arrive in Cairo within three or four days. As Egypt was, to all intents and
purposes, on a war footing, the officers were all dispersed at bases in various
parts of the country. Most of them had driven all night to get to the meeting,
but despite their tiredness, they were determined to be thorough in their
technical scrutiny.

Mubarak himself appeared briefly at the opening of the session to intro-
duce the officers to me. There was no doubt from his attitude that he was dis-
tancing himself from the game play; he just wanted the best possible equipment, from whatever source, to make his air force a match for the Israelis.

The officers put some very tough and pointed questions. They had all flown Mirages before; their concern was to quiz me on the enlarged profiles, to assess the value of the new weapons system and techniques which were part of the latest delivery. The strain of the responsibility placed on them at the meeting showed on some faces.

The most senior of them had to be satisfied before the deal could formally go ahead and I was put through my paces in no uncertain terms.

I enjoyed the session thoroughly. It was very pleasant to get away from all the intrigue and talk aviation with fellow experts, but the respite from the double-dealing did not last long.

The next day, I had another meeting at Heliopolis and there was even less attempt to conceal that the situation was turning sour.

It was made plain to me that total secrecy had to be maintained more than ever before. I could not assess where Ousmani stood, but the interested Sadats were clearly running scared at the enormity of deceiving Kissinger during the actual peace negotiations – and they were equally scared of losing the enormous kickback they stood to gain from the deal.

It was pretty plain, too, that the aircraft were not going to arrive as early as the Air Force expected them to. I had been told by the senior officer present that he was counting on me not to leave Cairo before the aircraft arrived as he wanted to start flying the acceptance missions immediately. I was quite happy to remain if the delay was to be a matter of a few days, but I had no wish to sit in Cairo indefinitely merely to be window-dressing for a deal that was falling apart.

There were growing indications, also, that I was being watched more and more closely. I discovered that my briefcase had been searched, fortunately by someone who had not noticed the tiny strip of tinfoil I had placed behind the lock to detect whether it had been tampered with.

Then, soon afterwards, there was an even more disturbing sign that I was being kept on a tight rein. There were a number of students in the building where my flat was located and I had struck up an acquaintance with one of them, a young Kuwaiti who was in Cairo to study law.

When I was satisfied that he had no connection with Khaled, I asked him to keep a friendly eye on my flat to let me know who was going in and out. Two days later, he was badly beaten up and neither he nor I ever found out whether it had been Khaled's men.

All in all, I wanted my own position clarified and the only person who could do that was Sheikh Ousmani. Dale Brinton was flying out to spend a weekend in Rome and I asked him to call Robert Hemsworth for me. My message to Hemsworth was simple – get Sheikh Ousmani to Cairo immediately, or I would pull out.

Brinton left and I was thrown back on the usual round of Arab hospitality, together with frequent and mostly pointless trips to the showroom, which seemed mainly designed to keep me under everyone's eyes. The only recreation to be had in the showroom was watching some of the extraordinary deals that were struck there, like the occasion when a Bedouin wandered in and bought two large, German-manufactured all-terrain vehicles and paid for them with thousands of pounds in banknotes which he produced from under his robes!

The tension continued to build up and I decided it was time to start planning my escape route. I was still seeing Anna during evenings at the Gizira Club and I had already mentioned that I might need her help with some last-minute arrangements. I went across to the British Airways office and told her that I wanted her to arrange a ticket very discreetly, one that could be paid for by my office in London, so that no one in Cairo could find any record that I was planning to fly out.

I had not told Anna anything about the deal but she could sense that I was in a dangerous situation and she had dropped several hints that I was mixing with people who were unhealthy company. She agreed to help and I managed to explain away my visit to the British Airways office by saying that I had wanted to see Anna to fix up another date.

It was as well I did take the precaution of warning Anna, because the situation came to a head with astonishing speed.

Brinton came back from Rome and confirmed that Sheikh Ousmani had agreed to come to Cairo within a couple of days. I decided to try to disengage from the wheeling and dealing as far as I could until he arrived and I had a good excuse as the weekend was coming up and I was able to arrange various tourist excursions with Dale. We went to the pyramids and took a trip in a dhow along the Nile, then on the Sunday evening we decided to have a little night on the town.

We began with drinks at the Sheraton, but the floorshow was pretty tame, so we decided to go to another nightclub which had been recommended to Dale. In that early part of the evening, I told Dale that I was expecting trouble getting out of Cairo and I might need his help. I had no exit visa and it did not seem likely that I would be able to get one, and I had not figured out a way round that. I told Dale that if I did get stuck in Cairo, I wanted him to fly out and call a number in London that I gave him, where I could get some help. Dale was not particularly fazed by all this. He has no experience himself of covert activities, he is very much the straightforward salesman whose main worry in life is how to get home regularly to his family in Boston between business trips. But he knew roughly what kind of life I led and some of the things I had been involved in, and he agreed to make the trip and the call if I asked him to.

Unfortunately, he was to get involved in my affairs much sooner than either of us realized – and in a much more brutal way.

We went to the second nightclub and stayed for about an hour, drinking and chatting as far as was possible with the noise of the music and the clatter of the dancers. When we decided to move on, Dale went ahead of me to have a pee and I stayed at the table to settle the bill.

The way out was down a short flight of stairs, through a door into a narrow, dark foyer, then out into the street.

I paid, then went down the stairs to look for Dale, and through the partly open door I could see three figures in the foyer. They were all men and two of them seemed to be holding the other, whom I could just make out as Dale. I thought at first that the police were questioning him but as I moved quietly down the stairs, I heard them speaking French. Dale speaks fluent French but with a strong American accent. The other two were native French speakers and looked French in appearance, but neither of them was the one I had run across in the backgammon parlour. They were both heavy-set but one was much taller than the other, and they both towered above Dale who was looking very scared indeed.

I hid behind the door and listened to the conversation. I couldn't make it out clearly, but I heard my name mentioned, then I heard Dale say loudly – clearly for my ears – 'I don't know what you're talking about.'

At that point the two men started to knock him about. One of them slapped him across the face with a half-closed hand and the other struck him a hard blow in the stomach. It winded Dale badly and the two men started to drag him towards the entrance. There was a sort of doorman at the exit, but he made no move to interfere and they hustled Dale out into the alley. I waited for a few seconds, then reached the door but I could see no sign of anyone in the street outside.

The street was narrow and dirty and very badly lit. There were cars parked all along the side where the nightclub was and over the years sand had blown from the roadway and banked up so that it was almost impossible to slip between the cars and the wall without fighting through a miniature sand-dune. I couldn't see down the street because there was a car parked immediately outside the door.

I waited for someone else to come down the stairs and leave so I could slip out unseen. It was not a long wait, but it seemed interminable. Then two men went out laughing and chatting and I went out behind them and crouched behind the parked car.

I could still see no one, so I crept along the row of cars until I came to an alley which led off the street.

It was narrow and dirty and smelled like a sewer. Because of the dim lighting, I did not see the alley until I was right on top of it, but as I looked down it I saw Dale lying on the ground. He looked to be in a lot of pain but he was conscious and trying to get to his feet. There was no doubt he had been left there as bait to get me into the alley, but I couldn't see either of the men or work out where they were hiding in ambush.

I watched as Dale managed to struggle to his feet, then I saw the smaller of the two Frenchmen coming out of the shadows towards him. They did not know I had come out of the nightclub and they didn't want their bait to get away, so the man closing in on Dale raised his arm to hit him again. Dale tried to struggle but the blow fell hard on the back of his neck and shoulders and he fell forward again onto the ground.

The Frenchman leaned over him to see if he needed to be hit again, which just gave me time to get up behind him. I hit him hard on the back of the neck, but he reacted like a professional and rode the blow, rolling off to the side, and I was forced to roll off to the other.

Dale lay in the alley, absolutely terrified, with his hands clasped around his face. As I looked across at the Frenchman, I saw a weapon being drawn. The only lighting in the alley was a streetlamp with a bulb so dim you could stare at it directly without being blinded, but I made out a heavy pistol with the barrel lengthened to a silencer.

He fired one shot and it came damned close. There was no report but I could smell it and hear it as the bullet passed my head and cracked into the wall. I drew the Beretta but there was no point in trying to hit him from where I was. A .25 Beretta is useless unless you get in close.

Instead of aiming, I relied on surprise and a bold move he could not have expected. I fired off one shot in his direction without aiming too closely, then I ran in behind it and shot him at close range before he could steady his aim. I aimed the second shot at the upper trunk and caught him in the shoulder. It didn't kill him but it knocked him backwards and he half fell, half slid to the floor. Dale, meanwhile, was just hugging the dirt, terrified and disorientated. As I started towards him to try to help I saw the second Frenchman coming into the alley. I guessed that he had been watching the nightclub entrance from the far side of the street and had missed me coming out but had heard the sounds of the fight in the alley.

He was coming in fast and drawing his weapon at the same time, and I dropped to one knee and got him with a head shot. Going for a body shot with a .25 is a waste of time. If I had had something heavy like a .357 Magnum, I would have blazed away at him, but I had only one .25 magazine against two adversaries and I had to fire sparingly and only from close up. The Frenchman was in too much of a hurry to get into the alley and I had the advantage of firing upwards. No matter how he weaved in the horizontal plane – and he wasn't paying much attention to evasive action – he could not alter the elevation of his head, which gave me the advantage in close combat.

The head shot killed him instantly, but the other Frenchman was still in a position to give trouble. He was hurting badly, but he still tried to raise his weapon so I strode across to him fast and drew a threatening bead on his neck.

He knew there was no choice and he opened his hand in the recognized sign of surrender. He let the pistol fall away into the dirt, but I still kept the Beretta trained at his head, and for a moment he thought I was going to kill him.

'Don't be crazy,' he yelled at me in French. 'If you kill me, they'll never let you get away with it.'

'You reckon the French are going to care enough about you to start a vendetta?' I asked.

The Frenchman started to splutter. 'Not the French. The Israelis. Mossad always hunts its killers.'

I was tempted to put another bullet in him, but I decided I had enough trouble in a foreign city as it was. I took his weapon, threw it into the darkness of the alley, then ran over to Dale.

I saw straightaway that he was much more badly hurt than I had realized. He hadn't been punched, he had been pistol-whipped and his whole face was puffed and bleeding. I felt really sorry for him. He was not paid as I was to get into situations like this; my only thought was to get him out of the alley to safety.

I dragged Dale to his feet, almost literally by the scruff of the neck, and forced him to run, with my arm supporting most of his weight, down the street and over the nearby bridge across the Nile. I did not know if there were any other Frenchmen acting as back-up and I wanted to get some distance between us and the alley.

Eventually, I found a taxi and I managed to get Dale to the Hilton and up to his room without causing too much commotion. I cleaned up the facial wounds but the bruising was still very ugly and he was obviously concussed. He was feeling very scared and miserable, and at one point he looked at me angrily and said, 'Gayle, I don't know what you're involved in but I don't want any part of it. I'm getting out of here tomorrow and if we ever meet again it will have to be in somewhere like Rome or London.'

I calmed him down as best I could. I told him everything would be fine as long as he could convince himself in his own mind that none of this had really taken place. 'Just leave town,' I said, 'and go back to your normal way of life and you'll be O.K.'

He wasn't convinced and I couldn't blame him. He was having the normal non-professional's reaction to a violent confrontation like that. He just wasn't tuned for it and no one could expect him to be.

He did leave Cairo the next day – and I did also, but I had a lot more trouble getting out than Dale.

The next morning, Khaled was furious. He knew about the Frenchman's death and he knew I must have done it, but he couldn't prove it and I just toughed it out. He got nasty and I got nasty and told him I didn't know anything about any goddamn Frenchman, all I was interested in was seeing Sheikh Ousmani.

I was told that Ousmani was coming in that afternoon and I said, 'I'm going to the airport to meet him.'

Khaled said sharply, 'You realize that you cannot leave Cairo without an exit visa.'

'I'm not interested in leaving Cairo,' I said. 'I just want to get this job finished. But I want some assurances from Ousmani first.'

After that, I went over to the British Airways office and invited Anna to come out for a coffee. Under this guise of a romantic tête-à-tête, Anna handed me the ticket, as promised – but she also gave me some help I hadn't bargained for. 'If you get into trouble when you leave,' she said, 'go to Swissair. I have lots of friends there. They know about you and they will help.'

I thanked her and promised to see her in London, then I went back to the flat. Khaled sent a message that I was wanted for a further meeting at the Ministry of Defence complex, but I sent one back saying I was going to the airport to meet Ousmani.

I was counting on Khaled not being willing to go all the way and physically restrain me. They were all running the risk of being exposed if they forced me into a showdown, but if they allowed me to leave, the Air Force might well scrub the deal anyway.

And I had other problems. The Israelis had obviously decided that the simplest way to sabotage the deal was to get rid of me. They could either come after me again, or they could shop me to the police for the murder of their Frenchman. Khaled was in no position to protect me without pulling strings which risked revealing why I was in Cairo.

I knew my best bet was Ousmani and I ignored all the pressures to have me wait for him at the showroom and drove out to the airport to meet his flight.

Ousmani came through the arrivals area looking a very worried man. He did his best to preserve his Arab dignity but despite his crisp linen robes and all his trappings of wealth, he looked like a man who was being hunted.

He was met by an enormous black Mercedes limousine and we talked sitting in it in an annexe to the airport parking lot, with the engine running and the air-conditioning going full blast.

He began by accusing me of talking too much about the deal and going beyond my mandate to organize the flight acceptance.

'You are fooling yourself,' I said. 'Your deal was exposed a month ago. The Israelis know about it and it won't be long before a lot of other people know too.'

At that point, he slipped into Arab impassivity but I wouldn't let him retreat into silence.

'Right now, you have only one choice,' I said. 'You have to get me out of Cairo.'

Ousmani protested that he could not do that and he revealed that he had already made a call from the airport arrivals lounge and knew about the Frenchman.

'That's none of your concern,' I said. 'Just take me back into the airport. Find an excuse. Say you've left a bag. I know you can fix the exit visa, and you'd better make sure you damned well do it.'

Ousmani sat for a while, staring out at the tattered billboards surrounding the parking lot. It was impossible to read his mind fully, but I could feel that he wasn't going to help.

I discovered later just how desperate Ousmani's own situation was at that point. I learned weeks afterwards that the deal had finally fallen through purely because of financial bickering. Ousmani had failed to provide enough funds up front to satisfy the Libyans and they had started stalling. Meanwhile, the Libyan leader, Colonel Qaddafi, had found out just how big the Sadat family interests commission was going to be and he had refused to go along with it and had vetoed the deal. The Saudis were already in a panic at having double-crossed the Americans. They realized that because of the financial row the deal could not be kept quiet; they wanted to get out from under and Sheikh Ousmani was the candidate for the blame.

Ousmani himself had other ideas. He was looking for a scapegoat of his own and it was me he had in mind. If I could be shown to have messed up the deal, he might just survive in the Saudi royal family's favour and he was perfectly willing to allow me to go down for the murder of the Frenchman if that would help.

I knew none of this as we sat side by side in the Mercedes. All I knew for certain was that he was not willing to get me out of Cairo.

At that point, I turned to simple, old-fashioned and well-tried methods. I told him calmly that Dale Brinton had already left Cairo that morning and he had taken with him a message from me to my associates. I told Ousmani that the effect of the message was that if I did not get out of Cairo that day, he would never be able to set foot in London again. To make quite sure he understood the implications, I spelled out in stark detail what fates could possibly befall him.

He didn't like any of them and, eventually, he gave the order for the Mercedes to return to the main entrance of the airport.

But my troubles were not yet over. As I had guessed we would, we got over the exit visa hurdle quite easily. Ousmani paid a hefty bribe – in the form of a special contribution on my behalf to saving one of Egypt's ancient monuments from damage by flooding – and I was allowed through into the departure area.

Because of the fear of Israeli attack, the airport was heavily defended with SAM missiles ranged on the runways and army patrols reinforcing the police, but there were extra police everywhere and it was obvious that they were looking for someone.

Once I had the exit visa, Sheikh Ousmani turned on his heel and walked away, without saying goodbye or looking back. I looked around and saw the British Airways ticket counter but I knew instinctively that it was useless to try to get out that way. I went to the toilet, came out again and headed for the departure area. There was a Swissair flight preparing to board, but there were police by the Swissair counter and I saw it was pointless to try to get help there.

I decided to gamble. The Swissair passengers were being bussed out to a DC8 sitting out on the runway and I went to the departure gate and simply bustled through.

The main check on boarding passes was being done at the plane and no one stopped me from getting on the bus. When I got out of the bus and walked to the foot of the aircraft steps, I saw a young stewardess standing at the boarding pass control which was being done by a male steward.

I walked up, motioned to the girl and discreetly produced the B.A. ticket Anna had got for me.

'I've had this ticket endorsed to Swissair,' I said, 'but I'm afraid I've dropped my boarding pass. Can you help me? My name is Rivers.'

The girl must have answered quite quickly but it seemed an awfully long wait before she smiled and said, 'That's fine, Mr Rivers. Just get on board the plane. Your seat is at the back.'

She allowed me to squeeze past between her and the steward and I walked up the steps. I thought I was home free, but I was not as near as I thought.

I took a seat near the back of the aircraft, fastened my seatbelt and picked up a copy of *Time Magazine* to allow me to look insignificant.

The plane was filling up fast and no one was claiming the seat I had chosen. Then I saw three policemen get on board, and I thought, 'Oh Christ, this is it.'

The senior of the three stood by the stewardess and I could see him asking her to count the boarding passes. I busied myself reading *Time* and tried to watch what was happening.

The stewardess came part way down the aisle and counted the heads one by one. Then she turned to the police officer and said, 'The number matches the boarding passes. You have the manifest.'

The policeman looked around. I could see him deciding whether it was worth the hassle of getting everybody off the plane and rechecking. He looked down again – then he turned his back and walked down the steps onto the tarmac.

The epilogue to the story can be told in a few lines. I got out safely but the deal was never completed. Many months later Egypt took delivery of some Mirages direct from France, by which time Sheikh Ousmani was already under an unofficial but absolute two-year banishment from his country.

Because I insist on being paid as I go, I still made money on the deal, but I have to admit that as the Swissair plane took off from Cairo that day, my mercenary instincts were well subdued. My only thought then was that, once more, I had survived.

NINETEEN

COMMANDO RAID IN THE GULF

'Remember, Gayle,' Colonel Abu Azed said, 'there are three objectives: cripple the merchant vessels, use them to block the port of Khorramshahr and make shipping in the Gulf uninsurable.'

Like many of the briefings for my missions for the Iraqis during the Gulf War, this one took place on horseback, riding Abu Azed's magnificent and fierce Arab hunters. It was early morning and we were on the island in the River Tigris that was the secret base of the Iraqi Special Forces unit he commanded.

I had known Abu Azed since my first combat missions in Iraq during the campaign against the Kurds in 1976, when I had been hired to train Iraqi paratroopers in S.A.S.-style tactics in the Kurdish mountains. Abu Azed, their commander, had become the hero of Kurdestan and been rewarded with the honour of forming Iraq's first Special Forces unit. As the S.A.S. was his model and as we had fought together successfully in Kurdestan, I was contracted to help set up his new unit. On and off for more than three years I helped to train men on the island and led missions against the Iranians to 'prove' my teaching in combat.

The mission being planned now during this early morning canter in the summer of 1982 was one of the most crucial of the Gulf War. It was to be the first use of attacks on international shipping as a tactic in the war; its other purpose was to avenge a humiliating defeat which Iraq had suffered through a betrayal by one of its own officers.

From the earliest days of the war, the Iranian port of Khorramshahr had been a vital strategic target. The Iraqis had captured it after a ferocious battle and held it successfully, causing serious dislocation to Iran's oil exports. Now, the Iraqis had lost it again because of the treachery of one individual – the Iraqi officer commanding the Khorramshahr garrison. The Iranians had mounted a massive counter-attack and the Iraqi commander had delayed his resistance to the last moment; finally, when the situation was already desperate, he had abandoned his men and had been airlifted by helicopter to Tehran, leaving Khorramshahr to fall with scarcely a shot being fired.

The humiliation of the defeat had burned deeply into the collective psyche of the Iraqi command. They wanted vengeance and they also needed to act quickly as the Iranians had moved at lightning speed to re-open the port to freighters and to tankers collecting Iranian crude at the head of the Gulf.

I had been asked to plan and execute a commando raid on some of the foreign vessels which were already using the Shatt-Al Arab waterways, and the three objectives Abu Azed had outlined were partly the result of my own proposals during earlier briefings relating to Khorramshahr.

I had already led several of these commando-style raids behind Iranian lines to hit at supply routes and communications posts, and to strike at oil pipelines and other installations. Despite the Iraqis' inexperience, we had had considerable success, but it was a very different style of warfare from the basic conflict between Iran and Iraq.

The West has never understood the Gulf War. It is probably one of the most under-reported and mis-reported conflicts in the history of war, partly because virtually no Western correspondents have got near the front and partly because American and European observers generally fail completely to understand the mentality of either side.

One thing is certain, though; the war is every bit as bloody and horrific as the very worst of the 'unconfirmed reports' have suggested. I have never seen such mass carnage anywhere. The sheer numbers of their dead bear comparison with the First World War rather than Vietnam, and the style of warfare, especially the Iranian human-wave attacks, are simply unimaginable to the Western mind.

I have flown in a Soviet-made Hinde helicopter over a battlefield near Dezful at 500 feet when, despite the blistering desert heat, I had to keep the cockpit closed to shut out the stench of death which seemed to fill the whole sky.

In these human-wave attacks, the Iranians drive hordes of children ahead of them to try to deter the Iraqi gunners. The children are armed only with placards carrying images of Ayatollah Khomeini. Many of the children are collected up in villages on the way to the battlefront, and their parents are told they are to carry water for the gallant troops at the front.

So that they do not slow down the attack, they are driven on from behind, like a cattle stampede, by fanatical Iranian militiamen who make up the second echelon of the attack, with the regular forces bringing up the rear. At first, the Iraqis tried to avoid killing the children, but the militiamen mingled with them and before long orders were given from Baghdad that all the attackers had to be targeted.

The Iraqis fired airburst shells over the attacking hoards, killing thousands of people in a single day's combat. The regular Iranian troops also die in huge numbers because they are often too lazy to march and so ride in clusters, like swarms of bees, on the top of French-made Panhard armoured cars and scores die with a single direct hit.

The casualty figures cause disbelief in the Western world and revulsion in the conservative Arab countries which are supporting Iraq, so Baghdad has learned to play down the figures. Some of the battles are like Flanders all happening in one day, instead of several months, with fifty and sixty thousand Iranians dying in one attack.

In such warfare there can be no evacuation of casualties; the wounded die or are shot by the Iranians themselves, and I have seen the Iraqis using flamethrowers to incinerate the dead just to be able to make a path through for their troops.

When reports or rumours of such fighting do reach the West one common reaction is that the Gulf War cannot last long at that pitch. Nothing could be further from the truth. Similarly, Western observers take heart quite wrongly when they hear that the war is draining Iraq's economy or that the Iraqis are failing to capture Iranian oil installations.

The reality is that this war is not about economics or oil; it is a religious war whose origins go back centuries. The enemy for the Iraqis is not Ayatollah Khomeini; it is 'the Persian'.

The Iraqis have always fought the Persians. The weapons may be modern but the cause is as old as the countries themselves. The balance of weapons is not the determining factor. Iran has a vast arsenal of modern weaponry built up during the reign of the Shah, but eighty per cent of it is unserviceable. That does not stop the human-wave attacks, and the Iraqis know that it is immensely hard to stop half a million men and children, whatever weapons they use against them.

The Iraqis fight with any weapons – including chemical ones – and they do so with a clear conscience. Anything that will kill the hated Persian is acceptable. Saying one should not use chemical weapons to kill Persians seems as unreal to an Iraqi as not wanting to use an insect spray.

Nevertheless, the Iraqis, who have one of the best led and best trained armies in the Middle East, know that they must use sophisticated techniques, including selective special warfare raids, to defeat the Iranians. The Iraqis are not fanatics, and anyway they cannot defeat the massive population of Iran in a war of attrition. Iraqi officers are generally highly politicized, motivated and conscious of the inseparability of politics and war in the region, and leaders like Abu Azed are well aware that although economic damage will not stop the Iranians, it can seriously impede their efforts to overrun Iraqi territory by depriving the Iranian forces of fuel, supplies and money.

The Special Forces base in the Tigris grouped together some of the best trained and motivated officers and men that Iraq possessed. At this time, there were about 2,000 people on the island which was virtually cut off from the outside world, and their absolute leader was Abu Azed. He is in his mid-forties, very stocky and muscular, about five foot six inches in height and immensely broad across the shoulders. He is very much a natural soldier who likes to lead from the front, but he also has a permanent compulsion to prove himself, which both inspires and puts a strain on those around him.

He left his family in Baghdad and lived in a small bungalow on the island. When he wasn't riding his hunters, he would drive around in a white Mercedes which had been given to him by President Saddam Hussein personally, but Abu Azed also used to run right round the island most days at the head of his men who all had to complete the circuit every day before breakfast. He was always dressed immaculately, whether in mess dress uniform or combat camouflage, and was totally dedicated to his Special Forces unit.

The island itself is about five miles long and fairly open and sandy, with patches of gum and bamboo here and there. You reach it from an unmarked turning off the main highway between Baghdad and Kuwait. There is just a cluster of huts and a battered filling station to tell you where to turn off, then a short drive down a desert road through scrubby farming country and across on an old twin-hulled ferry.

The camp is only about a hundred miles from the Iranian border and there are observation posts everywhere to warn Baghdad if Iranian Phantom jets are screaming over on their way to the capital, as well as tight security checkpoints all round the island.

A British firm was involved in building the security perimeter, which had electronic sensors, but no member of the firm was ever allowed onto the island itself during the whole construction project; it is probably the most sensitive military installation in the country.

The current in the Tigris is extremely fast there and the ferry has to aim off at an acute angle upstream to reach the opposite bank, but the waters are very good for training in various waterborne vehicles.

The main part of the island is like Special Forces training camps everywhere, with assault courses, ranges and roofless buildings for teaching asault techniques. There is also one tall structure which is used for teaching abseiling or rappelling, for use in attacking from a rope descent. I have reason to remember it very well as it was the scene of an incident which taught me a lot about Arab pride, a factor you have to take into account when leading Iraqi troops.

I was demonstrating a new rappelling device which I had designed myself and which has been adopted by Special Forces in several countries for rapid descent from a helicopter, or a rockface or a tall building.

All the previous designs had been based on classic mountaineering equipment and were attached by a clasp at the waist. My system lowered the centre of gravity by having the rope attached to the person at breastbone height below the weapon load which was carried on the chest, and had a system of straps under the crutch which made for faster release. With the old system, if you were wounded while you were coming down and let go of the rope, you would usually turn upside down because the centre of gravity was at the waist, always assuming you managed to stay on at all by a method known as 'locking on'. My system solved that particular problem and it also included a device which gave much greater control of the speed of descent.

I was demonstrating this system by coming down the tower in stages, kicking outwards from the building and stopping at each stage, to lecture the troops below on various positions and techniques.

Finally, I did a high-speed descent, then braked sharply using a device operated on the dead man principle, kicked backwards from the woodwork just above a window, then swung in through it, firing a burst from an automatic weapon before my feet had even touched the floor of the room, hitting selected targets and simultaneously releasing the rope.

It was a standard S.A.S. assault technique but Abu Azed was very impressed by it and wanted his men to be able to use it. One man, however, was not impressed: a big, burly Iraqi corporal who had won a lot of prestige in the unit as the champion rappeller using the old system. He did not like seeing me, a foreigner, outdoing his skills on the tower and he determined to go one better.

The corporal went up to the roof of the tower and rigged the old system. I stood below with Abu Azed, watching while two soldiers checked the knots as the corporal prepared for a descent.

The tower was about 150 feet high and the usual style was to come down in three jumps, kicking backwards off the side of the building after each one. The corporal obviously decided he would show me by doing it in two and kicking out with his back to the tower. I could see his eyes staring down at me as the preparations went on. He was determined to impress his commanding officer and the men, and he hurled himself frontwards off the building with an almighty yell. He made the first jump okay, kicked out with another huge screech and tried to make it all the way down in one final leap. In his enthusiasm, he managed to get his braking technique all wrong; he sped down towards the sand and just kept coming.

He crashed into the sand, leaving an imprint of his spreadeagled body like a character in a cinema cartoon, and I thought, 'Silly bastard.' He broke God knows how many bones and wrote himself off totally, but Abu Azed remained completely impassive. He turned to his men, then gestured down at the heap in the sand and said calmly: 'Let us hope you will learn from this man's mistake.' I took his cue, suppressing a chuckle, and added equally calmly: 'His braking technique was poor and I don't want to hear anyone screaming like that in what is supposed to be a silent attack technique.'

It was typical of Abu Azed not to be worried about the injury; his only concern was to make his unit into an elite fighting force. If he had any doubts about a man in the final stage of the selection process he had a technique for testing them which illustrates that reverence for life was not his strongest characteristic! He called the candidate to his office, handed him a pistol and ordered him to fire several times through the open door into the corridor. At the same time, he ordered another doubtful candidate to walk down the corridor and take the random risk of being shot. If either man refused, either to walk or fire, he was immediately thrown out of the unit.

Everyone on the island was furiously competitive – taking their lead from Abu Azed. For someone like me who doesn't need to go around proving himself, the atmosphere could get a bit wearing, but you had to set an example. When ping-pong was played in the mess, it was played with desperate earnestness, in the belief that it demonstrated co-ordination of hand and eye which would be helpful in shooting. Even rest and recreation were competition.

I have been a first-class shot since the age of eight because I was brought up with weapons in the country, but I detest ping-pong. Nevertheless, I had to join in and play as though it really mattered, so as not to let down the Colonel's example.

Generally, the Iraqis selected for the island made good Special Forces soldiers. They were tough and reliable and courageous; their main drawback was too much pride and a desire to go to Allah in style – often too early, in my judgment. A soldier is useless without courage but wanting to die a glorious and stylish death does not make for good special-weaponry technique and I had to curb this death-wish on many occasions.

My main concern on this particular mission against the shipping at Khorramshahr was that water skills were not the Iraqis' strongest point. I had selected twenty men to make up four teams of five – three teams for the attack and one in reserve. Technically, they were all qualified and several of them had attended civilian diving schools in France and Malta to learn skuba techniques, underwater swimming with breathing tanks, etc. But they were a long way from being experienced frogmen, and in the unfamiliar environment their bravery could be a drawback, making them try feats they were not really qualified to perform.

We had been training on the island for three weeks before the final briefing, and had also made expeditions up the Tigris to practise in more open water. They were pretty good, fast learners and the team leaders proved excellent officers, although still some way from S.A.S. or S.B.S. standards. Interestingly, you could always judge the importance of the mission by the number of officers assigned to it. In this case, one of the assault teams was led by a captain and the other two by full lieutenants – way over-ranked as compared with the S.A.S. In the S.A.S., it is unlikely there would be more than one commissioned officer with the whole force, and an individual assault team would, as like as not, be led by a trooper.

Partly it was because Abu Azed wanted his leaders to get the most varied combat experience possible, but there was also an element of prestige; if a mission was to be seen to be important, there had to be senior personnel in the teams. This mission would also satisfy various critical government observers as to his forces' marine capabilities.

For this assault, I had chosen to use semi-submersible silent-running inflatables which were particularly effective for this kind of operation. The vehicle is like a large rubber dinghy, except that when semi-inflated the bulk of it hangs just below the surface of the water. The explosives and weapons are carried on the craft, and the men swim beside it, holding onto loops on the sides. With a silenced outboard, it is capable of moving big loads at handy speeds. We had trained with them in the Tigris and we had practised placing the explosives on mock-ups of hulls – using Soviet-type limpet mines and some Spanish-manufactured submersible charges – but for most of the men it was their first experience in open water.

In the period leading up to the raid we had been receiving daily aerial reconnaissance photos of the port area and on the day of the assault there were three ships lying at anchor. One was German, one Greek and one had Panamanian registration, and they had only skeleton watch crews on board. The German vessel was a small tanker but the other two were freighters and one was suspected of having brought a cargo of weapons in for the Iranian forces. As soon as the port had been recaptured, the Iranians had opened channels through the scattered rusty hulls in the Shatt-Al Arab and had been shipping in weapons as fast as they could. There had been several consignments over the previous month, of a size to worry the Iraqis. The priority for sinking these vessels using Commando techniques was to ensure the hulls sank in exact locations. Sinking by artillery fire could not guarantee this.

In order to cover the minimum possible distance by water, I decided I had to launch the raid from inside Iranian territory and the first stage of the mission was a journey by truck all the way down to Basra and then across the southern corner of the border into Iran.

Theoretically, we were moving under the cover of Iraqi artillery but there was still a lot of Iranian movement in the area and there was a considerable risk of running into enemy patrols.

We reached our mission jumping-off point – a desolate stretch of beach partially shielded by low dunes – just before midnight and prepared to move nearer our targets. In the first stage, we inflated one submersible only – the one that was to carry the reserve team. It carried the other three craft uninflated and all the men swam behind as we moved silently along the shore to a point where we could prepare for the final assault.

The reserve submersible was camouflaged and left on the beach, with its team inside, ready to move off to support us if we ran into trouble. The other three were quickly inflated, the explosives and other loads distributed, and the assault teams took their positions.

Captain Abboud, the senior officer, led one of the teams but it was understood, as always, that I was in command of the operation.

At that point, we were about ten kilometres from the target, and the initial swim went off relatively well, except that physically it took too much out of some of the men. Endurance swimming is definitely not the Iraqis' strong point and with this type of semi-submersible the team has to assist the silent electric motor by kicking all the way to maintain speed.

They were not too encumbered. Their diving equipment was light warm-water gear – wetsuit, mask, flippers and light breathing tank – but many were clearly overcoming fear of the water, which creates tension and adds considerably to the fatigue.

My main worry was whether all three teams would place their charges properly. Once they had left the relative security of the semi-submersible and were operating alone in the darkened waters, I knew there would be a tremendous temptation to rush the work and they had not had enough training to do it unthinkingly. I was confident of Captain Abboud. He was a very durable individual who may well one day end up commanding the Special Forces unit, as Abu Azed's successor. I was with one of the teams led by a lieutenant but I was concerned about the third team which was to take the Greek freighter.

I gave the signal to disperse and led my own team towards the German tanker, towing the satchel charges behind us. It took fifteen minutes to place the charges correctly and I estimated that given the inexperience of the team dealing with the Greek freighter they would probably need double that.

But as we finished our part of the operation and turned to begin the swim to the rendezvous point four kilometres away, I checked to my left and realized that the team on the Greek vessel had already finished and had left the area! I knew instinctively it was not possible for them to have placed the charges correctly. I had worked fast, using all the experience and training I had acquired over many years. This was their first operation. Something had to have been skimped.

I signalled to the lieutenant and the rest of my team that we were returning to the Greek vessel. To put it bluntly, they did not want to go, but I gave a second order, in terms that made it clear I wanted obedience, and we turned back towards the middle target. I was not worried about the Panamanian ship, I was sure Captain Abboud would have done a thorough job, but two out of three vessels was not good enough.

When we were near the Greek ship, I left the semi-submersible and swam alone to inspect the work of the other team. Sure enough, I found immediately that it had been done far too hurriedly and one satchel of charges had detached itself completely and had sunk to the bottom of the Gulf.

At that point, I made a small mistake myself. I believed that we had an extra charge on our own semi-submersible and swam back to get it. The manoeuvre wasted a precious few minutes. We had in fact used all our explosives and my team were getting very edgy at the continuing delay as I swam back alone yet again to the freighter to reposition the charges already on the vessel's hull.

I could understand my team's fear. The longer we stayed close to the vessel, the more risk there was of being spotted by the deck watch, but I knew that the vessel would not be sunk by the charges if they were left as they were.

Still, it is not easy to move charges once they are underwater. These satchels are armed on the surface then deflated to allow them to be taken down and placed on the hull. There was no buoyancy left in the one I wanted to reposition and it was a tough haul to drag it aft and reset it where I wanted it to be.

I worked silently and steadily and after what seemed like an interminable quarter of an hour I had the satchel in its new, effective position. I swam back to rejoin a relieved team on the semi-submersible and we headed back towards the rendezvous point.

Here again, I was expecting trouble. Night swimming by compass is not the easiest of tasks. Each team had to swim from its target on a compass bearing to a point in open water, measuring the distance by the time taken. That meant trusting to judgment a drift factor and remaining calm in the very unfamiliar environment of the darkened water as well as keeping the dinghy at a constant speed. Once at the rendezvous, the teams were to tread water, using a landmark to keep their position and not drift away.

I was not surprised to reach the rendezvous point and find no one there. I left my semi-submersible in position and swam around, managing to locate Captain Abboud who was not very far off the mark. We joined up, but there was no sign anywhere of the third team which had botched the charges on the Greek vessel and eventually I ordered both teams to head back to the beach assembly point. We could not wait indefinitely in open water and, anyway, it was almost time for the firework display!

When they came, the explosions were almost simultaneous, and I knew immediately that we had a success. Fireballs rose from all three ships and the muffled sound of the explosions, which was like a giant cannon going off under water, echoed right across the Gulf.

The German tanker started sinking rapidly, as did the Greek freighter. Not all the charges placed by Captain Abboud under the Panamanian ship went off but there was one huge explosion in its stern and it swung and collided with the Greek freighter.

We paused for a few seconds to watch the initial explosions, but I signalled to Abboud to drive his men on, as there was no time to stay for the spectacle. We had more than an hour's swimming left and dare not lose momentum, given the exhausted and nervous state of many of the men. Occasionally, everyone would glance back to check on the vessels; the sight was truly spectacular.

The German ship went more or less straight down, and remained lodged on a shallow shelf, its superstructure jutting out of the water. The Greek boat went down much more slowly and it was still listing and sinking when we reached the beach, but the Panamanian vessel had by then keeled over and the two ships had crunched together to form a huge obstruction.

When we met up with the reserve team on the beach, there was still no sign of the third team. We deflated the semi-submersibles, packed our kit, and prepared to move inland across the no-man's-land between the shore and the Iraqi positions to join up with our truck.

While this was going on, I sent a search party down the beach and they found that the third team had landed some way along the shore. They had missed their bearing and gone for the nearest point on land and were sitting on the shoreline wondering what to do next.

I was not very impressed but I accepted that it was their first attempt and at least the mission had been completely successful.

We had only one casualty. The team that had strayed had lost a man who had gone adrift. While swim-assisting the dinghy, he had simply let go of the loop on the side and drifted away into the black waters, presumably to drown from exhaustion.

Abu Azed considered it a small price to pay for the success of the mission. We had almost totally blocked the port of Khorramshahr, and I gather the insurance rates were affected accordingly at Lloyds of London. The international shipping community had been given notice that trading with the Iranians was considered a hostile act by Iraq and amounted to taking sides in the war.

My own feeling after the mission was relief as much as satisfaction. They were good men I was training – but God, I wished they were better swimmers!

TWENTY

TRAPPED BEHIND IRANIAN LINES

Being caught behind enemy lines is never a comfortable situation but finding yourself on the wrong side of 20,000 fanatical Iranians has to be close to being every soldier's personal nightmare.

That was the situation I found myself in a year after the raid on the Gulf ships and I still have a few shudders when I think how close I came to having my head displayed on a pole in Tehran. Not a pretty sight, and I am sure the graffiti I would have attracted would not have been worthy of the effort taken to get it there.

In the year since the waterborne operations, the Special Force unit of Colonel Abu Azed had made considerable progress. They had carried out several successful missions on their own and I was being called in now only to sharpen up types of missions that had gone wrong. Endurance swimming, incidentally, had been dropped in favour of a different style of waterborne assault in which the teams were heli-lifted closer to the target and left to do only short distances in the water.

The war itself was in a kind of stalemate. Repeated threats of further huge Iranian attacks had not materialized but the Iraqi supply lines were fully extended and, at home, public opinion was growing concerned at the extent of Iraqi casualties. Much of the military attention was concentrated now on the city of Dezful; the Iraqis were debating whether to withdraw, after recapturing it for a second time.

Dezful, which lies well inland, north-west of Ahvaz, is the main commercial centre of its region and lies at a strategically valuable crossroads. The terrain is open, hard, tank country and before its original fall it had been an important Iranian military tactical headquarters.

Thousands of lives had been lost in the two battles to possess it and the Iraqis were now coming round to the view that they were in danger of being outflanked by the Iranians if they held on much longer.

The Iraqis had established a large garrison in Dezful but they were relatively safe only in the heart of the city. The Iranians had not bombed or shelled the city centre in order not to destroy their own installations, but they were already beginning to shell the outskirts and there was every sign that they would be able to bring about an encircling movement before long.

The Iraqi plan was to undertake a tactical withdrawal and establish new positions, still inside Iranian territory, but only about twenty to thirty kilometres from the Iraqi border, effectively shortening supply lines. However, it was decided that the Iranians should not be allowed to retake their city without cost and the Special Forces unit was charged with sending teams into Dezful to lay mines and booby traps to make the Iranian re-occupation as hazardous as possible.

Abu Azed mounted an operation involving fifty Special Forces men, divided into five teams of ten, who were to place as many and as varied devices as possible within Dezful before the completion of the Iraqi withdrawal. I led one of the teams and was given the task by Abu Azed of working on one particular building on the edge of the city which had been used by the Iranians as their military headquarters before the city fell. By the time we reached Dezful, we had three days to complete the task and get out with the last Iraqi units. The infantry had already pulled back and the remaining Iraqi force was made up of sappers, armoured units and forward gunnery observation posts.

On the first day, I spent a lot of time supervising other teams and helping them plan the type of device to be planted. The Iranians were reasonably familiar with booby traps and mines and I called in all my Vietnam experience to devise some tricks that would really give them a few headaches.

We established pressure-release devices, tension devices, trip wires and combination traps which are particularly difficult to deal with. We wired claymore mines to the electronic circuits, for example, so that as soon as someone switched on the overhead light, it would obliterate the room. We planted devices in air-conditioners and filing cabinets and slotted hand grenades in odd corners. We used especially a lot of double booby traps. One component could be a trip wire, linked to a hand grenade. If it was spotted and disarmed, the action of removing the trip wire would trigger a timing device which would set off a massive plastic charge several minutes later in another part of the room.

On the second day, we started work in earnest on the military headquarters building, this time concealing massive charges in the cellars and linking them to booby traps set in various parts of the upper floors of the building. A Toyota land-cruiser vehicle dumped the explosives at the entrance to the building and we ferried them down by hand and devised individual shaped charges to fit into the best places of concealment.

The operation took most of the day and for much of it we were out of touch with the other units. Radio communication was poor because of line-of-sight problems created by the tall buildings in the area and, anyway, we were in the cellar below ground for a lot of the time. It was a problem that was to cost us dearly, but I did not learn just how dearly until the following morning.

That night it was even hotter than normal and we slept on the roof of the building. We had a few hours' work left and my plan was to make a tour of the other Special Forces units during the early part of the day and complete our withdrawal by late afternoon.

During the night, we could hear the sound of constant movement through the city, but it did not strike me as unusual. The withdrawal had been continuing in phases over the whole two days and the plan was to have only one armoured section and the sappers' engineering vehicles left to complete the evacuation on the third day.

I awoke at dawn, looked over the parapet of the roof and had what can be described as a scrotum shock – the kind that gives you a jolt where you feel most sensitive. The street below was full of Iranian armour!

I stared for a moment in pure disbelief. Iranian tanks were passing in a column, followed by armoured personnel carriers with militiamen and regular troops riding on them. I had six men with me in the headquarters building and one by one they joined me on the parapet, staring wide-eyed at the movement below. It was a truly eerie moment and I could sense my men's fear. It was not just normal battle nerves but fear combined with shock and disbelief, and I knew that it was essential to get the team moving before paralysis set in.

The column was already passing the main entrance to the building and from our high elevation we could see that it was moving to join an even bigger Iranian concentration gathering to the west of us.

Our exfiltration route was to the west and it was already well compromised, but at least I could see the possibility of getting out of this building. It seemed virtually certain that the Iranians would again set up their headquarters there and it would only be a short time before they started coming inside it.

I led the team down to the ground floor and when the column had passed we slipped across the sandy street and into a side road leading away from the main thoroughfare. Of the buildings in the area, the safest-looking one was a four-storey stucco structure about three blocks away. It appeared to be the depot of a company selling technical equipment, with a warehouse below and offices above, and we managed to get up onto the roof without being seen.

As with most of the buildings in the city, the roof was flat with a five-foot parapet all round. There was also plenty of other cover as there were sacks of cement and assorted building materials everywhere which looked as though they had been left over from an earlier construction project. There were no signs that anyone made use of the roof in normal circumstances.

Down below, however, the situation was beginning to look appalling. There was no doubt now that the last of our own forces had gone and the Iranians were taking over in strength. We could hear some of our booby traps going off in various parts of the city, and in one direction we could see the Iranians beginning a mine-clearing operation on one of the broader commercial streets.

Our first priority was to make radio contact with the Special Forces command unit. Reception in this locality was still poor and we almost drained the radio batteries before getting in touch. When we did, the message was a straight shot in the gut. The Iraqi withdrawal had been brought forward by twenty-four hours; all units had been advised and had pulled out, including the other Special Forces teams. We were completely alone in Dezful which was once again an Iranian city!

Special Forces headquarters gave us 'extraction code blue' – the final emergency procedure when everything else was ruled out. That meant marching fifty-five kilometres westwards out of the city on a compass bearing and being picked up by helicopter three days hence. But that plan supposed that we could get out of the city limits. It was to have been used if our transport had failed. Moving westwards now was possible only if we could slip out of the city by stealth, but it was broad daylight, there were troops everywhere and Iranian civilians were starting to move back into the city centre after having taken flight during the Iraqi occupation.

I learned later that the order for the Iraqi withdrawal had been the result of poor command co-ordination and several units had had a last-minute scramble to join the main body of withdrawing armour. Also, the Iranians had moved back far faster than anyone expected. It was known that most of their forces were concentrated on the flanks, preparing to encircle Dezful, but once they learned that the Iraqis were leaving, the Iranians moved at lightning speed to achieve as big a propaganda victory as possible.

None of this information would have helped us as we sat crouched on our rooftop. It was clear to everyone that the position was virtually hopeless and the men's fear was beginning to turn into anger at me as leader. They were scared, but they were also disillusioned. I was in charge and in their eyes I should have known about the Iraqi withdrawal. I was responsible for their being caught in the town and I could feel their resentment burning as they muttered in Arabic among themselves. Of the six Iraqis, only one, the interpreter, spoke English. I understood very little Arabic and the men would huddle among themselves, and the interpreter would translate.

I could tell at least when they were talking about me because they referred to me usually as 'the Major' or 'English' and when I caught either word I would gesture to the interpreter to tell me exactly what was going on. The interpreter was scared of me but also of them and I had to threaten him several times to get the full story. I could see their anger at me but I could also see they were arguing among themselves and it took some very tense discussions with the interpreter to assess the full situation.

Among the six men, I had two supporters. One of them was particularly important because he was a massive, powerful sergeant who was determined to protect me and had considerable authority among the men. The other four were in a state of total panic but were divided about what to do. One plan was to kill me and then commit suicide, another was to go out guns blazing in a John Wayne suicidal shoot-out.

What they feared most was capture by the Iranians. Everyone knew that meant castration, disembowelment and other mutilations of a kind which would ensure that the soul of the victim would be unacceptable to Allah. They were desperate to avoid that fate, both from fear of the physical suffering and absolute terror of the religious consequences.

I grasped very quickly that if I was going to talk them out of it, I would have to institute a bit of terror myself.

I drew my knife and told the interpreter to say that anyone who moved without my permission would be the first to receive mutilations unacceptable to Allah. The battle of wills went on for almost an hour but eventually I achieved a kind of stand-off, partly because there were no signs of anyone coming up onto the roof, which restored a partial illusion of security, at least for the moment.

We sat crouched in a huddle, talking in hissed whispers and rough gestures for most of the day, and gradually I won them over to the idea that exfiltration by stealth was possible. I reminded them of Abu Azed's faith in me as their adviser and their pride as members of the elite Special Forces unit and by nightfall I had got them into a state where they were at least prepared to try.

When darkness fell we prepared to move out. There was a thick insulated electric cable linking our rooftop to the one opposite and from that building there seemed to be a route which bypassed the heaviest concentrations. But there was no safe route – there were troops and militiamen constantly in motion around the city and we knew there was not the remotest chance of reaching the western edge of Dezful without meeting some kind of resistance.

We crossed the overhead electric wire in commando style, and got down safely through the building opposite, then began the tense process of working our way westwards. We split into two teams – four men in one, and myself, the interpreter and one other in the second. One team advanced the length of a block or so, then took up position in doorways while the second team leapfrogged forward.

I had a street map of Dezful and had worked out an accurate route, but while I could establish the shortest distance to travel, I had no way of knowing which streets would be the emptiest. With so many troops about, we might just escape detection at a distance, but close up, there was no mistaking us for Iranians. We were wearing camouflage suits which did not resemble the Iranian regulars' tunics, and the Iranian militiamen wore an assortment of garb but usually nothing that looked much like ours.

Our first confrontation came after we had passed safely through three or four streets. As we turned the corner, we saw two Iranian militiamen. They were sitting on chairs in the doorway of a building, chatting and drinking tea, their weapons leaning up against the wall beside them. They saw us immediately so there was no point in pulling back. I marched straight towards them, signalling the sergeant quietly that we were going to take them out. I walked across the street, heading diagonally for a point just past them on the opposite pavement. I walked completely casually, as though I was barely aware of their existence, then, as we drew level, I turned suddenly and dived at the furthest one, threw him off balance and drove in a knife. The sergeant took the second one only seconds later and we dragged the two bodies into the doorway.

The move was a tremendous morale-booster for the men. Just for a few moments, we had managed to give the impression that the aggressive tactics we had learned could get us out, but I knew we still had a very long way to go.

We took the Iranians' jackets and their distinctive caps which can be pulled down like a balaclava at night for sleeping, or for cold weather. As I was the most conspicuous of our team, I took one cap and gave one to a man in the second group.

We moved off again, this time with just slightly more confidence, but our second encounter did not pass off as smoothly.

We were making our way down a narrow, deserted street, when we saw an Iranian armoured personnel carrier in the distance heading in our direction. At first it looked as though the vehicle might turn at a crossroads ahead, but it stopped and a dozen or so Iranian soldiers got out and started coming towards us down the street.

There were no alleyways we could run down and no doorways deep enough to provide cover so we ducked into the first open door we could see and found that it led to a kitchen which was dimly lit by a single naked bulb.

I reached up and tried to take the bulb out but it was rusted in and I had to cut the wire, giving myself a shock in the process. We crouched in the darkness, behind ovens and store cupboards, and just as we heard the first of the Iranians approaching down the street, two figures appeared in the kitchen doorway, a fat, heavy-bellied man and a boy of about sixteen. The man tried the light switch several times, then walked over to look at the bulb. He didn't seem to realize that the wire had been cut and he went back across the room to get some matches from a table near the stove.

All the time this was going on, we could hear the Iranian soldiers passing outside the window and I knew that if anything unusual appeared to be happening where we were, there was a good chance someone would come in to investigate.

The fat man got a chair, put it under the light fixture and climbed onto it to look at the socket.

I could not count on co-ordinated action by the other men and I decided it was safer to handle both of the Iranians myself. I found a thick piece of heavy metal on the floor beside me which was long enough to reach the chair. I hooked it under the leg of the chair and forced it forward like a lever to throw the man off balance.

While he was falling, I sprang up from my crouched position and punched the youth in the face, knocking him out cold. While the man was still entangled with his chair, I slit his throat from behind with my knife, then leaped back to the boy and sat astride him to prevent him from making any noise if he came to.

There can only have been twelve or fifteen soldiers in the street and one of them actually paused and looked in through our doorway, but their file seemed to take an eternity to pass. The boy did not stir and there were no other sounds inside the kitchen and we all managed to hold our breaths and our cramped positions long enough for the danger to pass.

So far we were surviving. We had killed three Iranians in as many streets, but the war on the nerves of my men was beginning to show and I did not know how long they would hold out before desperation would drive them back to the idea of a glorious suicidal rush at the enemy.

When I looked outside, though, I saw that the Iranians had left two soldiers posted at the end of the street. They were obviously supposed to be on some kind of sentry duty but luckily they looked pretty relaxed and for the moment they had their backs to us.

I gestured to one of the Iraqis to stay close to me and I walked up the street towards them, as casually as I could. They did not turn round until I drew almost level with them and I just grunted and continued as though I was not interested in them. As I passed the furthest one, I turned and grabbed his head in a necklock, pulling him back on to my knife, and the Iraqi behind me took three quick strides forward and drove his blade through the other Iranian's stomach.

At that point our only chance seemed to be to make a run for it, and we sprinted flat out, down the street, crossing and recrossing it in zig-zag fashion. We were now totally exposed, automatic weapons drawn. We heard another booby trap go off and then the sound of running feet in a side street where people appeared to be escaping from the exploded building. On a roof above us, someone started shouting something in Farsi. He was gesturing downwards but not pointing directly at us and we just had to try to find a quieter street.

In the process, we ran straight into an Iranian armoured personnel carrier. It was moving slowly down a street we turned into and there were four soldiers sitting on top. This time, there was no possibility of stealth or deception. The leading members of our team opened fire and I hurled a grenade which exploded on the turret. Three of the four men fell instantly and a second burst finished off the fourth. The turret was burning and the noise of the grenade had echoed down the street and there were figures running everywhere.

We still had a chance to escape but if we were not to be followed immediately by half the Iranian army we had to make some attempt to give the impression that the A.P.C. had hit a mine and not been knocked out in a firefight. I threw a second grenade, aiming directly at the section of the vehicle where the bodies were draped over the back of the turret and stayed just long enough to see the whole top of the vehicle split apart before we started running like hell again up the street.

When we regrouped at the first quieter street, I realized that I had another big problem on my hands. Several of the men were in a complete mental mess. Two of them were trembling with nerves and another looked as though he had gone into total shock. With men in that condition we could go no further and I look around desperately for a hiding-place.

There was only one suitable building: a large commercial garage which was locked and barred and which did not look as though it had been reopened since the Iraqis left the city.

I urged my men forward and we broke in and scrambled gratefully into the dark recesses behind piles of spares and bits of machinery.

When my eyes became accustomed to the darkness, I studied the layout of the garage and spotted an even better hiding-place. In the centre of the working area was a huge ramp, with an inspection pit beneath it, big enough for working on full-sized trucks. Most of it was covered in with wooden planking but there was a narrow gap at the end nearest the door and some steps leading down into a very deep working area below. It was filthy with oil and grease but in the darkness it was just about cool enough for us to pack our seven bodies in without suffocating.

The pit had two levels, with the deepest end furthest away from the door. That was the safer one, but it was the oil sump where vehicles were drained and it was thick with oil and slippery so we stayed at first in the shallower section. For the first two hours, there was no activity in the garage, then we heard sounds of shouting and arguing and a group of Iranian militiamen forced their way into the garage and started to look around.

It should have been the end of us, but they obviously did not really know what they were looking for and did not care much either; they had been given a section of streets to search and wanted to get finished. They poked around near the door but did not bother with the pit or even look behind the jumble of old machinery at the back of the workshop before leaving without closing the door behind them.

We waited in the pit until nightfall. No one else came then, and it was completely dark when we decided to chance moving up again into the main area of the garage.

We closed the outside door, set up observation posts at the two small windows looking out onto the street and settled down in hiding-places round the edge of the workshop floor.

No Iranians came during the night but no one slept and the tension was kept high by the failing nerve of the team. I did a lot of talking that night, through the interpreter, trying to find the right way to contain each man's fear.

These were strong men but they had come round to the idea that they were not going to get out of Dezful alive and they wanted to get it over with. It would be wrong to call them suicidal; the original idea of killing me and then themselves did not arise again. But they were prepared to die and their hatred of the Iranians kept erupting in waves. They would seem calm, almost meditative for a while, then someone would suggest a big assault, and the idea would catch on that we should head out and just kill as many people as we could – military and civilian – before being gunned down on the street ourselves.

I used several different approaches to contain them. I gave them lectures on endurance and the Special Forces will to survive and went over their training with them, trying to activate their pride. With some it worked, but with at least two I had to resort to my last threat – that if they wanted to go to their maker, I would be the first one to help them.

Although no one came into the garage, there was plenty of movement outside and the arguments were punctuated by bouts of crouching and hiding which added to the emotion. Each time anyone came near the building, the team readied itself for a firefight and if the mood was turning at that point towards a final shoot-out, I had to work extra hard to keep it suppressed, while at the same time maintaining their readiness if anyone should try to come in.

We survived the night, and eventually most of the men did agree to get some sleep, but dawn brought too much activity in the street and I ordered the men back into the pit.

We had barely taken up position when the garage doors were opened and three men came in. They were civilians and one looked like the owner of the garage, who had come to re-open it after the Iraqi departure.

We crouched down as low as possible and listened as they began their morning routines. It was a familiar scene. They made coffee and chatted first, then switched on various pieces of equipment and tuned a radio. Then they made more coffee, sending the smell drifting tantalizingly down into the pit, but our nightmare began in earnest when they opened for business for the day.

Their first customer was an Iranian military vehicle piled high with militiamen, which pulled up outside. The mechanics worked on it on the forecourt. It moved away and a second one arrived and this time it was brought inside and worked on beside the doorway.

Finally, the inevitable happened and they brought another militia A.P.C. right into the workshop and rolled it over our pit. We were suddenly in almost complete darkness except for a few cracks of light and we could actually hear Iranians inside the armoured vehicle who were presumably sitting waiting there for the repair to be completed.

Gingerly we edged our way into the deepest part of the pit and huddled in the sump hole, covering ourselves with oil and filth in the process. There were several inches of oil in the bottom and grease was caked all over the sides. It was not long before our clothes were streaked and our weapons slippery to hold, while the combination of fumes and confinement was almost becoming overpowering.

At one point the mechanic pulled away two of the planks from over the pit and walked down the top steps to allow him to work on the front axle. We stayed holding our breath, watching his legs from the knees down only a couple of metres away.

Meanwhile, oil and brake fluid was starting to drip quite heavily from above, forcing us to crouch down even further into the slime and sludge of the pit. While the mechanic worked, there was constant movement around the vehicle. People came to speak to him, and bring him a coffee, someone else slammed the vehicle door, and we could hear the agitation of the militiamen who wanted the job finished and to be on their way.

When my eyes were fully accustomed to the darkness I was able to look at my own men in the few strands of filtered sunlight from above. I could see that one of them was really beginning to crack up.

His hands were trembling and he was moving his head in odd jerky motions. I knew I had to do something there and then. I edged closer to him along the slippery edge of the pit, drew my pistol and put it right up against his face. I held it there for more than an hour. It was the only way I could be sure of keeping him in a frozen position. He was ready to blow and only the absolute certainty of receiving a bullet in the temple kept him steady.

The interpreter, who was himself showing serious signs of wear, was right next to us. He stared at the pistol, then at the man's head, and he kept putting his fingers to his mouth, silently urging the other man not to break down completely.

The armoured vehicle stayed above us for more than two hours and when it moved the respite was very brief.

We heard the sounds of the preparations for departure, then the engine was started and the vehicle rolled off the pit, leaving us suddenly bathed in light. It felt as though we were naked and exposed, but we were so far down in the oil-collecting end of the pit now that the light didn't expose us.

When the vehicle had gone, I inched my pistol away from the Iraqi's head and allowed the interpreter to move up close to him. The interpreter gently took the man's head between his hands and cradled it on his chest like a baby.

Almost immediately, another vehicle – a big commercial truck – was rolled over the pit. We made an extraordinary tableau, with the Iraqi staring wild-eyed over the interpreter's forearm at my weapon which I was holding so he could see that the threat had not gone away.

When work started on the truck, I really did think that, finally, we had come to the showdown. The mechanic pulled away three planks instead of two and I thought, oh Jesus, they're actually going to come down and work on the engine.

Our defensive position was hopeless. We were cramped and exhausted and our field of fire was very restricted. My weapon was so oily I could hardly keep a firm grip on it and I knew the men had virtually no resilience left.

But it was not an engine job. The truck had come in to have a bar welded on the back and within minutes we were showered with sparks as the welding torch crackled and popped above us.

This vehicle was also leaking quite badly and this time it was hot oil that was falling on us, the flecks burning our foreheads and cheeks as we tried to avoid them without stirring enough to make any noise.

Blinded by the sparks and concentrating only on the possible ways of firing an effective burst if anyone did come below the vehicle, I had to leave the interpreter to keep control of the man who was breaking down and the hour that followed was one of the most interminable of my professional life.

When the welding was done and the vehicle drove off, I looked across and saw that the man had almost fallen asleep on the interpreter's chest. He wasn't deeply asleep; it was more an emotional withdrawal, the act of a man who can no longer bear to look at what is going on around him. I left the two men undisturbed and tried to rally the rest of the team.

Morale had almost completely gone and I knew that we would not survive another night in the garage. Our best hope was to move out and just face any opposition as it came. If we stayed, the team was going to break apart anyway and they were more likely to hold up if we were in motion and geared up to actively face the enemy.

No more vehicles were put over the pit and the activity of the garage had quietened down by early evening but it did not close until almost nine o'clock. The wait seemed unending, but several of the men had followed the lead of the first man and were trying to control their nerves by taking snatches of sleep. Finally, the last mechanic left but unfortunately he closed the main doors by slotting a bar outside which had not been there before and sealing it with a massive padlock and chain.

We tried to free it, but from the inside it could be done only by breaking open panels in the door and the street was not quiet enough yet for that to go unnoticed. We waited another hour until there were no passers-by at all, then we took one of the windows completely out of its frame and climbed through into the street.

The sense of relief at being in the open air again was enormous but it was also short-lived. That street was quiet, but Dezful had come well and truly alive with the Iranian re-occupation. As we moved from street to street, the encounters multiplied, but several times we were able to avoid confrontation simply by waving and moving quickly on or by ignoring people in the darkness.

There were three moments in all which could have brought our possible escape to an end. In one, we came upon three garbage collectors but managed to kill them and dump them in their garbage truck before anyone else entered the street. In the second, we were forced to go through an occupied house, with people sitting having a meal in one room, while we walked down a corridor and out the other side. But it was the third that came closest to finishing us.

We had almost reached the edge of the city and were proceeding up a quiet street, with four of the team in front and three bringing up the rear, fifty yards behind, when without any warning at all two militiamen walked right into our midst. They came out of a side street and found themselves right up against the rear of our front section.

Neither knew what to do and my men were almost as bemused as the Iranians. Then one of the militiamen collected himself and started to run down the street to get away.

No one in our team moved fast enough and though I was the furthest away, I knew I would have to deal with him. I yelled to the interpreter, 'Get the other one,' and I set off down the street to give chase to the fleeing Iranian. I forced myself on, thinking furiously as I ran what a fucking nuisance the oil was. My combat fatigues were soaked in it and the oil was flicking up into my eyes and smearing my vision.

The Iranian obviously knew where to get help because he ignored the first turning that would have got him out of the field of fire and ran on, like a madman, towards the bigger crossroads further down the street.

I heard a shot behind me and I assumed that someone had despatched the other militiaman, but the fleeing man heard it too and he assumed he was being fired on.

He turned and looked back, saw me and tried to cock his weapon as he ran. I think he intended to get round the corner and then try a shot at me, but in his panic he turned too early and ran smack into the end of the cement wall. 'Got you, you bastard,' I thought. The Iranian's assult rifle went off and the bullet hit the wall. The man staggered back, stunned and disorientated, not even realizing what he had done.

In any other circumstances it would have been a moment of high comedy but my soldier's instincts were too strong to be thrown by the incongruity of the situation. He had panicked and lost his chance and all that mattered was that he had given me a chance to finish him before he could scramble round the corner and possibly give the alarm to other militiamen.

In his fear, the Iranian had dropped his weapon. As I closed in on him I noticed that it was a Soviet AK-47 assault rifle and I had time in one corner of my mind to register the change of allegiance in weapons supply to Iran.

The Iranian stopped to try to pick up his rifle and I aimed a kick at his head. He fell but he wasn't knocked out and he began to scramble frenziedly to make some kind of counter-attack.

He made a grab for my pistol and his fingers closed on my wrist. I deliberately allowed the pistol to fall onto his chest, knowing that it would make him relax his grip. He let go and tried to seize the pistol and I gave him a straight-arm fist into the nose. The blow alone almost killed him and I finished the job by taking his head in my hands and breaking his neck.

By this time, my team had regrouped and I saw that watching the combat had stiffened their resolve a bit. We still had a long distance to go, but we were almost out of the city and if I could just get them as far as the desert, there was a chance that we would survive after all.

That flight marked the beginning of a forced march that was to go on for the rest of that night and the whole of the following day, and of the seven men in the team, two came very close to failing their final test.

The man who had cracked first during the wait in the pit was by now useless as a soldier but killing him there and then would have had too bad an effect on the morale of the others. He was trembling and shaking and his eyes barely focused and he had to be virtually carried. One other had broken down too, though not quite as badly, and he had to be frogmarched and urged on through the desert march. What saved us, finally, was that the other four Iraqis realized that I had led them through a day and a night in occupied Dezful and they had suddenly become determined to try and follow my example.

They were saved really by my own determination not to end up with my head on a pole in Dezful or being dragged, mutilated, through the streets of Tehran as the first white mercenary captured and displayed by the Iranian propaganda machine.

One other factor, too, came to our aid at the end: the will of Colonel Abu Azed personally not to let me, his former co-fighter from Kurdestan, die because of a high command mix-up over the Iraqi withdrawal from Dezful.

We reached our code blue rendezvous point but we were more than two hours late and in those kinds of battle conditions I did not expect to find a helicopter waiting.

But Abu Azed had personally given the order to go beyond standard operating procedure and when we staggered into the rendezvous area, the Soviet-made Hinde chopper was there, still sitting it out.

It wasn't really equipped to carry us all, but we crammed ourselves in, and as we lifted off I saw that I still had one last lesson in Special Forces warfare to teach my Iraqi squad.

For them, the mission was over at the very second that the chopper left the ground. Relief flooded over them and I could feel the force of their excitement and jubilation. They started to talk and chatter, asking the interpreter to thank me for leading them to safety – and they got a considerable shock when I ordered them sharply to keep silent.

For me, the order was an essential act of discipline. The mission was almost over, but not quite. We were being lifted back behind Iraqi lines but we were still over enemy territory and they were still soldiers who needed to be ready for action.

I had seen it too many times in Vietnam. So often, American units believed their mission was over because they were out of denied territory, then they would suddenly be caught and wiped out because they were no longer in a state of preparedness.

I reserved my own release for much later – when I was sitting on a plane after taking off from Baghdad airport. In the debriefing stage, I remained tightly controlled even during an emotional scene back at the island when Abu Azed clasped me in a brotherly embrace. I was feeling the stress and I felt anger, too, at the way we had been forced into such a situation, but I kept it as inward anger and I did what I always do: quietly reviewed the events of the mission, noting lessons for the future.

Only when the civilian airliner was in the air did I finally allow myself to begin to relax. I ordered a drink and when the stewardess brought it she gave me a newspaper to read. The front page was full of news, but somehow it didn't seem all that relevant and I let it fall to my lap as I sat quietly, watching Iraq drift away beneath me.

I cannot help being introspective at such times, but I never indulge in soul-searching. When I think over events I mentally review them in a very logical and disciplined way – always combined with a sense of humour. There has to be laughter and my sense of humour rarely deserts me, even in extreme situations. What I try to do is to match what has happened against what was supposed to happen because I never go blindly into assignments.

When I am offered a mission, I examine it against very definite personal criteria. Am I certain I am not indirectly serving communism or terrorism?

Will the project undermine anything else I'm involved in? The bottom line, though, is always the same: Is it against the Queen?

By that I don't mean I judge my missions in the light of blind patriotism or loyalty to one country. For me, the Queen symbolizes a set of standards and a sense of honour and military tradition that I have built up over the years. It is a personal code which goes beyond any political dogma and I use it to judge assignments offered by countries that have nothing to do with the Queen, or Britain, or the Commonwealth. It is also a code that is based on healthy cynicism, a first-hand knowledge of human behaviour in extreme situations and a recognition of just how much crap there is in the world.

Certainly, I carry out assignments for money – money is, if nothing else, a measure of commercial value, a way of having your services assessed at the right price – but the assignments must also fit in with my personal principles and beliefs whch I describe, in shorthand, as loyalty to the Queen.

The same code has brought me up against enemies I respect, like the Kurds, and enemies I despise, like the pseudo-intellectual terrorists of E.T.A. In my experience, terrorists generally are people who serve their own self-interest under a phoney banner of idealism and in the process contribute nothing to the improvement of anything.

But once I accept an assignment, I go all the way. I am a perfectionist to a degree, which makes me laugh at myself sometimes. One consequence of this is that when I get into tight situations as in Dezful, I do not indulge afterwards in thoughts like, 'Christ, that was a close call'. I go over the ground, hacking away at means of improving my performance and the performance of my men.

At the same time, I am very aware of my limitations. It's a good job I do have a sense of humour, because it is easy enough to fall prey to a sense of futility. I have often come out of assignments with the feeling that it hadn't really mattered; that I was just a small element passing through a system that is going to continue whatever I do; that what I had done did not have a dramatic enough impact to prevent the situation from recurring.

In Dezful I was quite fatalistic about my predicament, but that certainly does not mean that I had a death wish. Over the years, I have developed a capacity to be resigned and detached so I feel no desperation, while at the same time fighting for survival with all the strength, energy and will-power I possess. I know that nothing in life is permanent, including life itself, yet I remain an optimist.

I set myself ferociously high standards, yet I don't consider myself or what I do important to other people. I suppose this is another aspect of the survival mechanism, a way of supressing the ego because ego is one of the great obstacles to success in special warfare.

Flying away from situations like Dezful, I inevitably start to reflect on events in a way that is totally impossible in the heat of action. I thought, for example, about the garbage men who had had to be killed to ensure our escape. It was unfortunate – as it always is in war situations – that they had found themselves in the wrong place at the wrong moment. It would have been easy to think about how I might have ended up in the dust beside them and yet, once again, I seemed to have managed – almost subconsciously – to carry through a sequence of actions which enabled me to get away with my life. I have several times had the feeling that my survival mechanism is functioning on automatic pilot, as it were. I can't explain it, even to myself. I have felt it in battle and I have felt it after a car crash, when I realized that even while I was crashing I was going through a series of actions that would allow me to walk away safely. I guess one day it will desert me.

Yet when I am going over a mission at times like this, it is easy to slip into deep depression. You can really bottom out. Your throat seems to be down in your bowels. You feel as though you do not belong where you have just been and yet you do not belong in the civilized capital you are heading for, either. If that feeling starts to come on, I have my own personal way of dealing with it.

I project myself forward and think ahead to some simple act, like greeting a dog when I get home, or taking my first shower in my apartment in Switzerland. If I choose the shower, I draw a simple picture of the shower room in my mind and I decide that the shower will mark the end of the depression. In the meantime, everything will be done automatically. I will get off the plane and go through immigration, passport control and baggage collection like a man on wheels. Then, when I take that shower, the book will be closed.

Occasionally, if something has really upset me, a shower is not enough and I will get into the Porsche and drive it very fast indeed. I don't drive in a hair-brained way. I drive with great deliberation but at another level where my mind is not giving the full attention required, as though it is designing its own form of escapism. This state of mind can be instantly reversed. It may take only the sight of something exhilarating in my surroundings that is detached from my way of life. It can be a scene, or a smell or an unexpected piece of music – the common denominator appears to be that it inspires a very basic feeling of freedom. But with me, it is essential medicine to tempt fate, if fate appears to be getting on top of me. Instead of backing off or slowing down, I will jump straight in and fight back head on.

Whatever I am feeling, though, on these flights at the end of missions, the people around me will never know. Even if I am feeling absolutely drained, I will make deliberate effort to conceal it. I perform for people. Other men in the same circumstances might say to hell with it, and slump into themselves, or get drunk. I always have to respond to whatever is coming at me – even when it is only a stewardess offering me dinner. The courtesies of life prevail.

In any event, the flight home is quite a convenient time to pass from the highly charged events of the assignment to the slower pace of normal life. On an assignment, I never even think about everyday matters. On the plane, my thoughts about the details of civilized life gradually move in to replace what I have just lived through and it becomes time to think about girlfriends and home, and the company of friends, but I have to rely on my sense of humour to fight off the negative aspects of introspection.

This time, I thought of one of my favourite fancies. I stretched back in my seat, closed my eyes, and went through the stages of buying a house and installing my donkey, which I call Greenfield, in the paddock beside it. Hearing a donkey bray first thing in the morning is a perfect way to start the day. The idiotic sound reminds me of the futility of so much in the human condition. I cannot talk to people about a situation like Dezful. There is no one I can describe it to and get the right response. Only Greenfield would understand.

INDEX